8/10

Hispanic American Biographies

Volume 7

Ponce de León, Juan—Seguín, Juan N.

GROLIER
an imprint of

www.scholastic.com/librarypublishing

First published 2006 by Grolier,
an imprint of Scholastic Library Publishing,
Old Sherman Turnpike,
Danbury, Connecticut 06816

Set ISBN-13: 978-0-7172-6124-6
Set ISBN-10: 0-7172-6124-7
Volume ISBN-13: 978-0-7172-6131-4
Volume ISBN-10: 0-7172-6131-X

Library of Congress Cataloging-in-Publication Data
Hispanic American biographies.
     v. cm.
   Includes bibliographical references and index.
   Contents: v. 1. Acevedo-Vilá, Aníbal - Bocanegra, Carlos -- v. 2. Bonilla,
Tony - Corretjer, Juan Antonio -- v. 3. Cortés, Carlos - Gálvez, Bernardo
de -- v. 4. Gamboa, Harry, Jr. - Julia, Raul -- v. 5. Juncos, Manuel
Fernández - Montez, Maria -- v. 6. Montoya, Carlos Garcia - Ponce, Mary
Helen -- v. 7. Ponce de León, Juan - Seguín, Juan N. -- v. 8. Selena -
Zúñiga, Martha.
   ISBN-13: 978-0-7172-6124-6 (set : alk. paper) -- ISBN-10: 0-7172-6124-7
(set : alk. paper) -- ISBN-13: 978-0-7172-6125-3 (v. 1 : alk. paper) -- ISBN-
10: 0-7172-6125-5 (v. 1 : alk. paper) -- ISBN-13: 978-0-7172-6126-0 (v. 2 :
alk. paper) -- ISBN-10: 0-7172-6126-3 (v. 2 : alk. paper) -- ISBN-13: 978-0-
7172-6127-7 (v. 3 : alk. paper) -- ISBN-10: 0-7172-6127-1 (v. 3 : alk. paper)
-- ISBN-13: 978-0-7172-6128-4 (v. 4 : alk. paper) -- ISBN-10: 0-7172-6128-
X (v. 4 : alk. paper) -- ISBN-13: 978-0-7172-6129-1 (v. 5 : alk. paper) --
ISBN-10: 0-7172-6129-8 (v. 5 : alk. paper) -- ISBN-13: 978-0-7172-6130-7
(v. 6 : alk. paper) -- ISBN-10: 0-7172-6130-1 (v. 6 : alk. paper) -- ISBN-13:
978-0-7172-6131-4 (v. 7 : alk. paper) -- ISBN-10: 0-7172-6131-X (v. 7 : alk.
paper) -- ISBN-13: 978-0-7172-6132-1 (v. 8 : alk. paper) -- ISBN-10: 0-7172-
6132-8 (v. 8 : alk. paper)
   1. Hispanic Americans--Biography--Encyclopedias--Juvenile literature. I.
Grolier Publishing Company.
E184.S75H5573 2006
973'.046800922--dc22
[B]
                                                           2006012294

For information address the publisher:
Grolier, Scholastic Library Publishing,
Old Sherman Turnpike,
Danbury, Connecticut 06816

FOR THE BROWN REFERENCE GROUP PLC

Project Editor:	Chris King
Editors:	Henry Russell, Aruna Vasudevan, Tom Jackson, Simon Hall
Design:	Q2A Solutions, Seth Grimbly, Lynne Ross
Picture Researcher:	Sharon Southren
Index:	Kay Ollerenshaw
Design Manager:	Sarah Williams
Production Director:	Alastair Gourlay
Senior Managing Editor:	Tim Cooke
Editorial Director:	Lindsey Lowe

ACADEMIC CONSULTANTS:

Ellen Riojas Clark,
Division of Bicultural Bilingual
    Studies,
University of Texas at San Antonio

Arnoldo de Leon,
Department of History,
Angelo State University

Printed and bound in Singapore

ABOUT THIS SET

This is one of a set of eight books chronicling the lives of Hispanic Americans who have helped shape the history of the United States. The set contains biographies of more than 750 people of Hispanic origin. They range from 16th-century explorers to 21st-century musicians and movie stars. Some were born in the United States, while others immigrated there from countries such as Mexico, Cuba, or Puerto Rico. The subjects therefore come from a wide range of cultural backgrounds, historical eras, and areas of achievement.

In addition to the biographical entries, the set includes a number of guidepost articles that provide an overview of a particular aspect of the Hispanic American experience. These guidepost articles cover general areas such as civil rights and religion as well as specific historical topics such as the Treaty of Guadalupe Hidalgo. These articles serve to help place the lives of the subjects of the biographies in a wider context.

Each biographical entry contains a box listing key dates in the subject's life as well as a further reading section that gives details of books and Web sites that the reader may wish to explore. Longer biographies also include a box about the people who inspired the subject, people the subject has influenced in turn, or the legacy that the subject has left behind. Where relevant, entries also contain a "See also" section that directs the reader to related articles elsewhere in the set. A comprehensive set index is included at the end of each volume.

The entries are arranged alphabetically, mostly by surname but also by stage name. In cases where the subject has more than one surname, he or she is alphabetized under the name that is most commonly used. For example, Héctor Pérez García is usually known simply as Hector P. Garcia and is therefore alphabetized under "G." Pedro Albizu Campos, meanwhile, is generally known by his full name and is alphabetized under "A." Both variants are included in the index. Where names are commonly spelled in a variety of ways, the most widespread version is used. Similarly, the use of accents is dictated in each individual case by general usage.

Contributors: Jorge Abril Sánchez; Holly Ackerman; Robert Anderson; Frank Argote-Freyre; Faisal Azam; Berta Bermúdez; Kelvin Bias; Erica Brodman; Hector Carbajal; Bec Chalkley; Eda Correa; Anita Dalal; Zilah Deckker; Stan Fedewa; Conrado Gomez; Leon Gray; Susan Green; José Angel Gutiérrez; Ted Henken; Nashieli Marcano; Luisa Moncada; Carlos Ortega; Teresa Palomo Acosta; Paul Schellinger; Melissa Segura; Iben Trino-Molenkamp; Alberto Varon; Chris Wiegand; Emma Young.

CONTENTS

PONCE DE LEÓN, Juan
Explorer

Juan Ponce de León was among the first Spanish explorers to visit the Americas. He later became the first governor of the Spanish colony of Puerto Rico. As the "discoverer" and the man who named Florida, Ponce de León is also celebrated as one of the first Europeans known to have set foot in territory that would later become the United States. Ponce de León's reputation, however, is tarnished by his brutal treatment of the Native people of Puerto Rico, the Taíno.

Modern knowledge of Juan Ponce de León's exploits largely depends on Spanish accounts recorded years after his death, such as that given by Antonio de Herrera y Tordesillas (1549–1625) in his history of the Spanish American colonies. His adventurous life story came to be colored by myth, most notably his long voyage around the Caribbean in search for the fountain of youth.

Sailing with Columbus
Juan Ponce de León was born in Santervás de Campos in León, part of the Spanish kingdom of Castile. The year of his birth is uncertain, although it seems to have been close

◀ Juan Ponce de León was the Spanish commander who set up the first European colonies on Puerto Rico and in Florida.

to 1460. He belonged to an aristocratic Leonese family, although Juan himself may have been illegitimate.

In 1469 the union of Castile with the neighboring kingdom of Aragon led to the creation of a powerful kingdom that would become modern Spain, the country that was to play the leading role in the coming conquest of the Americas. As a boy, Ponce de León served as a page in the newly formed Spanish royal court.

By 1492 Ponce de León was a soldier serving with the Spanish forces that conquered Granada, which was previously under the control of the Moors— Muslim people of North African origin. In 1493 he joined Christopher Columbus's second expedition to the Americas. Like many of the aristocratic young men who took part in the voyage, Ponce de León's motivation would have been to win honor and make a fortune. Ponce de León settled on the island of Santo Domingo, which had become the center of Spanish rule in the Caribbean. (Santo Domingo is now known as Hispaniola and is the location of Haiti and the Dominican Republic.)

Puerto Rican adventure
It was Ponce de León who led the Spanish invasion of the eastern region of Santo Domingo, and he was subsequently appointed that region's governor. His new base gave him the opportunity to explore the island immediately to the east of Hispaniola. Today this island is the U.S territory of Puerto Rico, meaning "wealthy port." In Ponce de León's day, the Spanish explorers knew it as San Juan Bautista (St. John the Baptist). On August 12, 1508, Ponce de León landed on the island and founded its first

---

KEY DATES

1460 Born in Santervás de Campos, León, Spain, at about this time.

1493 Accompanies Christopher Columbus on his second voyage to the Americas.

1508 Begins conquest of Puerto Rico.

1513 Claims Florida for Spain.

1521 Sets up first Spanish colony in Florida. Dies in Havana, Cuba.

INFLUENCES AND INSPIRATION

Juan Ponce de León is as much remembered for his search for a fabled fountain of youth as he is for his colonial deeds. According to the Spanish historian Antonio de Herrera y Tordesillas (1549–1625), the conquistador grew tired of the pursuit of wealth. Having heard stories from Puerto Rico's native Taíno people about a magical fountain that made anyone who drank from it young again, he decided to look for it and so rediscover the energy and optimism of his youth. The Taíno said the fountain was on the island of Bimini, located to the north of Cuba. According to Herrera y Tordesillas's account, Ponce de León began to wander around the Caribbean on his hopeless quest.

Neither the island nor the fountain existed. They were just stories. Recent research has shown that Ponce de León's quest is just a story as well, and never really happened. The story has entered folklore perhaps because people enjoyed the idea of a conquistador with motives less flagrantly mercenary than a simple lust for gold and power.

Spanish settlement, Caparra, in San Juan Bay. Installed as the governor, he oversaw the enslavement of the island's indigenous inhabitants.

The flowering land

Ponce de León did not enjoy the benefits of his new governorship for very long. In 1512 the Council of Castile restored Puerto Rico to the family of Columbus, who had first claimed the island, and Ponce de León was removed from office. Instead the Spanish Crown gave him permission to explore the islands north of Hispaniola. According to legend, Ponce de León's voyage was inspired by his quest to find a fountain of youth. However, while Ponce de León may well have heard tales of this miraculous spring, it is more likely that his primary purpose was to recover some of his lost prestige and glory and increase his wealth.

In March 1513, Ponce de León set sail from Puerto Rico with three ships—the *Santa Maria*, the *Santiago*, and the *San Cristobal*—and headed northward, eventually sighting what turned out to be the east coast of Florida on March 27, 1513. Instead of landing immediately, the expedition continued northward along the coast and dropped anchor near present-day St. Augustine, Florida. Ponce de León claimed the new land—which he thought was another island—for Spain and named it La Florida (The Flowery Land), either for the bountiful vegetation that blossomed there or because it was Easter Sunday—the beginning of a festival known as the Pascua Florida (Flowery Easter).

After six days, Ponce de León took his ships southward again, against a strong northern current. It was the first European encounter with the powerful oceanic phenomenon known as the Florida Current. This is a surge of warm water that rushes from the Gulf of Mexico through the Florida Straits between Cuba and the Florida Keys.

Ponce de León's expedition then rounded the southern tip of Florida and sailed up the western coast, perhaps as far as Cape Romano in the Everglades. After several more weeks of criss-crossing the Florida Straits, Ponce de León finally returned to Puerto Rico. The following year, he returned to Spain, where he was appointed governor of Florida and given permission to colonize it.

The lion-hearted conquistador

From 1515 to 1519 Ponce de León once again served as governor of Puerto Rico, and it was not until 1521 that he finally set out on another expedition to Florida. He took with him some 200 men and all the provisions he would need to start a new colony. The expedition landed on Florida's southwest coast, possibly somewhere in Charlotte Harbor. However, Ponce de León and his men soon found themselves under attack from local people, the Calusa. In the ensuing fight he was wounded, along with many other colonists. He was taken to Cuba, where he died of gangrene.

Ponce de León's body was later taken to Puerto Rico, where his tomb can be found in the cathedral of San Juan Bautista in the island's capital, San Juan. The Spanish inscription on his tomb makes a punning reference to his name: "In this sepulchre rest the bones of a man who was lion [león] by name and still more by nature." The seaport city of Ponce on the island's southern coast was named for the conquistador, and in 1882 a statue was raised in his honor in San Juan's Plaza San José.

Further reading: Fuson, Robert Henderson. *Juan Ponce de León and the Spanish Discovery of Puerto Rico and Florida.* Blacksburg, VA: McDonald & Woodward Pub. Co., 2000.
www.enchantedlearning.com/explorers/page/d/deleon.shtml (biography.)

PONCE DE LEÓN TROCHE, Juan
Politician

Juan Ponce de León Troche was the grandson and heir of the Spanish conquistador Juan Ponce de León (about 1460–1521) and, like him, one of the early governors of Puerto Rico.

The heir of a conquistador

Juan Ponce de León Troche was born around 1524 in San Juan, the Spanish settlement founded by his grandfather on Puerto Rico. His mother was Juana Ponce de León, the eldest daughter of Juan Ponce de León, who, after her father's death in 1521, managed the family estates. Juan Ponce de León Troche's father was Juan García Troche, the settlement's first treasurer.

The younger Juan Ponce de León was ambitious to follow in his grandfather's footsteps as an explorer and governor. In 1569, he attempted to found a colony on the island of Trinidad. The island's inhabitants had fiercely resisted Spanish attempts at colonization. Ponce de León fared no better than previous would-be governors. He remained on the island for just nine months, setting up a settlement but abandoning it the following year.

Ponce de León later became a priest, but remained an active and respected figure in Puerto Rican civic life. In

▼ **Juan Ponce de León Troche was the first native governor of Puerto Rico.**

KEY DATES	
1524	Born San Juan, Puerto Rico at about this time.
1569	Founds a Spanish settlement on the island of Trinidad.
1579	Briefly serves as governor of Puerto Rico.
1581	Compiles "La Relación de la Isla de Puerto Rico."

1579, he briefly served as Puerto Rico's governor—the first native Puerto Rican to do so. Ponce de León must also have been something of a scholar, for, in 1581, the Puerto Rican governor, Juan López Melgarejo, commissioned him "to gather the description of the island and of all the memorable things in it." The result, "La Relación de la Isla de Puerto Rico," was a short but invaluable overview of the island that became known as "Memorias de Melgarejo," or "Melgarejo's Memoirs."

Juan Ponce de Léon Troche died in around 1591 and was buried in San Juan.

See also: Ponce de León, Juan

Further reading: Fuson, Robert H: *Juan Ponce de León and the Spanish Discovery of Puerto Rico and Florida*. Blacksburg, VA: McDonald and Woodward Publishing Company, 2002.

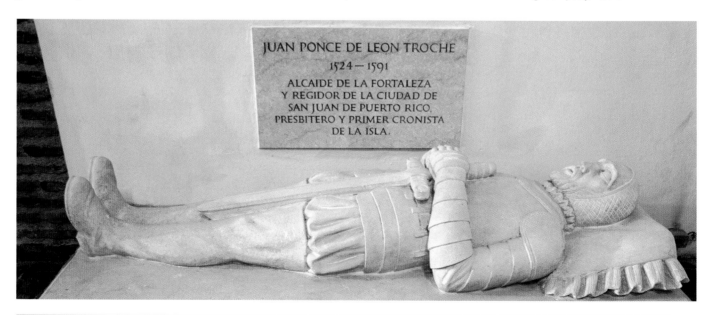

JUAN PONCE DE LEON TROCHE
1524 — 1591
ALCAIDE DE LA FORTALEZA
Y REGIDOR DE LA CIUDAD DE
SAN JUAN DE PUERTO RICO,
PRESBITERO Y PRIMER CRONISTA
DE LA ISLA.

PORTES, Alejandro
Sociologist

Alejandro Portes is a world-renowned sociologist who has a talent for making complicated social phenomena understandable. Portes has been a front–runner in identifying and conceptualizing social processes in five areas. In the 1970s, he was one of the first to investigate comparative migration and assimilation among different Hispanic groups. He proposed the "ethnic enclave" (a system of mutual aid) as a way to understand the success of Cubans in Miami, Florida. Portes's inquiries into the "informal economy" (a system of officially unrecognized labor such as street vendors) were among the first to scrutinize this sector of the global economy. His study of the second-generation children of immigrants has been useful for planning meaningful education and social welfare systems. More recently he has done work to explore "transnationalism" (the processes of living in multiple cultures and multiple places).

Early life
Born in Havana, Cuba, in 1944, Alejandro Portes left Cuba in 1960 because of his opposition to the new regime of Fidel Castro. Portes was inspired to study sociology as a reaction to his exile. He needed to explore why he was cast out of his homeland and to understand the various ways that migration takes place as well as how immigrants enter a new society. Portes's academic abilities were highlighted by his rapid rise from assistant professor at the

▲ *Alejandro Portes began his career as a social scientist after being exiled from his native Cuba.*

University of Illinois Urbana– Champaign in 1971 to full professor at Duke University four years later—a journey that usually takes ten years. Portes's proclivity for co-investigation has kept him in stimulating intellectual company, working with first-class researchers. Additionally, Portes's graduate students often publish with him, a mark of his engagement as a mentor.

Recent work
Since joining the faculty at Princeton University in 1997, as the chair of sociology, Alejandro Portes has founded the Center for Migration and Development, which explores the relationship between immigrant communities in the developed world and the growth and development prospects of the sending nations.

Further reading: Portes, Alejandro, and Alex Stepick. *City on the Edge: The Transformation of Miami.* Berkeley, CA: University of California Press, 1993.
http://cmd.princeton.edu/index.shtml (Portes's Center on Migration and Development at Princeton).

KEY DATES

1944 Born in Havana, Cuba, on October 13.

1960 Leaves Cuba as a political exile.

1971 Joins the faculty at the University of Illinois Urbana– Champaign as an associate professor.

1975 Moves to Duke University, North Carolina, as a full professor.

1995 His co-authored book, *City on the Edge,* wins the Robert Park Award for best book in urban sociology from the American Sociological Association.

1997 Moves to Princeton University as chair of sociology and director of the Center on Migration and Development.

1998 Elected president of the American Sociological Association.

PORTILLO TRAMBLEY, Estela
Writer

Estela Portillo Trambley is regarded as one of the first writers to publish a book concentrating on the experiences of Chicana women. Born and raised in Texas, she considered herself a Texas writer, and wrote about the lives of the people she knew and grew up with along the border between El Paso, Texas, and Ciudad Juárez, Mexico.

Early life
Estela Portillo was born in El Paso, probably in 1927, although many biographical sources give the year as 1936. Her father, Frank Portillo, was a railroad mechanic, and her mother, Delfina, gave piano lessons. At an early age, she went to live with her maternal grandparents in the Segundo Barrio of El Paso. They died when she was 12, and she then returned to live with her parents, two brothers, and a sister.

After high school, Portillo majored in English at the College of Mines, now part of the University of Texas at El Paso. In 1947, she married Robert D. Trambley, who worked in the automobile industry. The couple had five daughters and a son. She taught for several years at El Paso Technical High, and was head of the school's English department between 1959 and 1966.

Early life
Following the death in infancy of her only son, Portillo Trambley turned to reading, particularly philosophy, in an attempt to come to terms with the tragedy. She then wrote a book that combined Eastern and Western philosophies. As an unknown, however, she could not find a publisher. Portillo Trambley realized that the book was flawed, but she considered it a personal success, since it gave her a better understanding of life in general and how she wanted to live her own.

Portillo Trambley became involved in a bilingual theater group, the Chicano Theater, which was established in 1968 in El Paso. Although she had never previously attempted creative writing, when the group wanted material to perform, she volunteered to write a play. The resulting work was, by her own account, poor, but it gave her the theater and writing bug.

Breakthrough
In 1972, Portillo Trambley quit teaching to present a talk show for KIZZ, a radio station in El Paso. The success of her often controversial show brought her an invitation to write for *Cumbres* (Peaks), a cultural television show about the arts. When the show's funding ended, Portillo Trambley was happy to return to teaching. She continued to write plays, however.

A friend sent her play *The Day of the Swallows* to the Chicano literary journal *El Grito* (The Shout), which published it in 1971. The work won the 1972 Quinto Sol Award for literature, and established Portillo Trambley as a serious writer. Other plays followed; among them was *Sor Juana* (1983), about the 17th-century Mexican feminist and nun, Juana Inez de la Cruz.

Portillo Trambley also wrote prose fiction. Her work in the genre is notable for its depiction of borderland life during the 1940s and 1950s. Her collection of stories, *Rain of Scorpions and Other Writings* (1975), is widely regarded as the first work of the 1970s' Chicano literary renaissance. The nine stories examine women's pursuit of self-determination and the position of Chicanas in U.S. society. Her only novel, *Trini* (1986), is a Mexican American coming-of-age story. It tells of Trini's physical and spiritual journey as she travels from Mexico to a new life in the United States.

After the 1980s, Portillo Trambley did not publish any new work. Her theme of the position of women in a traditional macho society has continued to resonate, and some of her works were republished for a new audience at the start of the 21st century. Estela Portillo Trambley died in El Paso in 1998, at age 71.

KEY DATES	
1927	Born in El Paso, Texas, on January 16.
1947	Marries Robert D. Trambley.
1976	Publishes *Rain of Scorpions and Other Writings*.
1986	Publishes only novel, *Trini*.
1998	Dies in El Paso, Texas, on December 28.

Further reading: Portillo Trambley, Estela. *Trini.* Binghamton, NY: Bilingual Press/Editorial Bilingüe, 1986. www.enotes.com/twentieth-century-criticism/estela-portillo-trambley (biography).

POZO, Chano
Musician

Luciano "Chano" Pozo y Gonzalez was a conga drummer, dancer, singer, and composer. Influenced by West African rhythms in his native Cuba, he spent his early years participating in an Afro-Cuban religious cult, while at the same time developing his skills as a musician. He became well–known in Cuba as a choreographer, singer, and composer.

By the mid-1940s, Chano Pozo (as he was most often known) co–led the musical group Carabina de Ases with his brother, and worked with singer Rita Montaner, while his songs were recorded by Orquesta Casino de la Playa, Cuarteto Caney, Machito and his Afro-Cubans, Xavier Cugat, and Miguelito Valdes.

Pozo's associations with Machito and Valdes were especially important since both men had already achieved a level of musical success in the United States and convinced Pozo to move to New York City. Pozo did so in May 1946. On the night he arrived in the city, Pozo was introduced to Mario Bauzá, another Cuban musician who was experimenting with Latin rhythms and jazz. When Bauzá introduced Pozo to Dizzy Gillespie, the meeting marked a jazz milestone. Gillespie was searching for a Latin percussionist for his band. For the next two years, Pozo's contributions to Gillespie's band helped shape Latin jazz.

Work with Dizzy Gillespie

Pozo debuted with Gillespie's jazz band at a recording session in July 1946. Soon after, in February 1947, Miguelito Valdes arranged a recording session for Pozo and included Machito's Orquesta, Arsenio Rodriguez, and Tito Rodriguez, all of whom were important musicians at the time in New York. Pozo also played with Gillespie's band at a Carnegie Hall concert and in further recording sessions. The sessions proved important, as they included the successful "Cubana Be," "Cubana Bop," and "Manteca,"

▲ *In 1948, the year of his death, Chano Pozo (right) performs on stage with jazz saxophonist James Moody.*

which Pozo cowrote with Gillespie. In 1948, Pozo toured Europe with Gillespie's band and played a concert at the Pasadena Civic Auditorium in California.

Before the year was out, Pozo had also recorded four tracks with James Moody, including "Tin Tin Deo," which featured Pozo's vocals. In November 1948, Pozo began a tour of the South with Gillespie's band. Midway through the tour, however, his conga drums were stolen before a show in Raleigh, North Carolina. Pozo quit the tour and returned to New York.

Shortly afterward, Pozo, who had a famously short temper, was involved in a dispute over the sale of some drugs. During the incident, Pozo died of a gunshot wound he received. He was buried in Cuba.

See also: Bauzá, Mario; Cugat, Xavier; Machito

Further reading: Roberts, John Storm. *The Latin Tinge.* New York, NY: Oxford University Press, 1999.
www.bostonphoenix.com/boston/music/other_stories/documents/01982773.htm (short appreciation).

KEY DATES

1916 Born in Havana, Cuba, on January 7.

1946 Moves to New York; debuts with Dizzy Gillespie's band.

1947 Makes a series of influential New York recordings.

1948 Tours Europe with Dizzy Gillespie's band. Is involved in a drug dispute in New York City and dies from a gunshot wound on December 2.

PRADO, Pérez
Musician

▲ *Pérez Prado (right) was responsible for spreading the popular mambo music and dance craze.*

Known as "The Mambo King," Pérez Prado was at the forefront of the mambo music and dance craze of the 1950s. Instrumental in making Latin–American music accessible to mainstream American audiences, Prado had several hit records and wrote scores for many Hollywood films. His popularity waned in the 1960s with the introduction of rock and roll.

Early life
Dámaso Pérez Prado was born on December 11, 1916, in Matanzas, Cuba. His father worked for a newspaper and his mother was a schoolteacher. Prado studied classical piano at the Principal School of Matanzas, and played organ and piano in local nightclubs. In 1943, Prado moved to the capital, Havana, where he became pianist and arranger with the Orquesta Casino de la Playa, Cuba's leading orchestra. In 1947, he left Cuba for Puerto Rico and the following year settled in Mexico City. There, Prado recruited his own orchestra and they enjoyed great popularity, regularly appearing at the prestigious Club 1-2-3.

Prado's fortune lay in the mambo, which he described as a combination of Afro-Cuban rhythm with American swing. While it is commonly believed that two of Prado's Havana contemporaries, Arsenio Rodriguez and Orestes Lopez, created mambo, Prado undoubtedly developed and popularized it. He created an accompanying dance and was the first to market his music as "mambo." His recordings with Cuban singer Beny Moré led to a contract with record company RCA, which released his songs "Qué Rico El Mambo" and "Mambo No. 5" internationally in 1949.

Prado's first tour of the United States in 1951 was a huge success, the mambo replacing the rumba popular throughout the previous decade. Prado created a cha-cha version of "Cherry Pink and Apple Blossom White" that topped the charts in 1954. Featured in the 1955 film *Underwater!* it was one of the most successful instrumental tunes ever, remaining at number one for ten weeks. Prado attained a second number one in 1958 with "Patricia," which was later used in the movie *La Dolce Vita.* Following this, Prado enjoyed Top 20 hits with the theme from the Italian film *Anna* and the South African song "Skokiaan."

Late acclaim
Prado returned to Mexico in the 1960s and remained popular there until his death in Mexico City on September 14, 1989. He had posthumous success with his instrumental piece "Guaglione," Lou Bega's version of "Mambo No. 5," and Shaft's "Mucho Mambo (Sway)," which borrowed from Prado's "Quien Sera (Sway)."

Further reading: Story, Rosalyn M. *Life on the Hyphen: The Cuban–American Way*. Austin, TX: University of Texas Press, 1994.

http://www.laventure.net/tourist/prez_bio.htm (website about Pérez Prado and mamba).

KEY DATES	
1916	Born in Matanzas, Cuba, on December 11.
1951	Plays a mamba music tour of the United States.
1954	"Cherry Pink and Apple Blossom White" reaches number one in the U.S. charts.
1958	Has second number one with "Patricia."
1989	Dies in Mexico City, Mexico, on September 14.

PRIDA, Dolores
Playwright, Journalist

One of the United States's leading Latina playwrights, Dolores Prida uses comedy, farce, music, and soap opera to explore the problems and anxieties faced by Hispanic Americans as they struggle to reconcile two different cultures and languages. Prida writes sometimes in Spanish, sometimes in English, and in some plays switches between the two. Prida also works as a journalist, and is a senior editor on the New York–based magazine *Latina*.

First steps in playwriting
Dolores Prida was born in Caibarien, Cuba, in 1943, the eldest of three children in a working–class family. Soon after the Cuban revolution in 1959, her father fled to Miami, and was followed by the rest of his family in 1961. Prida moved to New York City, where she worked in a bakery while studying literature at night. In 1969, Prida earned a degree in Latin American literature from Hunter College and subsequently began her career in journalism, working for the New York Spanish daily newspaper *El Tiempo*.

Prida first became involved in theater in 1976, when she helped sell tickets at the Teatro Popular on New York's Lower East Side—one of several cooperative Hispanic theater groups at the time. She subsequently wrote her first play, the English–language *Beautiful Señoritas* (1977), a one–act musical in which she lampooned stereotypical views of Hispanic women.

Beneath the comedy
Music and comedy have continued to play an important role in Prida's works, from *The Beggar's Soap Opera* (1979) to 2000's off-Broadway hit *Four Guys Named José ... and Una Mujer,* a tribute to the Latino ballads of the 1940s and 1950s. Light-hearted as many of her works appear to be,

▲ *Dolores Prida's engaging writing uses humor to explore issues affecting Hispanic Americans.*

however, serious themes are never far beneath the surface. In the one-act *Coser y Cantar* (*To Stitch and to Sing;* 1980), for example, the internal cultural divisions and antagonisms experienced by Hispanic American women are dramatized as a conflict between two onstage characters— She and Ella—who live in the same New York apartment.

Controversy
Prida's feminist and left-wing views have not made her popular with many conservative Cuban Americans, and she has often found a more ready audience among the Puerto Rican community. In 1986, a production of *Coser y Cantar* was dropped from the program of Miami's Hispanic Theater Festival after the cast received threats from local Cuban American extremists, who accused Prida of working as an agent for Cuban leader, Fidel Castro.

Further reading: Weiss, Judith (ed.). *Prida, Dolores: Coser y Cantar, Beautiful Señoritas and Other Plays.* Houston, TX: Arte Publico Press, 1991.
www.repertorio.org/education/pdfs/prida.pdf (biography).

KEY DATES

1943 Born in Caibarien, Cuba.

1961 Settles in New York City.

1977 Her first play, *Beautiful Señoritas*, is produced at the Duo Theater, New York.

1981 *Coser y Cantar* is performed at the Duo Theater.

2000 *Four Guys Named Jose...and Una Mujer* performed off-Broadway.

PRINCIPAL, Victoria
Actor

Victoria Principal is a Latina actor best known for her role as Pamela Ewing in the popular CBS television soap opera *Dallas*, which ran from 1978 to 1991. She has also authored several health and beauty books and created a range of beauty products.

Early life

The daughter of Italian and Spanish Filipino parents, Concettina Ree Principale was born in 1945 in Fukuoka, Japan. The family moved frequently during her childhood, as her father was a sergeant in the U.S. Air Force. She was given a role in a commercial at age five, and as a child dreamed of becoming an actress. However, after studying at the Actor's Studio as a teenager, Principal decided to change course and study medicine at Miami-Dade Community College. Following a serious car crash at age 18, Principal reverted to her original plan, moving to New York City to work as a model while pursuing an acting

▼ **Victoria Principal is most famous for her role as Pamela Ewing in Dallas.**

career. After a period living in London, England, and studying acting privately, Principal moved to Los Angeles, California, in 1971.

Principal's first major role was in the movie *The Life and Times of Judge Roy Bean* (1972), with Paul Newman. The role earned her a nomination for the Golden Globe for Most Promising Newcomer in 1973. Principal's subsequent film roles included *The Naked Ape* (1973), *Earthquake* (1974), and *Vigilante Force* (1976). In 1978, Principal was offered the role of Pamela Barnes Ewing in the television soap opera *Dallas*, a part that she subsequently played for nine years. In 1983, the *Dallas* role earned her a nomination for the Golden Globe Award for Best Performance by an Actress in a TV Series.

Stardom and diversification

When Principal quit *Dallas* in 1987, she appeared in many television dramas and films, including *Mistress* (1987), *Naked Lie* (1987), *The Burden of Proof* (1992), *River of Rage* (1993), *Beyond Obsession* (1994), *Love in Another Town* (1997), *Michael Kael vs. the World News Company* (1998), and *Titans* (2000). Principal also appeared in theater, including *Time Flies, An Evening of Comic One-Acts* (1998) with LA Theater Works.

In 1991, Principal created a range of skin care and cosmetic products. She has written several best-selling health and beauty books, including *The Body Principal* (1983), *The Beauty Principal* (1984), and *Living Principal* (2001). She lives in Beverly Hills with her husband Harry Glassman.

Further reading: Brenna, Tony. *Victoria Principal*. New York, NY: St. Martin's Press, 1989.
http://www.victoriaprincipal.com (official Web site).

PRINZE, Freddie
Actor, Comedian

Freddie Prinze was a talented and influential comedian who found success at a very young age. He was the first Latino performer since Desi Arnaz to star in a television comedy series, which he achieved at age 20 as Chico in *Chico and the Man.* Prinze's career was cut tragically short when he committed suicide at the age of just 22.

Early life

Frederick Karl Preutzel was born in 1954 in New York City, the son of immigrants Karl and Maria Preutzel. Prinze's father was Hungarian Jewish, and his mother was Puerto Rican. Prinze would later humorously refer to himself as "Hungarican," although he identified himself as Puerto Rican. He would later change his name to Freddie Prinze. Raised in the Washington Heights area of New York's Upper West Side, Prinze initially attended a Lutheran private school. However, after taking an audition in secret, he was able to enroll at the Fiorello H. LaGuardia High School of Music and Art and Performing Arts. There he discovered and developed his comedic gifts, subsequently acquiring evening work as a stand-up comedian. He later dropped out of school to devote himself fully to stand-up comedy.

Prinze initially worked in the famous New York comedy clubs, The Improv and Catch a Rising Star, before moving to Los Angeles, California. He made his first television appearance on *The Jack Paar Show* in 1973, and at the end of the same year his breakthrough came on *The Tonight Show* starring Johnny Carson (NBC), which he was subsequently invited to guest host.

In 1974, Prinze was given his own television comedy series, *Chico and the Man.* He played Francisco "Chico" Rodriguez, whose catchphrase was "Looking good!" Prinze released a live comedy album in 1975 also titled *Looking Good,* and the following year appeared in the made-for-TV film *The Million Dollar Rip-Off.* Prinze also appeared several times on the *Dean Martin Celebrity Roasts* show.

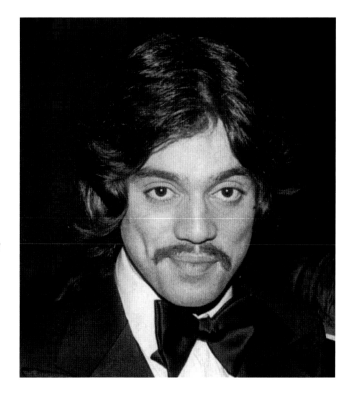

▲ *A very talented young comedian and actor, Freddie Prinze's life was cut tragically short.*

Premature death

Freddie Prinze married Katherine Cochran in 1975, and they had one child, Freddie Prinze, Jr., before divorcing the following year. Prinze found the pressures of fame and separation from his wife and child hard to tackle. He battled with depression, and became addicted to drugs. On January 29, 1977, shortly after performing at the inauguration ball for President Jimmy Carter, Prinze shot himself. Although his death was originally ruled a suicide, several years later it was reassessed and ruled an "accidental shooting due to the influence of Quaaludes."

See also: Arnaz, Desi; Prinze, Freddie, Jr.

Further reading: Pruetzel, Maria. *The Freddie Prinze Story.* Kalamazoo, MI. Master's Press, 1978.
http://geocities.com/chicoandtheman22/catcharisingstar.html
(tribute Web site).

KEY DATES	
1954	Born in New York City on June 22.
1973	Breakthrough appearance on *The Tonight Show.*
1974	Stars in his own show, *Chico and the Man.*
1977	Dies in Los Angeles, California, on January 29.

PRINZE, Freddie Jr.
Actor

Freddie Prinze, Jr., is a popular young film, theater, and television actor. He is well known for his roles in teen movies, including *I Know What You Did Last Summer* and its sequel, and is establishing himself as a writer and producer for film and television.

Early life

Freddie James Prinze was born in 1976, in Los Angeles, California. His mother, real-estate agent Katherine Cochran, is of Irish descent. His father was actor Freddie Prinze, a prominent comedian of Hungarian and Puerto Rican Catholic descent who committed suicide when Prinze was 10 months old. Soon after his father's death, Freddie Prinze, Jr., and his mother moved to Albuquerque, New Mexico, where Freddie revealed acting talents from an early age. He attended La Cueva High School, Albuquerque, and performed with the Albuquerque Children's Theater.

Tireless ambition

When he graduated from high school in 1994, Prinze moved to Los Angeles, and immediately began pursuing television roles. He worked tirelessly to achieve success as

▼ *Freddie Prinze, Jr., has developed a successful career in acting, screenwriting, and directing.*

KEY DATES

1976 Born in Los Angeles, California, on March 7.

1996 First movie role in *To Gillian on Her 37th Birthday.*

1997 First leading movie role in *I Know What You Did Last Summer.*

2003 Stars onstage in *This Is Our Youth* in London's West End.

2005 Stars in own television series, *Freddie.*

an actor, taking his first role in ABC's *Family Matters* (1995), followed by roles in ABC Afternoon Specials and made-for-TV movies. Prinze's film acting debut was in *To Gillian on Her 37th Birthday* (1996); the following year he had a featured role in *The House of Yes.*

A wealth of success

The project that attracted the most attention was *I Know What You Did Last Summer* (1997). The horror film, and its sequel *I Still Know What You Did Last Summer* (1998), established Prinze as a star and a teen idol. Prinze says that, in his early career, he was offered many stereotypical Latino roles, but he has avoided typecasting with lead roles in *She's All That* (1999), *Wing Commander* (1999), *Down to You* (2000), *Boys and Girls* (2000), and *Head over Heels* (2001). Other lead roles include *Hostage High* (2001), *Summer Catch* (2001), *Scooby-Doo* (2002), the sequel *Scooby-Doo 2: Monsters Unleashed* (2004), and *Shooting Gallery* (2005).

In 2005, Prinze produced and starred in the situation comedy *Freddie*, in which he played his first major role as a Hispanic character, a half-Italian, half-Puerto Rican chef. Prinze appeared in London's West End in 2003 in the successful comedy *This Is Our Youth*. He was given a star on the Hollywood Walk of Fame in 2004. Freddie Prinze, Jr., lives in Los Angeles with his wife, fellow actor Sarah Michelle Gellar.

See also: Prinze, Freddie

Further reading: Jordan, Victoria. *Freddie Prinze, Jr.: A Biography.* New York, NY: Simon Spotlight Entertainment, 2000. http://www.freddieprinzejr.com (fan Web site).

PUENTE, Tito
Musician

Percussionist, bandleader, composer, and arranger Tito Puente was one of the world's most celebrated Latino musicians. His long and remarkable career enabled him to develop a style that has crossed the boundaries of culture, race, and generation.

Early life

Puente was born in 1923 in New York, his parents having recently arrived from Puerto Rico, and grew up in Spanish Harlem. His musical talents were apparent at an early age, and his mother arranged piano lessons for him from the age of seven. Puente started to learn percussion, playing the drums and the timbales that would enable him to join the Afro-Cuban rumba bands popular in the 1930s.

Puente started playing professionally from 1939, as a percussionist in the bands of the pianists Noro Morales, José Curbelo, and, in 1941, of Frank Grillo (Machito) in Machito and His Afro-Cuban Boys. During World War II (1939–1945), Puente served in the U.S. Navy for three years, for which he received a presidential commendation. While in the Navy, he played drums in the ship's band and learned the saxophone. After the war, Puente used the provisions of the GI Bill to further his musical education, enrolling at the Julliard School of Music, where he studied composition and orchestration between 1945 and 1947. In the late 1940s, Puente became increasingly in demand by the big Latin bands both as an arranger and composer and as a timbales player. His performing style, standing front stage, was considered revolutionary for a percussionist and it soon became his trademark. He performed and recorded mainly as a member of the orchestras of Pupi Campo and Curbelo until he formed his own group, The Piccadilly Boys,

Puente and His Orchestra

In 1949, Puente's band was renamed Puente and His Orchestra. It was characterized by its emphasis on the brass section, a sound that was seminal to the fusion of Latin and jazz styles. It became one of the great mambo

▼ *Tito Puente performs live on stage at a 1980s concert in Pittsburgh, Pennsylvania.*

INFLUENCES AND INSPIRATION

Tito Puente epitomized Latin music in the United States and was acclaimed as the "The King of Latin music." His versatility as a performer, composer, and bandleader enabled him to survive among the various genres of popular music and contribute to bringing Latin Music to an international audience without succumbing to passing trends. It is known that Puente disliked the term "salsa," as he considered its meaning of "sauce" a derogatory term for a musical genre. He was not only an inspiration to young musicians but also provided training in his ensembles for many younger and newer arrivals to the United States. Puente strongly believed that music had to be studied seriously, and believed that studying at Julliard was the best decision of his life. To that end, he left a foundation to assist children with their musical education.

bands of the 1950s, based mostly at the Palladium Ballroom, which was known as New York's "Home of the Mambo." *Dance Mania*, recorded in 1958, became Puente's best-selling album

At the Palladium, great jazz names such as trumpeter Dizzy Gillespie mingled with leading contemporary Latino musicians. Puente also played in jazz clubs and recorded with jazz players: *Puente Goes Jazz* (1956) was a commercial success, *Night Beat* (1957) was recorded with trumpeter Doc Severinson, and *Herman's Heat Puente's Beat* (1958) was recorded with saxophonist Woody Herman. Puente also experimented with various genres of music from Latin America, including Brazilian bossa nova on the album *Bossa Nova by Puente* (1962). He also often performed and recorded with the Cuban singer Celia Cruz.

The recording of Puente's song "Oye como va" (1962) by Carlos Santana in 1970, which became a chart hit, brought Puente to the attention of a young audience and greatly revived his popularity in the 1970s. Santana recorded Puente's "Para los Rumberos" (1956) in 1972, and the pair also appeared together in concert in 1977. In 1979, Puente received his first Grammy Award for the album *Homenaje a Beny*, in honour of the Cuban singer Beny Moré.

In the 1980s, Puente developed his style into a Latin jazz format; he dissolved his traditional band to create the Latin Percussion Jazz Ensemble with Carlos "Patato" Valdez and Johnny Rodriguez. With this group, he performed throughout the 1980s at jazz festivals such as those at Montreux and Monterey. As the term Latin jazz became more recognizable and established in the 1990s, the ensemble was renamed the Latin Jazz Ensemble. Puente received three Grammy awards with this ensemble, for *Tito Puente and His Latin Ensemble on Broadway* (1983), *Mambo Diablo* (1985), and *Goza Mi Timbal* (1989).

Continuing achievement

In the 1990s, Puente continued to perform and record, celebrating his 100th album with the release of *The Mambo King: 100th* (1991), widely considered a return to his traditional style. Puente also was featured in several Hollywood films, such as *Radio Days* (1987), *Salsa* (1989), and *The Mambo Kings* (1992). Puente received numerous awards, including honorary degrees from Hunter College and Columbia University, the Eubie Blake Award (1990), the National Medal for the Arts (1997), and a last Grammy for *Mambo Birdland* (1999). Puente completed his last recording, "Obra Maestra/ Masterpiece" with Eddie Palmieri, just before his death in May 2000; it was released posthumously in July 2000. Puente left two scholarship funds, the Tito Puente Scholarship Foundation, which he created in 1980 to assist talented children, and the Tito Puente Memorial Scholarship Fund for Latino Outreach. Tito Puente recorded a total of 120 albums, published 450 songs, and had more than 2,000 arrangements to his name.

KEY DATES	
1923	Born in New York on April 20.
1945	Begins studies at the Julliard School of Music.
1948	Forms his first band, The Piccadilly Boys.
1958	Releases the best–selling album *Dance Mania*.
1977	Appears in concert with Carlos Santana.
1990	Forms the award–winning Latin Jazz Ensemble.
2000	Dies in New York on May 31.

See also: Cruz, Celia; Machito; Palmieri, Eddie; Santana, Carlos

Further reading: Loza, Steven J. *Tito Puente and the Making of Latin Music*. Urbana, IL: University of Illinois Press, 1999.
http://www.musicofpuertorico.com/en/tito_puente.html

QUEEN, Ivy
Musician

Popular musician Ivy Queen, also known as "La Diva" and "La Caballota," emerged as an important Latina artist in the 1990s and quickly earned the title of "Queen of Reggaetón." Reggaetón is a form of music associated with Puerto Rico's underground club scene that draws heavily on Jamaican reggae, hip-hop, salsa, and bomba. The *New York Times* called Ivy Queen the only "significant reggaetón rapper."

Early life
Born in Añasco, Puerto Rico, on March 4, 1972, Martha Ivelisse Pesante (who would later give herself the name Ivy Queen) spent her early years in New York City. Her family then moved back to Añasco when she was a teenager. Queen's father was a guitar player, and she grew up listening to salsa and nueva trova music. From an early age she showed talent as a musician, writing and performing her own songs while still at school. After hearing Vico C (Armando Lozada Cruz), the man credited with bringing hip-hop to Puerto Rico, Queen decided that this was the type of music that she wanted to write and perform.

Following a dream
Despite being discouraged from performing what many thought of as "men's music," Queen pursued her dream of performing rap and reggaetón. When she was 18, she met DJ Negro who was looking for a female vocalist to join his rap/reggaetón group, The Noise. He offered Queen the position, and she became one of a handful of female lead rappers at the time. Queen had her first hit, "Somos Raperos Pero No Delincuentes" ("We're Rappers But Not Delinquents"), with the band.

▲ *Puerto Rican Ivy Queen has found international success as a reggaetón rapper.*

Signed to Sony Records, Queen released her debut album *En Mi Imperio* (In My Empire) in 1997. Several leading musicians and producers worked on the album, including Domingo Quiñones and Sergio George, and Queen quickly became established as both a leading rapper and an important reggaetón star. She was praised for her political and socially aware lyrics that highlighted such issues as the abuse of women and female empowerment. Queen went on to collaborate with several key musicians, including former Fugees star Wyclef Jean, who performed with her on the duet "In the Zone," featured on her second album, *The Original Rude Girl* (1998).

In 2000, Queen began working in New York. In 2003, she released *Diva*, followed by *Diva Platinum Edition* in 2004. In 2005, Queen released a greatest hits album, *Flashdance*, and set up her own label, Imperio Records.

Further reading: http://www.mysanantonio.com/entertainment/music/stories/MYSA112005.5Z.burr.1af21d97.html (article on Queen's life and work).

KEY DATES	
1972	Born in Añasco, Puerto Rico, on March 4.
1997	Releases debut album, *En Mi Imperio*.
1998	Releases album *The Original Rude Girl*.
2000	Moves to New York to work and perform.
2003	Releases *Diva*.
2005	Releases *Flashdance* and sets up own recording label.

QUINN, Anthony
Actor

An exceptionally powerful actor with Mexican–Irish roots, striking looks, and a formidable frame, Anthony Quinn enjoyed a long but uneven international career in the movie industry. It took him many years to earn his stripes in Hollywood, as he persevered with the sort of unimaginative and one–dimensional roles typically offered to Latino actors at the time. Oscar success in the 1950s and his performance in the Italian arthouse film *La Strada* (1954) sealed his fame, but Quinn's choice of projects often veered between the sublime and the ridiculous. Still, he emitted such authority that he shone in even the smallest of roles. He won an Academy Award for just a few minutes of screen time in *Lust for Life* (1956).

Early struggles
Quinn's colorful life story has many of the ingredients of a matinee movie. He was born Antonio Rudolfo Oaxaca Quinn on April 21, 1915, in Chihuaha, Mexico. His parents were committed Mexican revolutionaries who followed Pancho Villa. When Anthony was young, the Quinn family left Mexico and migrated to the United States, living first in Texas and then in California. Anthony Quinn took on a wide variety of employment at a young age. He worked in a factory, shined shoes, picked fruit, dug ditches, and mixed cement among many other short–lived professions. He also considered becoming a priest or an architect. Quinn had skilled hands. He proved himself a talented boxer and also revealed a flair for art, sketching portraits of film stars and winning accolades for his sculptures.

Road to Hollywood
Quinn's passion for the cinema was born when his grandmother took him to see a movie starring Spanish–born idol Antonio Moreno. In his 1995 autobiography, *One Man Tango,* Quinn recalled that his grandmother prophetically told him "Someday, you'll be bigger than Antonio Moreno." This would prove no easy feat, however. First, Quinn had to overcome a troublesome speech defect. He initially tried acting as a means to resolve this problem and worked with a theater group before moving into films in his early 20s.

Quinn was hardly an overnight success. One of his first roles was as a Native American in a western about Buffalo Bill. *The Plainsman* (1937) was directed by Hollywood legend Cecil B. DeMille, who would direct Quinn in two more movies. *The Plainsman* set box-office cash registers ringing, but Quinn only made a fleeting appearance. Off the screen, he romanced the director's adopted daughter, actress Katherine DeMille. The pair quickly wed and had a son in 1939, but the boy tragically drowned at a young age. Quinn and his wife would remain married until 1965.

◀ *A Mexican American, Anthony Quinn struggled with typecasting as an actor. Despite the restrictions, he played his roles with panache, and won two Oscars.*

INFLUENCES AND INSPIRATION

Anthony Quinn enjoyed watching the work of several actors, including Spencer Tracy, but his favorite star was perhaps the less widely known but highly respected Walter Huston (1884–1950). Quinn once remarked that he considered Huston "one of the greatest actors that ever lived."

After many years on the stage, Walter Huston made an impact with one of his earliest movies, starring as Abraham Lincoln in D. W. Griffith's 1930 film of the same name. Huston's career in Hollywood lasted for 20 years and he enjoyed success with movies such as *The Outlaw* (1941) and *Duel in the Sun* (1947).

Like Quinn, who starred opposite his own children in a handful of productions, Walter worked on several occasions with his actor–director son, John Huston. These included the classic adventure film *The Treasure of the Sierre Madre* (1948), which won Academy Awards for both father and son.

Memorable roles

Quinn's physical size and Latino looks resulted in him being typecast throughout much of his career, even after he had made a name for himself in Hollywood. This typecasting meant that Quinn played a motley procession of villainous characters such as bandits, cutthroats, gangsters, henchmen, heavies, and pirates—including a one-eyed vagabond in the buccaneering swashbuckler *The Black Swan* (1942). Despite such roles, Quinn managed to play most of the characters with style, and turned in a particularly memorable performance as a wronged Mexican in *The Ox-Bow Incident* (1943), one of his many Mexican characters. Quinn later earned a Best Supporting Actor Oscar as the brother of Mexican guerrilla leader Emiliano Zapata in *Viva Zapata!* (1952). The years between these roles saw Quinn becoming a United States citizen and portraying a vigorous Stanley Kowalski in a stage production of *A Streetcar Named Desire.*

Quinn also stood out as the hulking Zampano, an itinerant circus performer with a dismal repertoire of tricks, in Federico Fellini's bittersweet road movie *La Strada* (1954). The character was a full–blooded, pig–headed, and two–fisted bully, victimizing his innocent assistant (played by Giulietta Masina), but Quinn

spectacularly succeeded in making him a tragic figure. He also managed to film another movie at the same time as *La Strada,* playing Attila the Hun in the French-Italian coproduction *Attila* (1954). A brief turn as the acclaimed painter Paul Gauguin in *Lust for Life* (1956) earned Quinn a second Best Supporting Actor Oscar, which was remarkable since he spent only eight minutes on screen. However, with *The Buccaneer* (1958), his first and only film as a director, Quinn faltered.

Undeterred, Quinn stepped back in front of the camera. He was perfect for the part of a successful man torn between loyalties to his best friend and his murderous son in the superior western *Last Train from Gun Hill* (1959). He appeared in David Lean's epic *Lawrence of Arabia* (1962) and played the larger-than-life title role in *Zorba the Greek* (1964), the pope in *The Shoes of the Fisherman* (1968), a mysterious magician in *The Magus* (1968), and a dogged police captain in *Across 110th Street* (1972), which he also executive-produced. Quinn also threw himself into a personal project, *The Children of Sanchez* (1978), adapted from a novel about a Mexican family battling poverty.

Later years

Quinn remained active in film and television into his 80s. He won a Golden Globe nomination for the television mafia drama *Gotti* (1996) and also excelled in a recurring role as the mighty Zeus in a run of popular TV films about Hercules. He continued to work as a painter and sculptor, his creations as an artist sometimes eclipsing his acting performances. Quinn died in 2001, leaving behind a mammoth body of work that is sure to be embraced by legions of new fans in the future.

Further reading: Quinn, Anthony, and Daniel Paisner. *One Man Tango.* New York, NY: Harper Collins, 1995. http://www.imdb.com/name/nm0000063/ (full filmography).

KEY DATES

1915	Born on April 21 in Chihuaha, Mexico.
1937	Marries Katherine DeMille.
1953	Wins a Best Supporting Actor Oscar for *Viva Zapata!*
1956	Wins a second Oscar for his small role in *Lust for Life.*
1996	Nominated for a Golden Globe for TV drama *Gotti.*
2001	Dies on June 3.

QUINTANA, Ismael "Pat"
Musician

Singer, composer, and hand percussionist Ismael Quintana was a founding member of and original singer with Eddie Palmieri's band, La Perfecta, a group that was widely popular in New York in the early 1960s. Quintana then joined the Fania All Stars, becoming further renowned as a voice of the salsa genre.

Early life

Born in 1937 in Ponce, Puerto Rico, Quintana moved with his family to New York City when he was two weeks old. While attending high school in the Bronx, he played the bongos in a band he formed with his neighborhood friends. After graduating from high school, Quintana held regular jobs playing in a variety of venues in the Bronx. Eddie Palmieri, a bandleader of a salsa and Latin jazz orchestra, heard Quintana sing at an audition and was impressed with his style. In 1961, Palmieri formed a band named La Perfecta, and invited Quintana to join. Quintana accepted and became the lead vocalist from 1961 to 1971. The combination of Quintana's voice and Palmieri's powerful sound inspired by Cuban charanga became a sensation in New York. During this time they wrote many songs together and performed memorable hits such as "Adoración," "Puerto Rico," "Vámonos Pa'l Monte," "Tirándote Flores," "Ritmo Caliente," "Lo Que Traigo es Sabroso," "Bomba del Corazón," "Sujétate la Lengua," and "Bilongo," among others.

In 1966, Quintana won a trophy for the Most Popular Latin Singer of the Year, awarded at the Palladium Ballroom in New York. In the early 1970s, while still singing with Palmieri, Quintana also made his solo recording debut under the United Artists label with *Punto Y Aparte. Dos Imágenes*, which he recorded a year later, included many boleros that gave Quintana the opportunity to show the versatility of his voice. Although he was known as a salsa singer, Quintana proved he could also perform other genres.

▲ *A leading voice of salsa music, Ismael Quintana is also a talented composer.*

In 1973, after 12 years with La Perfecta performing some of his finest works, Quintana decided to leave the band and launch a solo career. He signed with Vaya Records and issued five albums between 1974 and 1983. The first album included his hit single "Mi Debilidad." In 1981, Quintana reunited with Palmieri to perform "No Me Hagas Sufrir" and "Ven Ven," compositions they cowrote.

From 1975 to 1984, Quintana performed with the Fania All-Stars, a group of leading salsa musicians and singers under the record label Fania Records. In 1976, he made an appearance in the movie *Salsa*, with Celia Cruz and Tito Puente. Today, Quintana remains an active member of the Fania All-Stars.

See also: Cruz, Celia; Fania All-Stars; Palmieri, Eddie; Puente, Tito

Further reading: Larkin, Colin (ed.). *The Encyclopedia of Popular Music.* 3rd edition. New York, NY: Muze, 1998. http://www.findarticles.com/p/articles/mi_m0FXV/is_6_15/ai _n15387331 (article about Ismael Quintana from *Latin Beat Magazine*, August 2005).

KEY DATES	
1937	Born in Ponce, Puerto Rico, on July 3.
1961	Starts performing with Palmieri's band, La Perfecta.
1973	Launches solo career.
1975	Becomes a member of the Fania All–Stars.

QUINTANA, Leroy V.
Poet

Leroy V. Quintana is one of the best-known poets to have written about the Hispanic contribution to the Vietnam War. A winner of the American Book Award on two occasions, Quintana says that he still sees himself as a "small-town New Mexico boy carrying on the oral tradition."

Early life

Born in Albuquerque, New Mexico, in 1944, Quintana never knew his father. He was raised by his grandparents until third grade, when he went to live with his mother and stepfather. Quintana spent his childhood moving around small northern New Mexico towns such as Ratón and Questa. As a young child, he was kept entertained by his grandparents' traditional Mexican folk tales (*"cuentos"*). The tradition of oral storytelling had a great effect on Quintana and heavily influenced his later poetry.

After graduating from high school in 1962, Quintana worked as a roofer with his stepfather before entering the University of New Mexico (UNM) in 1964 to study anthropology. Between 1967 and 1969, Quintana's studies were interrupted by a tour of duty in the U.S. Army during the Vietnam War. On his return, Quintana wrote about some of his own and his friends' experiences.

The road to writing

In 1969 Quintana returned to the University of New Mexico; he switched his major to English. He married in 1970, and he and his wife had three children.

After graduating in 1971, Quintana worked as an alcoholism counselor in Albuquerque before moving to Denver to study for an MA. He then worked as an assistant professor at New Mexico State University, where he came under the guidance of Professor Keith Wilson, a noted poet, who encouraged him to start writing again. Quintana completed his MA in 1974. He published his first collection of poetry, *Hijo del pueblo: New Mexico Poems*, two years later. The influence of Quintana's early years spent listening to *cuentos* is apparent in the rhythms of the poems included in the volume.

Within New Mexico the book was well reviewed, and that encouraged Quintana to continue writing. In 1975 he moved with his family to Texas, where he worked at El Paso Community College and finished his second collection of poetry, *Sangre,* although the book was not

KEY DATES	
1944	Born in Albuquerque, New Mexico, on June 10.
1967	Goes to Vietnam with the U.S. Army.
1971	Graduates with a BA from the University of New Mexico (UNM).
1976	Publishes first book of poetry, *Hijo del Pueblo*.
1990	Publishes *Interrogations*.
1993	Publishes *The History of Home*.
1999	Publishes *Great Whirl of Exile*; wins American Book Award.

published until 1981. Quintana's poetry also appeared in various publications; it was included in the 1980 *Hispanics in the United States* anthology, edited by Gary D. Keller and Francisco Jiménez.

Moving home

In 1980 Quintana and his family moved back to Albuquerque, where he taught at the University of New Mexico. During the 1980s he stopped writing poetry and concentrated instead on his newspaper columns for the *Albuquerque Tribune*. He also trained to be a psychologist.

The Quintana family relocated again, this time to San Diego, California, where they still live. Quintana believes his training as a psychologist has helped his writing. His book of poetry about the Vietnam War, *Interrogations* (1990), distilled his memories and experiences about the war and is a plea for peace.

The volume *The History of Home* (1993) reflects Chicano history during the 1950s, while in his 1996 volume, *My Hair Turning Gray among Strangers*, he attempts to recapture the period of his youth. In 1999 Quintana published *Great Whirl of Exile*. The collection was critically acclaimed. A licensed marriage, family, and child counselor, Quintana practices in California; he also teaches English at San Diego Mesa College.

Further reading: Quintana, Leroy. *Interrogations.* Chevy Chase, MD: Burning Cities Press, 1990.
www.ou.edu/worldlit/authors/quintana/quintana.html (short biographical detail about Quintana and his work).

QUINTERO, José
Theater Director

José Quintero was a renowned theater director and the first Latino to win a Tony Award for Best Director. He was cofounder of the Circle in the Square Theater in New York, which established Off-Broadway as a serious theatrical movement. Quintero was most acclaimed for his staging of the plays of Eugene O'Neill, which initiated a widespread revival of the playwright's works.

Early life
Quintero was born in 1924 in Panama City, Panama. He was sent to the United States in 1943 to study medicine, but changed to theater, a decision that led to his estrangement from his wealthy family. Quintero received a bachelor of arts degree from the University of Southern California, Los Angeles, in 1948. After training at the Goodman Theatre School in Chicago, Illinois, from 1948 to 1949, he went to Woodstock, New York, where he formed the Loft Players with a group of friends, and directed *The Glass Menagerie* by Tennessee Williams in the summer of 1949. The following year, Quintero and Theodore Mann relocated to New York City and transformed a nightclub in Greenwich Village into a

▼ *A visionary theater producer and director, José Quintero championed the plays of Eugene O'Neill.*

KEY DATES

1924 Born in Panama City, Panama, on October 15.

1951 Cofounds the Circle in the Square Theater in New York City.

1957 Wins a Tony Award for Best Producer for Eugene O'Neill's *Long Day's Journey into Night.*

1973 Wins a second Tony Award for Best Director for O'Neill's *A Moon for the Misbegotten*.

1999 Dies in New York on February 27.

theater. There they developed the concept of three-quarter staging, where the audience sat on three sides of the stage. They called their theater the Circle in the Square.

The Circle in the Square became the first Off-Broadway theater to receive widespread critical attention when it revived Tennessee Williams's *Summer and Smoke* (1952). The play also established Quintero as an outstanding theater director. Quintero developed an interest in Eugene O'Neill, who had died in 1953 virtually forgotten, and secured permission to stage *The Iceman Cometh* (1956). His production was a great critical success, and ran for nearly two years. Quintero then premiered O'Neill's autobiographical drama, *Long Day's Journey into Night* (1956), for which he won a Tony Award in 1957.

Although Quintero directed other writers, he became known as the premier interpreter of O'Neill, staging 19 productions of his work. *A Moon for the Misbegotten* (1973) brought him a second Tony Award. Quintero also directed a Hollywood movie, *The Roman Spring of Mrs Stone* (1961), based on a novel by Tennessee Williams.

In 1987, Quintero underwent surgery for cancer of the larynx and resumed his career using a mechanical voice device. He staged a revival of *Long Day's Journey into Night* in 1988. He also became a professor of acting and directing at the University of Houston, Florida State University, and New York University. He published his autobiography, *If You Don't Dance, They Beat You,* in 1972.

Further reading: Little, Stuart W. *Off-Broadway: The Prophetic Theatre.* New York, NY: Coward, McCann & Geoghegan, 1972.
http://info.lib.uh.edu/dev/libed/1998/summer/summer98.htm
(collection of Quintero's papers at University of Houston).

RAMIREZ, Manny
Baseball Player

The Dominican Republic has produced some of the best baseball players in major league baseball history. American League (AL) slugger Manny Ramirez is a leading example, carving his own niche in the long line of Dominican stars. Ramirez was named an All-Star nine times, topped 100 runs batted in (RBIs) and 30 home runs in 10 out of 11 successive seasons, and crushed 20 grand slams—the most ever by a Latino player. To Boston Red Sox fans, however, Ramirez will always be remembered for his most valuable player (MVP) performance in the 2004 World Series. Boston swept the St. Louis Cardinals four games to none to win its first World Series title since 1918. Ramirez hit one home run and scored four runs in the series, helping the Red Sox end one of the longest droughts in major league history. Overall in the postseason, Ramirez hit safely in all 14 games, with 11 RBIs and eight runs. The Red Sox's World Series win capped off a banner year for Ramirez: 43 home runs (the best in the AL), 130 RBIs, and 108 runs scored.

Early life

Manny Ramirez was born in 1972 in Santo Domingo, the Dominican Republic. When he was 13, Ramirez's family moved to New York City, where his father worked as a taxi driver and his mother as a seamstress. Ramirez attended George Washington High School in the Bronx. While there, he was named the New York City Public Schools High School Player of the Year in 1991, after he hit 14 home runs in 22 games. In 1999, Ramirez was inducted into the New York City Public Schools Athletic Hall of Fame, along with fellow professional baseball players Bobby Thomson,

▲ *Manny Ramirez helped lead the Boston Red Sox to World Series glory in 2004.*

John Franco, and Shawon Dunston, as well as National Basketball Association (NBA) star Nate "Tiny" Archibald.

The Cleveland Indians drafted Ramirez straight out of high school in the 1991 amateur draft. After nearly three seasons in the minors, the Indians made Ramirez a late–season call–up in September 1993. Following his debut, Ramirez went on to play seven more seasons with the Indians, leading the team to the 1995 and 1997 World Series. In those World Series, Cleveland lost to the Atlanta Braves and Florida Marlins respectively, but in the process Ramirez solidified his position as one of the AL's top players.

On December 12, 2000, Ramirez signed as a free agent with the Red Sox, and in his fourth year with the team propelled them to their historic 2004 World Series victory. The Red Sox had made it to the World Series by coming back from a 3-0 deficit to defeat their fierce rivals, the New York Yankees, in the AL Championship Series.

Further reading: Shaughnessy, Dan. *Reversing the Curse.* New York, NY: Houghton Mifflin, 2005.
http://www.mannyramirez.com (official Web site).

KEY DATES	
1972	Born in Santo Domingo, Dominican Republic, on May 30.
1993	A late–season call–up, he makes his major league debut with the Cleveland Indians on September 2.
2000	Signs as a free agent with the Boston Red Sox on December 12.
2004	Helps the Red Sox win the World Series for the first time since 1918.
2005	Named an AL All–Star for an eighth consecutive season (his ninth overall).

RAMÍREZ, Martin
Artist

Martin Ramírez was a Mexican American artist who belonged to the category of so-called naive or self-taught art. His work was unique among naive artists for its modern aesthetic quality and for its intrinsic "Mexicanidad," or Mexican spirit. Ramírez is celebrated both as a Latino and as one of the finest of all self-taught artists.

Ramírez was born in 1885 in Jalisco, Mexico, and came to California between 1900 and 1910 with the wave of refugees and migrants displaced in the run-up to the Mexican Revolution. He is believed to have worked for the railroad, but, by 1915, traumatized by life in the United States, he stopped speaking, and was picked up in 1930 as a destitute in Los Angeles. Ramírez was diagnosed with chronic paranoid schizophrenia and committed in 1935 to De Witt State Hospital, Auburn, California, where he spent the remainder of his life.

Therapeutic art

Ramírez started drawing in about 1945 using scraps of paper; he had to hide his drawings to prevent them being thrown out by the hospital cleaning staff. In 1948, he showed some of his drawings to the psychiatrist Tarmo Pasto, a professor from Sacramento State University. Pasto, recognizing the quality of Ramírez's work, provided him with art materials to develop his art and provide him with therapy. He also collected the artist's work, and gathered information about his life. From his mute and destitute world, Ramírez devised images that were both naive and powerful, and had an aesthetic quality that went beyond so-called "psychic art." His drawings, mostly in colored pencil on paper, consist of series of parallel lines that form the perspectives of the structures of buildings, roads or tunnels, and figures within them. Ramírez's "Mexicanidad" was expressed in his subject matter, much of which was

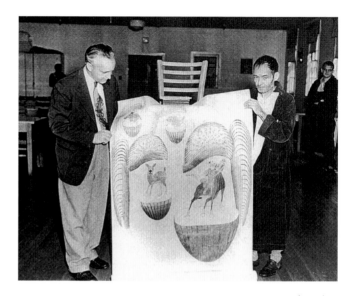

▲ *Martin Ramirez (right) spent most of his life in hospital, where he produced widely acclaimed art.*

taken from what he had known before he came to the United States: guerrillas from the Mexican Revolution, female figures reminiscent of the Virgin of Guadalupe, and animals that resemble popular wooden toys. *Soldado with American Flag* (about 1955) is an outstanding example of his work.

It was long after his death in 1960, however, that Ramírez's work became known in the art world through the artist Jim Nutt and the art dealer Phyllis Kind, who, with Pasto, organized an exhibition at Sacramento State University. Ramírez was included in the "Outsiders" exhibition at the Hayward Gallery, London, England, in 1979, and had his first major exhibition, "The Heart of Creation: The Art of Martin Ramírez," at Moore College of Art, Philadelphia, in 1985. Ramírez's work was also included in the seminal "Hispanic Art in the United States: 30 Contemporary Painters and Sculptors" at the Houston Fine Art Museum in 1987. Ramírez's reputation is now firmly established as one of the best self-taught artists of the 20th century.

KEY DATES

1885 Born in Jalisco, Mexico, on March 31.

1930 Committed to De Witt State Hospital, Auburn, California, suffering from schizophrenia.

1948 Artistic talent recognized by psychiatrist Tarmo Pasto.

1960 Dies in Auburn, California.

1985 First major exhibition of his work.

Further reading: *Martin Ramírez: Pintor Mexicano.* Mexico City, Mexico: Centro Cultural Arte Contemporáneo, 1989.
http://www.janesaddictions.com/ramirez01.htm

RAMÍREZ, Sara Estela
Poet, Activist

Poet and activist Sara Estela Ramírez spent the last 12 years of her relatively short life serving her community as a teacher, writer, and spokeswoman for the Partido Liberal Mexicano (PLM), the political party of Mexicans and Mexican American intellectuals in support of what would become the Mexican Revolution.

Early life
Born in Villa de Progreso, Coahuila, Mexico, in 1881, Sara Estela Ramírez was brought up by her father; her mother died when she was a young girl. As a child, Ramírez lived in northern Mexico; she completed public school in Monterrey, Nuevo León. Ramírez studied to become a teacher at Ateneo Fuentes in Saltillo, Coahuila. In 1898, when she was 17 years old, Ramírez obtained a position as a Spanish teacher at the Seminario Laredo in Laredo, Texas. She spent the rest of her life in the border city.

Activism
Ramírez was a friend of Ricardo Flores Magón, the PLM leader, and she became a leading party spokesperson in South Texas. She sometimes stood in for Magón and other PLM leaders, who were under surveillance by law enforcement authorities.

In June 1901, Ramírez became the publisher of the journals *La Corregidora* and *Aurora*. With the poet, journalist, and radical Juana Belén Gutiérrez de Mendoza, she collaborated on *Vesper: Justicia y Libertad*, a newspaper for women and Mexican American workers. Gutiérrez de Mendoza had founded the paper in 1901 to protest the foreign domination of Mexican business and the increasing impoverishment of local people.

KEY DATES	
1881	Born in Villa de Progreso, Coahuila, Mexico.
1898	Takes position as Spanish teacher at Seminario Laredo, Laredo, Texas.
1901	Becomes publisher of *La Corregidora* and *Aurora*.
1908	Her 21 known works are published in *El Demócrata Fronterizo* and *La Crónica*.
1910	Dies in Laredo, Texas, on August 21.

Women's movement
Ramírez was involved with Regeneración y Concordia (Regeneration and Harmony), an early women's organization. Along with Gutiérrez de Mendoza, Elisa Acuña y Rosetti, and Dolores Jiménez y Muro, Ramírez is regarded as one of the founders of modern Mexican American feminism. Moreover, Ramírez's political activities on behalf of PLM and women's causes made her a forerunner of the founders of important contemporary Mexican American women's organizations such as the ladies branch of the League of United Latin American Citizens (LULAC), the American GI Forum Women's Auxiliary, and Mujeres por la Raza (Women for the People).

Between January 8, 1908, and April 9, 1910, Ramírez published her work in *El Demócrata Fronterizo* and *La Crónica*, two leading South Texas newspapers owned by the activist and journalist Nicasio Idar. Ramírez was a good friend of Nicasio's wife, Jovita, also a prominent civil and women's rights activist. Among Ramírez's best known works are *"Surge"* ("Rise Up"), an anthem in praise of women's strength, *"Diamantes Negros"* ("Black Diamonds"), *"A Juárez"* ("To Juárez"), and *"Huye"* ("Flee"). In addition to poems, Ramírez wrote a play, *Noema*, and published the speeches that she made to the members of the Sociedad de Obreros (Workers' Society). One of these talks, "Igualdad y Progreso" (Equality and Progress), reflected her participation in local labor organizing efforts among Mexican Americans. Through her literary works, Ramírez evoked the bicultural nature of Mexican American culture and history along the U.S. and Mexican border.

Ramírez died of unknown causes on August 21, 1910, at approximately 29 years of age. Jovita Idar eulogized Ramírez in *La Crónica* as "La Musa Texana" ("The Texan Muse"). Ramírez left an important legacy for writers of Mexican origin in the United States, many of whom have carried on her commitment to Hispanic cultural and human rights through their writing and personal involvement in political activism.

See also: Flores Magón, Ricardo; Idar, Nicasio

Further reading: http://www.tsha.utexas.edu/handbook/online/articles/RR/fra60.html (Handbook of Texas Online biography of Ramírez).

RAMOS, Basilio
Revolutionary

Basilio Ramos was one of the leading conspirators in the so-called Plan de San Diego, a plot to bring about a Mexican uprising across the U.S. Southwest in the early months of 1915. Although relatively little is known about the lives and motivations of the plotters, including Ramos, historians continue to debate and write about the circumstances that led to the plan's discovery and its consequences.

Unrest

In 1848 Mexico and the United States signed the Treaty of Guadalupe Hidalgo, by which Mexico ceded more than 55 percent of its land to its neighbor. The area lost consisted of most of the present-day states of California, Arizona, New Mexico, Utah, and Nevada and parts of western Colorado. Many Mexicans living in these areas became disgruntled by the treatment that they subsequently received. In particular, many were upset at the U.S. Senate's refusal to guarantee Mexican land grants. Over the next decades, many Mexicans conspired to reclaim their lost territory.

The plan

In the midst of the Mexican Revolution (1910–1920), Basilio Ramos, a native of Nuevo Laredo, Mexico, came to national attention after he was arrested by U.S. authorities on January 24, 1915, in McAllen, a small town in South Texas close to the Mexican border. Among Ramos's personal papers was a document, the Plan de San Diego. It told of a planned mass uprising of Texas-domiciled Mexicans living along the border. The revolt was planned for 2:00 A.M. on February 20, 1915, and called for the formation of an army made up of Hispanics, blacks, Japanese, and Native Americans, with the eventual aim of seizing control of all the territory ceded by Mexico to the United States. The reclaimed land would be used to form the basis of an independent republic annexed to Mexico; the six neighboring states would then be captured and made into a republic for African Americans. The document stated that the rebels must use any necessary means to secure their goal, including executing all white Texans aged 16 and over.

Taken to a jail in Brownsville, Texas, for questioning, Ramos revealed that he and his six or seven conspirators had first hatched the plan in December 1914, while in

KEY DATES

1848   Treaty of Guadalupe Hidalgo signed; Mexico cedes 55 percent of its territory to the United States.

1910   Mexican Revolution breaks out; President Porfirio Diaz resigns.

1914   Basilio Ramos meets with other Mexicans to conspire against the U.S. government and plan a revolution to reclaim the territory lost by Mexico in 1848.

1915   A deputy sheriff arrests Basilio Ramos in McAllen, Texas; the Plan de San Diego is discovered, revealing details of a revolt due to occur on February 20.

prison in Monterrey, but had put their names to the actual document in San Diego in South Texas.

When February 20, 1915, came and went without incident, a federal judge commented that Ramos deserved to be tried for "lunacy, not conspiracy against the United States." He was released on bail pending trial and disappeared.

Aftermath

In the following months, however, bands of armed Mexicans took part in almost daily attacks on the Anglo-Texan community. They raided post offices and stores, destroyed bridges, and attacked and killed individuals, particularly members of the hated Texas Rangers. Whether the attacks were related to the Plan de San Diego or not is unclear, but most Anglo-Texans believed that they were. Some took part in extremely brutal vigilante attacks on Mexicans and Mexican Americans, resulting in the deaths of more than 300 Hispanics.

Some commentators believe that the Plan de San Diego originated with Mexican dictator General Victoriano Huerta. Others claim that Venustiano Carranza, who ousted Huerta from power in 1914, was responsible. The United States recognized Carranza's presidency in 1915.

Further reading: Johnson, Benjamin Heber. *Revolution in Texas: How a Forgotten Rebellion and Its Bloody Suppression Turned Mexicans into Americans.* New Haven, CT: Yale University Press, 2003.
http://www.tsha.utexas.edu/handbook/online/articles/ PP/ngp4.html (Handbook of Texas Online).

RAMOS, Jorge
Journalist, Anchorman

Mexican-born Jorge Ramos is one of the United States's most respected, influential, and well-known Hispanic broadcast journalists. With Maria Elena Salinas, he is co-anchor of *Noticieros*, the popular early-evening news program broadcast by the Spanish-language television network Univision. Ramos is also the author of several best-selling nonfiction books, and writes a weekly column that appears in Spanish-language newspapers nationwide.

Voice of the voiceless

The eldest of five children, Jorge Ramos was born in Mexico City on March 16, 1958. After high school, he earned a degree in media and communications from Mexico City's Ibero-American University, and subsequently worked as a radio journalist. Ramos soon became frustrated with the rigorous censorship that the Mexican government imposed on the media at that time and, in 1983, he moved to California. Despite being warned that there was no future in Spanish-language broadcasting in the United States, in 1984 Ramos took a job as a reporter with a Univision-affiliated station in Los Angeles.

In 1986, at age 28, Ramos became the anchorman of Univision's *Noticieros*, on which he has worked ever since. Ramos has also worked extensively as a correspondent, and became well known for his reports from New York City in the aftermath of the 9/11 terrorist attacks in 2001, during which he drew attention to the large number of undocumented—and mainly Mexican—aliens who had lost their lives in the attacks.

Throughout his career, Ramos has been concerned with how historical events affect the lives of ordinary people—a focus that has earned him the byname "the voice of the voiceless." The high regard in which Ramos is held by

▲ *Jorge Ramos is a well-known television news presenter and an incisive journalist.*

most of the Hispanic community has helped win him interviews with world leaders, including Cuban president Fidel Castro and President George W. Bush. Ramos has become well known for his hard-hitting interview style. He once received death threats after asking former president of Colombia Ernesto Samper how much of his political funding came from his country's drug "barons." Such fearless, principled journalism has won Ramos wide recognition, earning him eight Emmy awards and a Maria Moors Cabot Award.

Other activities

In addition to his work in television, Ramos has written several books, including *Dying to Cross* (2005), an account of a 2003 incident in which 19 illegal Mexican immigrants died while being smuggled to Houston, Texas, in a tightly sealed trailer.

See also: Salinas, Maria Elena

Further reading: Ramos, Jorge. *No Borders: A Journalist's Search for Home.* New York, NY: Rayo, 2002.
www.jorgeramos.com (Ramos's own Web site).

KEY DATES	
1958	Born in Mexico City, Mexico, on March 16.
1983	Immigrates to the United States.
1986	Becomes co-anchor on *Noticieros*, Univision's main news program.
2001	Wins a Maria Moors Cabot Award for excellence in reporting on Latin America.
2005	Publishes *Dying to Cross*.

RAMOS, Tab
Soccer Player

Tab Ramos is widely regarded as one of the United States's best soccer players. A midfielder, Ramos played on three consecutive World Cup soccer teams (1990, 1994, and 1998). He was the first player ever to sign with the newly formed Major League Soccer (MLS) on January 3, 1995, and scored the league's first All-Star goal. Despite being hampered by numerous injuries, Ramos scored eight goals in 81 international appearances for the U.S. national team. During his seven-year MLS career (all with the New York/New Jersey MetroStars), Ramos was twice named an All-Star.

Early life

Born in 1966 in Montevideo, Uruguay, Ramos immigrated to the United States with his family in 1978, at age 11. He grew up in northern New Jersey, and attended high school at St. Benedict's, which was renowned for its soccer. Ramos was twice named an All-American, and was the Parade National Player of the Year in 1983. Ramos attended

▼ *Tab Ramos represented the United States in three soccer World Cup tournaments.*

KEY DATES	
1966	Born in Montevideo, Uruguay, on September 21.
1994	Starts every game for the U.S. in the 1994 World Cup.
1995	Becomes the first player to sign with Major League Soccer on January 3.
2005	Inducted into the National Soccer Hall of Fame.

North Carolina State University in Raleigh, where he was a three-time All-American.

In 1988, Ramos played the first of two consecutive seasons in the now defunct American Soccer League. In January that year, he also made his first appearance with the U.S. national team, against Guatemala.

Ramos played his first World Cup game for the United States in Italy in 1990. In 1994, the United States hosted the World Cup for the first time. Ramos started all four games, but suffered a fractured skull in the United States's 1–0 quarterfinal loss to Brazil after being elbowed by Leonardo. After scoring a memorable qualifying goal in September 1997 against Costa Rica, Ramos also played in the 1998 World Cup finals in France.

Before joining the MLS in 1995, Ramos played five seasons in the Spanish soccer league with Figuere and Real Betis. He retired from the MetroStars after the 2002 MLS season, having scored eight goals and adding 36 assists.

Life off the pitch

Today, Ramos passes on his soccer expertise to youths through several programs in his name. He founded and serves as president of Tab Ramos Soccer Programs, which conduct camps, clinics, and coaching in New York, Pennsylvania, and his home state of New Jersey. He also founded the the Tab Ramos GOAL! Foundation, a non-profit organization helping inner city children through soccer and other sports. Ramos also helped found the New Jersey Soccer Academy.

Further reading: Allaway, Roger, and Colin Jose. *The United States Tackles the World Cup.* Haworth, NJ: Saint Johann Press, 2002.
http://www.soccerhall.org/famers/Tab_Ramos.htm (Soccer Hall of Fame Web page).

RANGEL, Irma
Legislator, Lawyer, Teacher

Irma Rangel was the first Mexican American woman to be elected to the Texas House of Representatives and the first woman to become chair of the Mexican American Legislative Caucus. A respected legislator, attorney, and teacher, Rangel helped pass a law in 1997 to give mandatory college and university admission to students in the top 10 percent of their high-school graduation classes.

Early life

Born in Kingsville, Texas, on May 15, 1931, Rangel was the daughter of Presiliano M. Rangel, a cottonpicker who went on to own several businesses, and Hermini Lerma. Rangel's mother emphasized the importance of education and encouraged her three daughters to go to college. Rangel's sister, Minnie, became a pharmacist and owned the only pharmacy catering to Mexican Americans in Kingsville. In 1970 Minnie became the first woman elected to the local school board.

From teaching to law

Influenced by her father's friend, the renowned attorney Gus García, Rangel wanted to study law, but with family bills to help pay, she chose instead to study business at Texas A&I University. After graduating in 1951, Rangel became a teacher. She joined the Peace Corps, working as a bilingual teacher in Caracas, Venezuela, for seven years. Following her return to the United States, Rangel taught in California before returning to Texas to enroll at St. Mary's University School of Law in San Antonio. Graduating in 1969, Rangel clerked for U.S. District Judge Adrian Spears. By 1973 she and Gus García had opened a law office, García and Rangel, in Kingsville. At the time, she was the only Mexican American female lawyer working in the state.

▲ **Irma Rangel had three successful careers: She was a teacher, lawyer, and state legislator.**

An important legislator

In 1976 Rangel, a Democrat, became the first Mexican American female to be elected to the Texas House of Representatives. Rangel immediately began to concentrate her skills on working to improve education and resources for the state's minority groups, poor, and the disenfranchised. In 1993, she closed her law practice to devote herself to politics full time. Rangel was responsible for sponsoring a great deal of influential legislation, including a bill that created the Texas grant program to assist low-income students with tuition for college. Her career was cut short by cancer, however. When undergoing chemotherapy, Rangel took to wearing a different hat each day to cover her baldness. In a show of solidarity, several members of the 78th legislative session donned hats similar to those worn by Rangel. She received many awards and honors before her death in 2003, including being inducted into the Texas Women's Hall of Fame.

See also: García, Gustavo C.

Further reading: http://www.abanet.org/publiced/rbir.html (obituary on the American Bar Association Web site).

KEY DATES

1931 Born in Kingsville, Texas, on May 15.

1969 Receives law degree from St. Mary's University School of Law in San Antonio.

1976 Becomes first Mexican American woman elected to the Texas House of Representatives; serves for 26 years.

1994 Inducted into Texas Women's Hall of Fame.

2003 Dies on March 18.

REBOZO, Charles
Banker

A shrewd Cuban American financier who turned his flair for making political connections into a fortune, Charles "Bebe" Rebozo is best known as President Richard M. Nixon's friend and adviser. While there is no doubt that Rebozo played a key role in the Watergate scandal that forced Nixon from office, the extent of any criminal involvement remains unclear.

Natural businessman

Charles Gregory Rebozo was born in Tampa, Florida, in 1912. He was the son of a Havana cigar maker. As the youngest of nine children, Charles was soon nicknamed "Bebe"—an Anglicized version of the Spanish for "baby."

Rebozo was a natural businessman. He made his first real-estate investment while still in high school. Although he made a loss on the venture, the experience awakened his passion for making money.

After graduating from high school in 1930, Rebozo decided to see the world, and became one of Pan-American Airways' first air stewards. He saved his wages, always keeping an eye out for lucrative opportunities. Rebozo eventually invested in inexpensive Florida real estate and a service station that sold retread tires.

Making it pay

In 1941, when the United States entered World War II (1939–1945), Rebozo profited from the increased demand for tires. Another big payoff came when his real estate investments soared during the postwar land boom.

The now-wealthy Rebozo entered Miami high society. By the late 1940s, as his fortune grew, he had become the central figure and guiding influence of a set of wealthy investors who poured their money into real estate. He

▲ *Charles Rebozo was a loyal supporter of and financial fixer for the administration of the disgraced U.S. president Richard M. Nixon.*

became acquainted with some of the most influential people in U.S. society. Among the contacts he made was the then congressional representative Richard M. Nixon.

Rebozo began to operate as Nixon's financial adviser and remained a faithful friend as Nixon became a U.S. senator, vice president, and then president in 1968. In 1974, Nixon resigned from office after the Watergate scandal, in which his supporters were found spying on his Democratic opponents during the 1972 presidential election. Rebozo's role in the scandal came under the scrutiny of a congressional committee. Despite evidence that he received secret donations on behalf of Nixon, and was also involved in many suspect financial dealings, Congress did not link Rebozo to any criminal wrongdoing. He died in Miami in 1998.

Further reading: http://foia.fbi.gov/foiaindex/
rebozo_charles_g.htm (FBI papers on Rebozo).

KEY DATES	
1912	Born in Tampa, Florida, on November 17.
1930	Becomes air steward for Pan-American Airways.
1950	Meets future president Richard M. Nixon.
1964	Founds a bank in Key Biscayne, Florida.
1974	Investigated by Congress for an alleged role in the Watergate scandal.
1998	Dies in Miami, Florida, on May 8.

RECHY, John
Writer

John Rechy is a Mexican American writer who continues to define contemporary gay literature from his double minority perspective as a gay male and a Chicano. Rechy's award-winning novels, plays, and essays have paved the way for many other gay male writers, especially those from Latino backgrounds.

Troubled youth

John Francisco Rechy, the youngest of five siblings, was born in the border city of El Paso, Texas, in 1934. His parents—Roberto Sixto Rechy, an aspiring but failed musician of Scottish-Spanish descent, and Guadalupe Flores Rechy, a Mexican who would become Rechy's muse—struggled to raise their children during the later years of the Great Depression (1929–1939).

Rechy's early life was plagued not only by poverty but also by a violent and distant father. As a refuge from that difficult relationship, Rechy pursued his artistic longings by becoming involved in acting and creative writing in high school. As a teenager, Rechy longed to escape El Paso by attending college in another city.

He failed in that ambition, however, and studied at Texas Western College (now the University of Texas, El Paso). On completing his undergraduate degree, Rechy enlisted in the U.S. Army. There his homosexuality, which he kept a strictly guarded secret, was further repressed. After his honorable discharge from the military, Rechy returned to college, this time to Columbia University in

▲ *John Rechy's infamous experiences as a hustler on the underside of New York life have inspired much of his unflinching and skillful writing.*

New York, the city that would shape his life and career. In Manhattan, Rechy became a male hustler (prostitute), a role that would later inspire and inform the action of his first major novel.

Life in New York

After years of earning money from sexual encounters with strangers, Rechy began to write about his experiences, at first in the form of a letter to a friend. The letter eventually became a short story, which was published in the radical magazine *Evergreen Review*. Its success inspired Rechy to develop the work further. The result was a novel, *City of Night,* which was published in 1963. With a cutting edge and street-smart prose, Rechy's full-length fiction debut broke new ground with its guileless narrative of explicit sexuality in the semifictionalized world of hustling. It sparked a revolution in gay literature, and created intense controversy over its portrait of one young man's sexual journey in a bleak urban underworld.

City of Night received a mixed critical reception on its first appearance. Some reviewers claimed that the work could not have been written by Rechy because he was a hustler, and as such must be "less than intelligent." Despite such reservations, the novel topped the best-seller list, and was later translated into eight languages. It turned

KEY DATES

1934 Born in El Paso, Texas, to Roberto Sixto and Guadalupe (Flores) Rechy.

1951 Aged 17, Rechy writes his first novel, *Time on Wings,* a historical narrative.

1963 Grove Press publishes Rechy's classic debut novel *City of Night.*

1977 Rechy writes *The Sexual Outlaw: A Documentary.* The novel marks the public declaration of Rechy as an outspoken gay activist.

1997 Rechy receives the PEN-USA-West Lifetime Achievement Award.

2004 Carroll & Graf publishes Rechy's collection of essays titled *Beneath the Skin: The Collected Essays of John Rechy.*

INFLUENCES AND INSPIRATION

Despite the unusually bold and gritty realism of many of his books, perhaps Rechy's most inspired work has been *Memories and Desire: Searching the Worlds of John Rechy*. Produced on CD-ROM, this work challenges the borders between autobiography, memory, and history. Drawing themes from *Autobiography, a Novel* (a work in progress) and passages from Rechy's published writings, it assembles a network of personal memories and family documents, setting them against larger collective histories of Chicano culture and the gay world. Combining drawings and family photographs, historic documents, film footage, taped interviews, word games, and representations of the male body, and rearranging them into three interrelated realms, it provides a wide range of interfaces that can be used to solve mysteries or generate new fictions.

the male prostitute into an award-winning author who was soon in demand as a lecturer in colleges throughout the United States.

Prolific novelist

During the late 1960s and early 1970s, Rechy produced a rapid succession of novels, including *Numbers* (1967), *This Day's Death* (1969), *The Vampires* (1971), and *The Fourth Angel* (1973). Each of the works examined loneliness, faith, death, sexuality, identity, and loss. *The Fourth Angel* was particularly moving, because it was inspired by the death of Rechy's mother.

Despite his continuing success as an author, Rechy continued to work as a street hustler. His experiences were angrily poured into *The Sexual Outlaw: A Documentary* (1977), an experimental nonfiction account of the relationship between desire, homosexuality, and the law. The book became a celebrated work of gay literature, and was named as one of the 100 Best Nonfiction Books of the 20th Century by the *San Francisco Chronicle*.

Broadening themes

During the 1980s and early 1990s, Rechy broadened his range with novels such as *Bodies and Souls* (1983), *Marilyn's Daughter* (1988), and the outstanding *The Miraculous Day of Amalia Gomez* (1992). The last-named work earned the author recognition in the world of Chicano literature through its semiautobiographical portrait of life in Los Angeles from the perspective of a Mexican American woman.

In his later writing, Rechy often revisited previously established themes. *The Coming of the Night*, for example, echoes his debut novel, both in title and in plot; on its publication in 1999, the work went straight to number two on the *Los Angeles Times'* best-seller list. Yet he did not restrict his range too tightly. In the following year, he broke new ground with *Memories and Desire: Searching the*

Worlds of John Rechy, a CD-ROM that explored the nature of memory, autobiography, narrative, and imagery. The innovative work was launched at the Museum of Modern Art in Los Angeles, and then became a traveling exhibition that was shown across the United States and Europe. The experiment further enhanced Rechy's growing reputation. The year 2002 saw the publication of *Outlaw: The Lives and Careers of John Rechy*, a detailed and explicit biography of the author by Charles Casillo.

Rechy's later works include *The Life and Adventures of Lyle Clemens* (2003), a novel, and *Beneath the Skin: The Collected Essays of John Rechy* (2004).

A literary legacy

City of Night was greeted with skepticism and hostility on its original publication, but it is now widely regarded as a literary classic. That development may be attributed in part to the fact that Rechy has in the meantime become a prolific author. The large body of subsequent work has confounded critics who predicted that he would find no more to say after his controversial debut. As his confidence as a writer has grown, Rechy has branched out from autobiographical prose to explore the lives and experiences of a range of Mexican Americans in urban settings. His writing has earned him numerous honors, including the 1997 PEN-USA-West's Lifetime Achievement Award and the 1999 Publishing Triangle's William Whitehead Award for Lifetime Achievement. He has lectured at Harvard, Yale, and Duke universities, and currently teaches on the Master of Professional Writing Program at the University of Southern California.

From humble beginnings, John Rechy has become an icon of both gay and Mexican American literature.

Further reading: Casillo, Charles. *Outlaw: The Lives and Careers of John Rechy*. Los Angeles, CA: Advocate Books, 2002. http://www.johnrechy.com (tribute Web site).

RELIGION

The overwhelming majority of the United States's 40 million Latinos and Latinas are Roman Catholic Christians. In 2000, according to that year's census, between 70 and 75 percent of all Mexican Americans, Cuban Americans, and Puerto Ricans above age six were members of the Catholic Church. Of the remainder, the largest group was Protestant (22 percent); there were also Jews, and a small number of Muslims (about 15,000).

Historical background
Catholicism was first introduced into the Americas in 1519 by Hernán Cortés, who was accompanied by priests on his voyage from Spain to Mexico. The territories colonized by Spain were conquered in the name of Jesus as well as that of the Spanish monarchs. The Spanish authorities forced many natives to convert to Christianity. One consequence of the Spanish approach to empire-building was that the church

became strongly associated with the ruling orders. Whenever the people came into conflict with the government, there was often a related loss of confidence in the state religion.

Catholicism dislodged the pre-Columbian religions, but it did not entirely displace them. There is plentiful evidence that Latino

Catholics attend a service at the Cathedral of Our Lady of the Angels in Los Angeles, California.

MARÍA DE JESÚS DE ÁGREDA

Although she probably spent her whole life in Spain, and certainly never visited the New World, María de Jesús de Ágreda played a prominent role in the religious history of the U.S. Southwest.

Born in Ágreda, Spain, in the early 17th century, María Coronel y Arana was a gifted child who longed to journey to the New World to preach. As a female, however, she was not permitted to travel. Instead, she decided to devote her life to Christ as a nun. In 1620, she took the name Sister Maria of Jesus, and entered a convent.

One day, while at prayer, she imagined herself on a visit to Native Americans. Her vision helped create an unusual legend.

In 1629 a delegation of 50 Jumano Native Americans visited the Franciscan mission at Isleta, near Albuquerque (modern New Mexico). They claimed that a "Lady in Blue" had taught them about Christianity, and told them to seek baptism at the local mission. The Jumanos described in detail the woman's facial features and attire.

The Catholic church then investigated the Lady in Blue. Alonso de Benavides, in charge of missions in New Mexico, interviewed the Jumanos. When he later returned to Spain to deliver his mission report, the *Memorial of 1630*, he learned of a nun who told her superiors about visiting America in a vision to convert the Jumanos. After interviewing Sister Maria, Benavides concluded that her descriptions of the Jumanos, their chief, and the New Mexico terrain, were accurate, and that the Jumanos' description of her was also accurate.

Sister Maria wrote several spiritual books, and began a lengthy biography of Mary, mother of Jesus, entitled *Mystical City of God*. King Philip IV of Spain heard about the extraordinary author, and visited her in 1643 on his way to war on the Spanish frontier. They began a correspondence that produced more than 600 letters, which have survived.

The Lady in Blue died in 1665, but her legend and reputation remain undimmed by the passage of time: *Mystical City of God* is still in print, and has sold 210,000 copies since 1978 in the United States alone.

Catholicism combines the conventional Christian doctrine put forth by the Vatican (the religion's world headquarters in Rome, Italy) and older, traditional, pagan observances. For example, Mexican Americans may still employ the services of *curanderos* (folk healers), in spite of the hostility of the church to what it regards as a superstitious practice. Further examples of the phenomenon are the popularity of the Virgin of Guadalupe (*see box on page 36*) and the ritual celebration of the Day of the Dead (*see box on page 38*).

Three-way struggle
In Spain's colonial territories, the church and the state were in theory a single entity, and attempted to speak with one voice. In practice, however, their aims were often conflicting. Both wanted the greater say in government, each was envious of the other's influence, and neither was willing to renounce its title to property. As a result, throughout much of the period of Spanish rule in the Americas, there was a three-way struggle between politicians, priests, and people. The tension was particularly intense in Mexico, and when the country gained independence from Spain in 1821, the new republic introduced measures to limit the power and influence of the church, which by that time owned between one-quarter and one-half of all the land, and controled most of the nation's schools and hospitals.

In 1833 the Mexican government took the education system out of church control. It also ended compulsory tithes, an ancient system that required all citizens to give one-tenth of all their earnings or produce to the church. Mexico then lost more than half of its territory to the United States in the Mexican War (1846–1848). Thereafter the church was divided in two, and each part developed along different lines.

Mexican American Catholicism
The 1848 Treaty of Guadalupe Hidalgo that ended the Mexican War turned approximately 100,000 Mexican Catholics overnight into U.S. citizens. Their relationship with the church into which they had been baptized was often

strained—many of them were routinely exploited by the religious authorities—but under the new flag their plight deteriorated even further. Many Mexican Americans were alienated from the U.S. Catholic church by a variety of factors, principally its failure to combat the injustices to which they were subjected.

English scripture

Another problem was language. Christianity is to a large extent a graphocentric religion—in other words, it is dependent on an understanding of written texts. Since most poor Mexicans were illiterate, they depended for their knowledge of the Bible on sermons and homilies delivered

The church of San José de Laguna was formerly the focal point of a Spanish mission in New Mexico.

by their priests in their own language. For as long as their homes had been in Mexico, they had been accustomed to communicating with church authorities in their native Spanish. However, as vacancies occurred in Southwest parishes, the U.S. Catholic church gradually filled them with Anglo-American priests,

most of whom spoke only English. Mexican Americans thus derived little benefit from going to church.

Unconventional worship

The development of religion in the U.S. Southwest after 1848 reflected the fact that, while Roman Catholicism was imposed on all Spanish conquests, the

KEY DATES	
1492	Christopher Columbus reaches the New World.
1519	Hernán Cortés conquers Mexico for Spain.
1821	Mexico becomes an independent republic.
1833	Mexican government wrests schools from Roman Catholic control.
1848	Defeated in the Mexican War (1846–1848), Mexico cedes more than half its territory to the victorious United States by the Treaty of Guadalupe Hidalgo.
1952	Separation of church and state enshrined in commonwealth constitution of Puerto Rico.
1961	Revolutionary dictator Fidel Castro closes all religious schools in Cuba.

THE VIRGIN OF GUADALUPE

According to legend, the Virgin of Guadalupe appeared to Juan Diego in December 1531 on Tepeyac Hill, outside Mexico City. The young man, who had been known by his Nahuatl name, Cuautlatohuac, before his conversion to Catholicism, spoke no Spanish, but the apparition spoke to him in Nahuatl.

The meaning of the tale is widely debated. In the Catholic interpretation, the apparition is the Virgin Mary come to welcome Native Americans into her protection. An alternative version sees her as the Aztec goddess, Tonantzin, disguised. (Tepeyac, where she appeared to Juan Diego, was the site of an Aztec temple to Tonantzin that had been razed by Hernán Cortés.)

The legend is an enduring example of the cross-fertilization that has continually occurred between indigenous North American religious practices and the Catholicism imported from Europe in the 16th century.

The Virgin of Guadalupe was painted in 1824 by Isidro Escamilla. It is housed in the Brooklyn Museum, New York.

converts had not been entirely passive recipients of the new creed. As it became clear to Mexican Americans that the church represented the interests of the ruling elite rather than their own, they increasingly adapted the religion for their own spiritual purposes. While the Vatican combated such heresy when it occurred in Europe, it was poorly positioned to intervene effectively in a vast and sparsely populated territory on the far side of the Atlantic Ocean. The Catholic church in the U.S. Southwest was thus free to develop a distinctive character, which was at once Roman and Latino. In the late 19th century, many Mexican American Catholics greatly reduced the number of times they went to church services. They did not lose their faith, however. They maintained religious observances, such as holy days, in small groups away from the established church.

The church authorities were dismayed by the rapid increase in unsanctioned practices, such as secular marriage. They particularly disapproved of the proliferation of *altarcitos* (home altars), and domestic *retablos* (painted wooden panels depicting religious or intimate personal stories). According to conventional church doctrine, such icons should only be displayed on consecrated ground.

Yet Mexican Americans did not reject U.S. Catholic institutions and sacraments entirely; rather, they picked and chose those they wanted. Attendances at Mass dwindled, but absentees typically returned for baptisms, confirmations, and funerals.

Cuba and Puerto Rico

The evolution of the church in the U.S. Southwest was reflected to some extent in Cuba. The Spanish imposed Catholicism in the 1500s, and the religion became predominant throughout the island. It was never exclusive, however, and its character was altered in the late-16th century through the arrival of African slaves, who brought with them, mainly from Nigeria, various Yoruba traditions that became synthesized with Catholicism.

Until 1959, most Cubans described themselves as Roman Catholic, despite the fact that only a minority of them attended church regularly. After that year's takeover of the island by Fidel Castro, the revolutionary government became increasingly anticlerical. In 1961 it took control of education, and closed all religious schools. Many priests left the country or were deported. The Pope, in protest, withdrew his ambassador, the papal nuncio. Gradually, however, relations between church and state improved, and in 1974 the Vatican

restored diplomatic links with Havana. After more than a decade of suppression, religion was again practiced openly, and became attractive to many Cubans as a focus of opposition to the regime (political opposition was largely suppressed). The Catholic church introduced classes in democracy. In a controversial 1995 pastoral letter, the Church suggested that any denial of individual will was a violation of human rights. Both actions were openly hostile to Castro's government.

The Catholic Church thus increased both its popularity and its membership, but it was not the only beneficiary. Large numbers of Cubans also joined Protestant denominations, including the Methodists and the Presbyterians, and evangelical sects, such as the Pentecostalists and the Seventh-day Adventists.

Another religion that grew in influence at about this time was Santería, a synthesis of Catholicism and various West and Central African religions that had been brought to Cuba by slaves in the 1800s. A minority cult for more than a century, Santería grew in the antireligious climate created by Castro into an integral part of Cuban—and later of Cuban American—culture.

In Puerto Rico, the constitution of 1952 demands complete separation of church and state. Perhaps as a result, the influence of Roman Catholic customs and traditions has remained consistently powerful on the island, with few of the ebbs and flows witnessed in the U.S. Southwest and in Cuba. Nevertheless, Christianity in Puerto Rico has also been influenced by slaves from Africa.

Modern trends

Even before Mexico gained independence from Spain, the Catholic Church in the country had been moving away from its European counterpart. This move was accelerated in the Southwest after the U.S. conquest by linguistic and cultural factors. Under U.S. rule, Mexican Americans held tenaciously to their own brand of Catholicism, which they had forged to meet their particular needs, specifically as a consolation for their poverty and oppression, and as a focus for their sense of racial identity. They remained Catholics on their own terms, and used their religion to sustain and celebrate their existence.

In the 1990s, the number of Latinos in the United States increased by 10 percent to 31 million. Church attendances rose dramatically, but the figures partly reflected the massive influx of new Hispanic immigrants from Latin America. Substantial numbers of longer-established Hispanic Americans had not just quit going to church, they had abandoned Catholicism altogether. According to some surveys, the proportion of Catholics among Mexican Americans falls from a starting point of about 75 percent to 72 percent in the second generation, and 62 percent in the third. Research into the causes of the decline is sketchy, and the findings inconclusive. One possible contributory factor was the secular spirit of the age: Significant numbers of U.S. citizens of every heritage became detached from religion, which they came to regard as irrelevant. Some Catholic church policies—such as the refusal to ordain women and the

THE DAY OF THE DEAD

Despite its name, el Día de los Muertos (the Day of the Dead) is not a morbid occasion, but a holiday during which Mexican families honor the deceased and celebrate the continuity of life. The original celebration can be traced back thousands of years to native Mesoamerican traditions. In the Aztec calendar, the ritual was held at the end of July or the beginning of August. In the Spanish colonial era priests changed the date to November 1 to bring it into line with All Saints' Day (*Día de todos santos*). They hoped thus to supplant the indigenous observance by creating a sympathetic link between it and a Christian holiday. In fact, the Catholic church succeeded in persuading Mexicans to postpone their Día de los Muertos celebrations until November 1, but still could not eradicate the original spirit of the celebration.

In the 21st century, the Day of the Dead is characterized by a blend of Christian theology and folk traditions, such as the widespread use of skull motifs. The holiday is celebrated differently in various regions, but generally consists of rituals in which families welcome and honor the dead. In the United States and in Mexico's larger cities, altars adorned with flowers, candles, pictures of the deceased, and burning candles are set up in people's homes. In rural Mexico, people visit cemeteries to decorate the graves of loved ones with brightly colored flowers and candles. In the belief that the souls of the dead have returned and are near to the living, a warm atmosphere, complete with food and drink, is created to receive them. While feasting with the dead, the revellers are reminded of their own mortality.

ban on the use of contraception—sparked crises of faith among progressive and liberal communicants. Another reason for the decline may be the increasing urbanization of what was formerly a mainly rural population: Sociologists have frequently observed that organized religion is more important to country folk than to city-dwellers.

Faith and worship

Latino attendance at church remains relatively low. At the start of the 21st century, only 53 percent of all Hispanic Americans were regular parishioners, against 71 percent of Anglo-American Catholics. Among Mexican Americans, the figures were even lower: While 70 percent identified themselves as Catholics, 46.8 percent claimed never to attend religious services. That is a continuation of a strongly established historical trend: Latino Catholicism can seldom be measured by the size of church congregations, which never fully recovered from their decline in the late 19th century. More reliable indicators of faith are the massive public rituals in which Latino Catholics express their devotion to Christ, the Eucharist, the Virgin Mary, and particular patron saints. In New York, Miami, Los Angeles, Washington, D.C., and other areas with significant Latino populations, Catholic feast days are celebrated and religious traditions marked by street processions, outdoor masses and prayer services, and other public manifestations of faith that have altered the character of numerous U.S. communities.

The future

For more than 150 years, Latino Catholicism was intricately linked to notions of Hispanic American identity. At the start of the 21st century, however, many U.S. Latinos and Latinas appeared to be moving away from the church in numerous directions, not all of which have been charted. The impact, if any, of that development on U.S. society as a whole is hard to predict with any certainty.

See also: Guadalupe Hidalgo, Treaty of; Immigration and Immigration Law

---

Further reading: Dolan, Jay P., and Gilberto M. Hinojosa (eds.). *Mexican Americans and the Catholic Church, 1900–1965*. Notre Dame, IN: University of Notre Dame Press, 1994.
Poole, Stafford. *Our Lady of Guadalupe: The Origins and Sources of a Mexican National Symbol, 1531–1797*. Tucson, AZ: University of Arizona Press, 1995.
Redinger, Matthew. *American Catholics and the Mexican Revolution, 1924–1936*. Notre Dame, IN: University of Notre Dame Press, 2005.

REYES, Guillermo
Playwright

A first-generation Chilean American, Guillermo Reyes is a playwright best known for such witty and provocative plays as *Men on the Verge of a His-Panic Breakdown* (1994) and *Deporting the Divas* (1996). While he uses his work to explore a wide variety of themes associated with the experience of Hispanic immigrants, Reyes, who is gay, also writes about the particular problems facing homosexual and bisexual Latino men. Since 1996 Reyes has been an assistant professor at Arizona State University at Tempe, where he directs the playwriting program.

Early life
Guillermo Reyes was born in Chile in 1962. His father left the family home and his mother, Maria Cáceras, moved to the United States in 1970 in search of work; Reyes followed her a year later. They eventually settled in Los Angeles, California, and Reyes became a U.S. citizen. After high school, Reyes studied Italian at the University of California at Los Angeles. In 1987 he was accepted into a postgraduate playwriting program at the university's San Diego campus.

Making a name as a playwright
In 1990 Reyes returned to Los Angeles, and from 1992 to 1996 he was literary manager at the Los Angeles Bilingual Foundation for the Arts, an organization that promotes Hispanic plays. He first won acclaim with *Men on the Verge of a His-Panic Breakdown*; first performed by a gay theater

group in Los Angeles in 1994, it later transferred to play Off-Broadway. The play takes the form of nine monologues, in which seven gay Hispanic men from different backgrounds recount their experiences as homosexuals, Hispanics, and immigrants. A recurring character is a poor young immigrant named Federico; he finds himself turned away by the very same Anglo men who had sought out his company in his native country. The play earned Reyes an Emerging Playwright award. His 1996 play *Deporting the Divas*, the story of a Mexican American border patrolman who falls in love with an undocumented Mexican immigrant, was also a critical success.

In 1996 Reyes moved to Arizona to become an associate professor at Arizona State University. Since then, Reyes has continued to write prolifically for the theater, sometimes premiering works with the Phoenix-based Hispanic troupe Teatro Bravo, of which he is a founding member along with Trino Sandoval and Daniel Enrique Pérez. Among his more recent plays are *Mother Lolita* (2000) and *Places to Touch Him* (2002), the latter the tale of a gay Hispanic lawyer and politician.

Hispanic, gifted, and gay
In his portrayal of gay Latinos, Reyes examines how it is often not so much sexuality that makes their lives difficult but a combination of factors, such as being gay, Hispanic, and poor. Reyes's works are full of Hispanic references and slang, and this sometimes makes them difficult for Anglo audiences to appreciate. His supporters claim that he has also been largely overlooked by Latino theater companies because they do not know what to do with his material, and favor more traditional expressions of Latino culture. His primary audience is still largely gay. Reyes says, "You'd think if art is done well, it should reach beyond one particular group."

Reyes has won two Ovation Awards from Theater L.A. for *Men on the Verge*, the National Hispanic Playwrights' Contest for *A Southern Christmas*, and the 2002 AriZoni Award for Original Play Production for *Miss Consuelo*.

KEY DATES	
1962	Born in Chile.
1971	Immigrates to the United States.
1987	Begins MA at UC-San Diego.
1994	Premiere of *Men on the Verge of a His-Panic Breakdown* in Los Angeles.
1996	Appointed assistant professor at Arizona State University, Tempe; wins Emerging Playwright Award for *Men on the Verge*.
2002	Wins the AriZoni Award for Original Play and Original Play Production for *Miss Consuelo*; forms Teatro Bravo with colleagues Trino Sandoval and Daniel Enrique Pérez.

Further reading: Nelson, Emmanuel S. (ed.). *Contemporary Gay American Poets and Playwrights: An A-to-Z Guide*. Westport, CT: Greenwood Press, 2003.
http://andrejkoymasky.com/liv/fam/bior2/reye1.html (short biography.)

REYNA, María Torres
Businesswoman

The Houston busineswoman María "Mary" Torres Reyna is best remembered for her efforts to improve American and Mexican relations, which were acknowledged by the Mexican president, José Lopez Portillo. She was also actively involved in many charities and community organizations.

Early life

Born on January 13, 1911, in Piedras Negas, Coahuila, Mexico, María de Torres was one of seven children. Her parents owned a vaudeville theater. Having completed her education in her hometown, Torres married José Ángel Reyna, a car mechanic, at the age of 16.

Soon after the wedding, the couple moved to Houston, Texas. Once he had sufficient funds, José Ángel Reyna set up a car garage business. Reyna and her husband eventually had five children, and adopted a further three. Reyna took various jobs despite the growing demands of her family. In the 1930s, she sold clothes door-to-door and later ran a fruit stall. She carefully saved money to fulfill a long-held ambition of becoming a florist. She worked for free in local florists in order to learn the business.

◀ *María Torres Reyna was a leading businesswoman who donated money to a wide range of charities, and became active in the civil rights movement.*

Success

In 1947 Reyna finally opened her own shop. It became a very successful enterprise, a rare achievement for a woman at the time, let alone one of Hispanic origin. Reyna soon became known as the "Queen of the flowers" because of her readiness to donate her services free to poor families and charities. Reyna also became increasingly involved in politics. She was a founding member of a women's council attached to the League of United Latin American Citizens (LULAC). She also worked with the Hispanic Business and Professional Women's Club. Reyna assisted many charities, including a Mexican orphanage and the American Cancer Society.

Rewarding the community

In 1975 Reyna organized "The Day of Appreciation" to recognize all those who had made a contribution to the Mexican American community. She presented awards to noteworthy individuals in front of more than 1,000 people. In the same decade she contributed a weekly column on local issues to the Spanish-language newspaper *El Presente*. She also spoke about Mexican American affairs on Spanish- and English-language radio and television programs. Between 1980 and 1984, Reyna was president of Comité Patriótico Mexicano, aiming to improve relations between Mexico and the United States. The recipient of many honors and awards, María Torres Reyna died in 1987.

Further reading: http://www.tsha.utexas.edu/handbook/online/articles/RR/fre59.html (Handbook of Texas Online biographical article on Reyna).

KEY DATES	
1911	Born in Piedras Negas, Mexico, on January 13.
1927	Marries José Ángel Reyna.
1947	Opens first florist shop.
1935	Helps to found LULAC's Ladies Council 22.
1980	Becomes president of Comité Patriótico Mexicano.
1984	Comité Patriótico Mexicano names her Houston's Ambassador of Good Faith.
1987	Dies in Houston, Texas.

RICHARDSON, Bill
Governor, Congressman, Ambassador

Bill Richardson is a respected and influential U.S. congressman. He was elected governor of New Mexico in 2002, having previously served as U.S. ambassador to the United Nations and secretary of energy. Some political commentators consider Richardson to be a likely Democratic candidate for a future presidential election.

Bicultural roots
Born in 1947 in Pasadena, California, William Blaine Richardson was the son of William Richardson and Maria Louisa Lopez Collada, a Mexican national. Richardson's father was an executive with Citibank who transferred to work in Mexico City, where Richardson and his sister,

▼ *Bill Richardson is viewed by many political commentators as a possible future U.S. president.*

Vesta, enjoyed a privileged upbringing. Richardson attended Middlesex, a prep school in Concord, Massachusetts, as a teenager. He excelled as a baseball pitcher. After graduating in 1966, Richardson went to Tufts University, Massachusetts, majoring in political science and French. After earning a BA in 1970, Richardson began his graduate studies at the university's Fletcher School of Law and Diplomacy. On finishing his MA, Richardson spent seven years obtaining valuable experience as a staff member on the U.S. House of Representatives, the State Department, and Senator Hubert Humphrey's powerful Foreign Relations Committee. During that time he married antiques dealer Barbara Flavin in 1972.

New Mexico becomes home
Richardson entered business in 1978 as a trade consultant based in Santa Fe. His first attempt at elective office came in 1980; he took on entrenched incumbent congressman Manuel Luján for the job of representing the 1st congressional district of New Mexico in Washington, D.C., but lost by a narrow margin. Two years later, Richardson ran again and won with 67 percent of the vote in the newly drawn 3rd congressional district that covered a widely diverse population of Native Americans, Latinos, and whites living in northern New Mexico.

A popular politician
Richardson's bicultural upbringing, his exceptional academic credentials, and his broad experience in Washington, D.C., served him well, not only in convincing voters to elect him, but also in enabling Richardson to effectively represent them. Richardson proved so popular with his constituents that they elected him to serve eight two-year terms.

While in the U.S. House of Representatives, Richardson served on several important committees, and rose in the ranks of the House Democratic leadership, earning the post of chief deputy majority whip in 1992. In that role, Richardson lined up votes among his Democratic colleagues for passing key legislation in the administration of President Bill Clinton. Richardson traveled to world trouble spots, such as North Korea, Haiti, Cuba, and Iraq, where he successfully represented U.S. interests. Richardson's work as an emissary resulted in his nomination for the Nobel Peace Prize in 1995.

Bill Richardson has said that one of his biggest influences is his family. Richardson's parents, William and Luisa, taught him to respect both his U.S. and Latino heritages. His father talked with him in English, and his mother in Spanish. Richardson learned to speak and think fluently in both languages.

When Richardson first ran for Congress in 1980, an adviser suggested that he take his mother's maiden name, Lopez, to attract the Hispanic vote. He refused, claiming that it was too obvious a ploy. Richardson has had a successful career without having to resort to such tactics. He claims that having an Anglo name and speaking fluent Spanish provided him with an advantage in relating to his own diverse constituency in New Mexico. Richardson's upbringing also taught him to be more aware of and sensitive to different cultures. An effective diplomat and peacekeeper, Richardson helped to negotiate the release of two U.S. pilots shot down in North Korea; he also persuaded U.S. military leaders to meet with the Burmese civil rights leader Aung San Suu Kyi.

Key posts in Clinton administration

Following his reelection in 1996, President Bill Clinton appointed Richardson to replace Madeleine Korbel Albright as U.S. ambassador to the United Nations. In that post, Richardson capitalized on his wide experience in foreign relations, promoting peace, democracy, and human rights.

In 1998, Clinton appointed Richardson to his cabinet as secretary of energy, a post that he held until the end of the president's term in 2000. In that position, Richardson advised the president on all matters related to energy, including its production, distribution and regulation, and oversaw the Department of Energy.

One of the most controversial issues that arose when Richardson was secretary of energy occurred at the Los Alamos National Laboratory, which falls under the supervision of the Department of Energy. The laboratory had acquired a reputation for lax security, and Taiwanese-born nuclear scientist Wen Ho Lee became the focus of a government inquiry into alleged Chinese espionage. Believing that Lee might present a threat to U.S. national security, Richardson fired him. After a two-year fight, Lee eventually managed to clear his name, and Richardson was criticized for his involvement in Lee's dismissal.

New Mexico's governorship beckons

Richardson returned to New Mexico to run for governor. He beat John Sanchez in 2002 to become the only Hispanic governor serving in the nation. A dedicated self-publicist, Richardson set a world record for the number of hands shaken in one day during the 2002 race. After his election Richardson was almost immediately at the forefront of the news: A group of North Korean diplomats visited him to ask for his help in preventing a nuclear standoff with the United States. The press gathered at Richardson's mansion to report on the phone calls between the new governor and Secretary of State Colin Powell.

In 2004, Bill Richardson was reelected for a second term. In addition to governing the state, Richardson has served as chairman of the Democratic Governor's Association, and was chairman of both the Western Governor's Association and the 2004 Democratic Convention. In 2006, many media commentators speculated that Richardson might stand as the Democratic Party candidate for the 2008 presidency.

See also: Luján, Manuel, Jr.

Further reading: Richardson, Bill. *Between Worlds: The Making of an American Life*. New York, NY: Putnam Publishing Group, 2005.
http/www.governor.state.nm.us/index2.php (information on Richardson and policies on the governor of New Mexico's site).

KEY DATES

1947 Born in Pasadena, California, on November 15.

1971 Receives MA from Tufts University's Fletcher School of Law and Diplomacy.

1972 Marries Barbara Flavin.

1983 Becomes Democratic U.S. congressman from New Mexico until 1997.

1997 Becomes U.S. ambassador to United Nations, secretary of energy through 2000.

2002 Elected governor of New Mexico.

2004 Reelected for a second term of office.

RIOS, Alberto
Writer

Alberto Rios is best known as the award-winning author of hundreds of poems, three collections of short stories, and a memoir, but he has also written nonfiction and drama. His work closely reflects his experience of growing up in the United States near the Mexican border.

Publication

Rios was born in the small town of Nogales, Arizona, in 1952, to a Mexican father and an English mother. Most of his family spoke only Spanish. Their home was full of books, and Rios started to read at an early age. By second grade, Rios was writing for pleasure, and by junior high school it had become his main pastime. Rios loved the fantasy and escapism that books could offer.

After high school, Rios studied English literature and creative writing at the University of Arizona in Tucson. Unsure how to become a writer, he took a degree in psychology to help his chances of getting into law school.

Rios quit law school after a year, and went on a creative writing course in 1979. While there, he won the highly respected Walt Whitman Award, which included publication as part of the prize. Rios's first book, a collection of poetry entitled *Whispering to Fool the Wind,* was published to acclaim in 1982.

▼ *Alberto Rios is an acclaimed Chicano writer, combining Mexican and Anglo influences in his work.*

KEY DATES

1952   Born in Nogales, Arizona, on September 18.

1979   Wins Walt Whitman award.

1982   Publishes *Whispering to Fool the Wind,* an award-winning collection of verse.

1984   *The Iguana Killer: Twelve Stories of the Heart* wins the Western States Book Award.

1986   Wins the Pushcart Prize for fiction.

2000   Receives Latino Literary Hall of Fame Award.

2002   Finalist for the National Book Award; winner of the Western Literature Association's Distinguished Achievement Award.

Many volumes of poetry and short story collections followed, including *Five Indiscretions* (1985) and *The Lime Orchard Woman* (1988). Rios's work has been included in more than 90 international collections, including *The Norton Anthology of Modern Poetry.*

Themes and inspiration

Much of Rios's writing uses the oral traditions of his Latino heritage, and draws deeply on stories he was told by his father about growing up in Mexico. Rios's work also features a blend of fantasy and realism inspired by fables about kings, castles, and rolling countryside told to him as a child by his English mother. *The Iguana Killer: Twelve Stories of the Heart* (1984) reveals both these influences.

Capirotada (1999) is a memoir about growing up in Nogales. Religion, sin, and salvation are regular themes. Rios was raised as a Catholic, but also celebrated the Mexican festival, the Day of the Dead, and believed that the spirits of dead family members return one day a year.

As well as winning numerous awards, Rios has received various fellowships, including one from the Guggenheim Foundation. He is a Regents Professor of English at Arizona State University, and teaches creative writing and literature. He lives in Chandler, Arizona.

Further reading: Rios, Alberto. *Capirotada: A Nogales Memoir.* Albuquerque, NM: University of New Mexico Press, 1999. http://www.public.asu.edu/~aarios (Alberto Rios's Web site).

RIVERA, Chita
Singer, Dancer, Actor

For more than 40 years, Chita Rivera helped shape the face of American theater. Rivera's achievements on the stage have provided inspiration to many young Latinas.

Early life

Dolores Conchita Figueroa del Rivero was born in 1933 in Washington, D.C. Both her parents were from Puerto Rico: Her father, Pedro Julio Figueroa, was a musician, and her mother, Katherine Anderson del Rivero, worked for the Pentagon. After her father died, her mother encouraged the 11-year-old girl to study at the Jones-Hayward School of Ballet.

A talented dancer, Rivera was picked at age 15 by an American Ballet scout for an audition in New York City. Her performance led her to be accepted into the George Balanchine School of American Ballet on a scholarship. By the age of 19, Rivera had won a role in *Call Me Madam* on Broadway. She was later cast in several more theater productions.

Groundbreaking achievements

Rivera worked with several well-known artists such as the "Rat Pack" member Sammy Davis, Jr., and actor and singer-dancer Liza Minnelli. In 1957, she won critical acclaim for her performance in Leonard Bernstein's 1957 Broadway stage show, *West Side Story*. Based on William

▲ **Chita Rivera received critical acclaim for her performance as Anita in** West Side Story.

Shakespeare's play *Romeo and Juliet*, the musical transposed the romance to modern-day New York, and examined racial tensions between white Americans and Puerto Ricans. Rivera played Anita, a role later performed by Rita Moreno in the 1961 movie version of the same title. Rivera met her future husband, fellow dancer Tony Mordente, in the show: The couple married later that year.

Rivera also appeared in movies and on television: She won praise for her performance as Nickie in the movie *Sweet Charity*. She also made guest appearances on popular TV shows, such as the *Judy Garland Show*.

Rivera received two Tony awards, one in 1984 for her role in *The Rink*, and the other in 1993 for her performance in *Kiss of the Spider Woman*. She also received six Tony Award nominations. In 2002, Rivera became the first Hispanic female to receive the Kennedy Center Honors Award. Four years later, she immortalized her life in the biographical show *Chita Rivera: The Dancer's Life*.

See also: Moreno, Rita

Further reading: Kantor, Michael, and Laurence Maslon. *Broadway: The American Musical*. New York, NY; Bulfinch Press, 2004.
www.chitarivera.com (official Web site)

KEY DATES

1933 Born in Washington, D.C., on January 23.

1944 Enters Jones-Hayward School of Ballet.

1952 Wins a role in the Broadway production *Call Me Madam*.

1957 Stars as Anita in *West Side Story*.

1984 Receives first Tony Award and six additional nominations.

1993 Receives Tony Award for Best Leading Actress for *Kiss of the Spiderwoman*.

2002 Becomes the first Latina to receive the Kennedy Center Honors Award.

2006 Puts on the biographical show *Chita Rivera: The Dancer's Life*.

RIVERA, Geraldo
Journalist, Attorney

A masterful self-promoter, champion of the oppressed, popular talk show host, and journalist, Geraldo Miguel Rivera is a complex and contradictory figure.

Early life
Born in 1943 in New York City, Rivera is the product of a bicultural union between Cruz Rivera, his Puerto Rican father, and Lilly Friedman, his Jewish mother. After graduating from school, Rivera earned a BS from the University of Arizona in 1965, after which he received his law degree from Brooklyn Law School in 1969. He also studied at Columbia University School of Journalism.

A career in the public eye
After Columbia, Rivera began working as an attorney. He represented the Young Lords, a group of Puerto Rican activists. When the group occupied an East Harlem church in 1970, Rivera was interviewed on WABC-TV. He was subsequently hired as a reporter by the station's news director. In 1972 Rivera broke an important story about the horrific abuse of thousands of mentally challenged patients at New York's Willowbrook State School. His story helped spawn a class-action lawsuit against the state of New York and the passage of the Civil Rights of the Institutionalized Persons Act of 1980.

Rivera went on to work for ABC's *Good Morning America* and *20/20*, helping to produce hard-hitting stories. In 1985, however, Rivera was fired by the station after publicly criticizing ABC's cancellation of a sensationalistic piece about the relationship between President John F. Kennedy and Marilyn Monroe. Undaunted, Rivera hosted

▲ *Geraldo Rivera's confrontational style of journalism has occasionally resulted in violence.*

a highly publicized special about Al Capone's secret vault the next year. When he opened the notorious gangster's safe at the climax of the show, it contained nothing but a dusty old whiskey bottle.

Moving to daytime television in 1987 with a self-titled talk show, Rivera used tabloid journalistic techniques to boost his ratings. He was often criticized for encouraging the violence and conflict often witnessed on his show. In a highly publicized program on Nazi skinheads, Rivera taunted his guests and contributed to a violent brawl that resulted in his nose being smashed by a flying chair. A November 1988 cover of *Newsweek* carried a close-up shot of his bashed face, accompanied by the headline: "Trash TV: From the Lurid to the Loud, Anything Goes."

In 1997, however, Rivera moved back to news reporting when he joined NBC. After the 9/11 terrorist attacks of 2001, Rivera moved to the Fox News Channel as a war correspondent, covering Afghanistan, Israel, and Iraq.

KEY DATES

1943 Born in New York City on July 4.

1969 Receives JD from Brooklyn Law School.

1972 Reports groundbreaking story on abuses at Willowbrook State School, New York.

1983 Fired by ABC for criticism of the cancellation of a show on John F. Kennedy and Marilyn Monroe.

1987 Hosts syndicated show, *Geraldo*.

2001 Becomes a war correspondent for Fox News Channel.

Further reading: Rivera, Geraldo. *Exposing Myself*. New York, NY: Bantam Books, 1991.
www.geraldo.com (official Web site).

RIVERA, Tomás
Writer, Academic

Educator and writer Tomás Rivera was the author of the landmark Chicano novel *... y no se lo tragó la tierra* (*And the Earth Did Not Part*). Rivera drew on his own experiences, writing about the harsh reality of the lives of Chicano migrant workers and their families. Rivera was also a respected academic, and was chancellor of the University of California from 1979. After Rivera's death in 1984, several collections of his work were published posthumously, including *The Harvest/La Cosecha*, *The Searchers: Collected Poetry,* and a complete edition of his work in English. Rivera received several honors, including the establishment in his name of a children's book award at Texas State University (1995), a writing award at the University of Oklahoma (2000), and professorship of creative writing at the University of California–Riverside (2004). The Tomás Rivera Policy Institute was also founded to continue Rivera's work as an educator and scholar (*see box on page 47*).

Early life
Born on December 22, 1935, in Crystal City, Texas, Rivera was one of the five children of Mexican migrant farmworkers, Florencio and Josefa. He worked in the fields with his parents, following the harvest of crops from West Texas to the Red River Valley in the Dakotas. Rivera returned late each fall to catch up with his high-school classes. An intelligent boy, Rivera dreamed of going to school full time and of someday attending college. He managed to graduate from high school, and went on to study at the area junior college in Uvalde, Texas.

Achieving a dream
Rivera achieved his dream of further education. He enrolled at Southwest State University, where he received a bachelor's degree in English in 1958 and a master's degree in English education in 1964. After teaching in public schools and at Southwest Texas Junior College in Uvalde, he went on to study for a doctorate in romance languages and literature at the University of Oklahoma. He received his PhD in 1969. After graduating, Rivera taught at several universities, including Sam Houston State University.

Rivera also began to write during this time, drawing on his own experiences growing up in a family of Mexican migrant workers to create his first novel. In 1971 he published the highly acclaimed *... y no se lo tragó la tierra*, later translated into English as *And the Earth Did Not Part*. The plot explores the grim reality of the lives of Mexican migrant workers in the 1950s, as seen through the eyes of a young Mexican boy, Marcos. Critically well received *... y no se lo tragó la tierra* won the Quinto Sol Award in 1971, establishing Rivera as a leading and influential Chicano writer.

Rivera also contributed to several journals, including *El Grito*, a journal of contemporary Mexican American thought, and published several essays on education, literature, and Chicano-related issues. In 1973 Rivera published *Always and Other Poems*.

Administration
Rivera also excelled as an educator and administrator. He had a talent for dealing with people. Rivera rose through

▼ *Tomás Rivera longed to attend school full time when he was a child but the lifestyle of his migrant-worker parents made that impossible. He later wrote about the children of migrant laborers in his books.*

LEGACY

Tomás Rivera was an influential educator. From a young age Rivera realized the importance of education. He worked hard to give Hispanics better educational opportunities and to improve the role of Latinos in U.S. society. He envisioned a world in which Hispanic Americans could play an integral part in establishing a better life for their community through their positive contribution to government, education, and business.

Rivera died in 1984, but his legacy in education lives on.

Before his death he was instrumental in setting up the Tomás Rivera Policy Institute (TRPI). Established in 1985, the TRPI is a nonprofit, independent research group. It is dedicated to examining and researching key issues relevant to the Hispanic community, such as education, health care, voting, the media, immigration, and the economic well-being of Latinos.

The TRPI has its headquarters at the University of Southern California and a satellite office at Columbia University in New York.

It has produced several hundred reports and policy briefs. In 2002 it established the Center for Latino Educational Excellence (CLEE) to help improve Hispanic education. The TRPI also founded the Center for Latino Health Policy in 2003, and began an annual series of conferences focusing on key issues in 2004.

The TRPI's findings are regularly cited by the media. The *Wall Street Journal,* the *LA Times,* Telemundo, CNN, and Univision are among the journals and broadcasters that use its research.

---

the ranks of education. At the University of Texas at San Antonio he went from departmental chair to dean, and finally to vice president of the university. While in that capacity, Rivera was recruited to head the University of Texas at El Paso in 1978.

KEY DATES

1935 Born in Crystal City, Texas, on December 22.

1958 Receives bachelor's degree in English from Southwest Texas State University; receives a master's degree in English education in 1964.

1969 Receives PhD in romance languages from the University of Oklahoma.

1971 Publishes *...y no se lo tragó la tierra* (*And the Earth Did Not Part*).

1979 Becomes the highest-ranking Chicano in education as chancellor of University of California at Riverside.

1984 Dies in Fontana, California, on May 16.

1985 Tomás Rivera Policy Institute founded at the University of Southern California.

1992 *Complete Works* published.

1995 Texas State University establishes the Tomás Rivera Mexican American Children's Award.

2000 University of Oklahoma establishes the Tomás Rivera Writing Award.

2004 University of California–Riverside establishes the Tomás Rivera Endowed Chair of Creative Writing.

In 1979 Rivera became the highest-ranking Chicano in public and private education, when he was appointed chancellor at the Riverside campus of the University of California. During his tenure Rivera fought hard to improve the quality of education that was available to Hispanics, believing that it would create "stronger individuals, and in turn a stronger community.... We can only insure this education if we lead, if we become involved in getting it, ... and most importantly, if we make it part of our prophecy."

Organizations

Rivera belonged to several important professional and education-related organizations. He was a founding member of the National Council of Chicanos in Higher Education and was president of the American Association of Teachers in Spanish and Portuguese in Alamo Valley. He also sat on the board of the Carnegie Institute. Rivera was also the first Mexican American to be made a distinguished alumnus at Texas State University–San Marcos.

Rivera died, aged 49, in 1984, leaving behind his wife, Conchita, and three children. His contribution to education was acknowledged after his death: The school board in his hometown of Crystal City, Texas, named an elementary school in his honor and the University of Texas at Austin established a professorship in his memory.

Further reading: Olivares, Juan (ed.). *Tomás Rivera: Complete Works.* Houston, TX: Arte Público Press, 1998.
http://www.tsha.utexas.edu/handbook/online/articles/RR/fri34.html (biography).

ROBLES, Belén
Federal Official, Activist

A government official and activist, Belén Robles became the first female chief inspector at the El Paso port of entry to the United States. She was also the first woman president of the League of United Latin American Citizens (LULAC), the nation's oldest and largest Hispanic civil rights organization.

Early life
Robles was born in 1936 in El Paso, Texas, to Mexican parents. In 1954, she graduated from Bowie High School, and in 1957 she began her government career, first as a clerk-typist with the Immigration and Naturalization Service, and then in different positions in the U.S. Customs Service. Among the posts Robles held were supervisor of El Paso International Airport, chief inspector of Bridge of the Americas, chief inspector for cargo operations, and deputy assistant district director for inspection and control.

In 1994, Robles was elected national president of LULAC, a position she held until 1998. As the head of the organization, she was recognized for her strong support of Hispanics seeking to obtain civil and social justice. Before assuming the presidency, Robles had been an active member of the organization for about 40 years, and served at both local and national levels.

Range of involvements
In other organizations, during four decades, Robles has served as the director of the El Paso Hispanic Chamber of Commerce, vice chair of the National Hispanic Leadership Agenda, vice chair of SER–Jobs for Progress, an executive committee member of Foundation Solidaridad Mexico–American A.C., and a board member of the National Hispanic Corporate Council.

KEY DATES	
1936	Born in El Paso, Texas.
1957	Begins professional career with the U.S. Immigration and Naturalization and Customs Service.
1967	Receives a bronze Chamizal Medallion from President Lyndon Johnson.
1994	Becomes president of LULAC.
1999	Retires from United States Customs Service.

▲ *In 1994, Belén Robles became the first female president of LULAC.*

Robles has been recognized for her work with the Hispanic Achievement Award. She also received a bronze Chamizal Medallion from President Lyndon Johnson (in recognition of her efforts at the cabinet-level hearings on Mexican-American Affairs in El Paso, Texas, in 1967), has won a National Hero Award, and a McDonald's Hispanos Triunfadores (triumphant Hispanics) award. Robles was the 2004 inductee of the El Paso Women's Hall of Fame, and was named as one of both the "10 Outstanding Women in Federal Service" and the "100 Most Influential Hispanics in the United States."

Since her retirement in 1999, Robles has continued serving as an adviser to the Hispanic Cultural Institute, the El Paso Group, the Paso Al Norte Immigration Museum, and the El Paso Museum of History. She is married to Ramiro Robles and has three children: Ramiro Jr., Carlos Francisco, and Mary Helen LoPresti. Robles's notable contributions to the Latin American community have made her one of the most esteemed Texas leaders.

Further reading: http://www.lulac.org/about/history/history.html (historical survey of past presidents of LULAC).

ROCHE-RABELL, Arnaldo
Artist

Arnaldo Roche-Rabell is a major contemporary painter in Puerto Rico who has also made a mark in the U.S. art scene. His work, which expresses his Spanish-African-Antillean heritage, has been categorized as neo-expressionist with a Latin American sensibility that is close to magical realism.

Early life
Roche-Rabell was born in 1955 in Santurce, Puerto Rico, to parents of French and mulatto descent. During his childhood, he suffered the trauma of witnessing his mentally disturbed older brother shoot dead his sister. This haunting event and other experiences in Roche-Rabell's youth shaped his attitudes to life, and directed his artistic perspective from an early age toward realism.

Art education
Roche-Rabell studied at the School of Architecture in the University of Puerto Rico in San Juan from 1974 to 1978. He then went on a James Nelson Raymond Fellowship to the United States to study visual art at the Art Institute of Chicago, Illinois. There, Roche-Rabell received a fine arts bachelor's degree in 1982 and a master's in 1984. He remained in Chicago until 1994, when he returned to Puerto Rico.

During his artistic training, Roche-Rabell developed a technique of layering his canvases with different colors of paint, and working them using various techniques, including wrapping his models in the canvas itself. The results are a fascinating profusion of shapes, textures, reliefs, colors, and intriguing images.

Some of Roche-Rabell's earliest works are self-portraits in which he studies mixed identities. One of them, *We Have to Dream in Blue* (1986), is a close-up of a face with strong African features and bright blue eyes. As well as exploring identity and soul in the 1980s, Roche-Rabell also established continuing themes of life, death, and consciousness in such works as *Mother* (1985), *At the Edge of My Door* (1985), and *Dreams Are Real* (1986).

Developing an artistic voice
In the 1990s, Roche-Rabell's work became increasingly political, depicting the difficult nature of U.S.-Puerto Rico relations. In *Under a Total Eclipse of the Sun* (1991), for example, the Capitol building in Washington, D.C., appears

KEY DATES

1955   Born in Santurce, Puerto Rico.

1984   Qualifies as a Master of Fine Arts from the School of the Art Institute of Chicago, Illinois.

1980   Produces his first major work, *The Spirit of the Flesh, Carving the Spirit of the Flesh, Burning the Spirit of the Flesh*.

1997   Stages major U.S. solo traveling exhibition.

surrounded by exuberant Puerto Rican foliage. In *Father Tell Me If You Love Me* (1995), U.S. political imagery is interspersed with depictions of traditional scenes and native faces from Puerto Rico.

In *Five Hundred Years without an Ear*, Roche-Rabell depicted Vincent Van Gogh drowned in sunflowers. One aim of the work was to establish a link between the 19th-century Dutch painter and Puerto Rican artists such as José Campeche Y Jordán and Francisco Oller. His indebtedness to Oller may also be seen in two 1995 still-lives with fruit: *Campeche, Oller and Roche*, and *Even If I Try I Can't Forget You, Oller*.

Exhibitions
Since 1983, Roche-Rabell has had solo shows in the United States and Puerto Rico. "Arnaldo Roche-Rabell: the Uncommonwealth" was a major traveling exhibition organized by the School of the Arts, Virginia Commonwealth University, Richmond, in 1997. Roche-Rabell has been included in Hispanic art surveys, such as "Hispanic Art in the United States: 30 Contemporary painters and Sculptors" (Houston Fine Art Museum, 1987), and in U.S. art surveys such as "Chicago Artists in the European Tradition" (Museum of Contemporary Art, Chicago, 1989). Roche-Rabell's series of self-portraits has become an icon of Puerto Rican identity, and details have been used for the covers of several books on the subject of cultural identity.

See also: Campeche y Jordán, José; Oller, Francisco.

Further reading: Hobbs, Robert. *Arnaldo Roche-Rabell: The Uncommonwealth.* Seattle, WA: University of Washington Press, 1996.
http://www.arnaldoroche.com (official Web site).

RODRIGUEZ, Abraham, Jr.
Writer

Abraham Rodriguez, Jr., is a Nuyorican (New York-Puerto Rican) author whose fictional portrayal of a violent and troubled South Bronx (a New York City neighborhood) has won wide critical acclaim. In his novels and short stories, which are inspired by his own experience, Rodriguez focuses on Latino and Latina teenagers whose lives have been marred by poverty and racism, and who are led into drug abuse, early pregnancy, gang culture, or crime.

Life in the Bronx

Much of Rodriguez's work reflects his own upbringing in the Mott Haven neighborhood of the Bronx, where he was born in 1961. By the 1960s, much of the Bronx had become degraded: High-density housing, lack of investment, and prejudice against Hispanic and African communities had turned many of its neighborhoods into crime-ridden ghettos. However talented or determined, many ethnic minority members growing up in the Bronx in the 1970s and 1980s found it hard to break out of a cycle of poverty and poor education.

Determination

At school, Rodriguez was confronted by the ignorant prejudice of teachers who told him that there was no such thing as a Puerto Rican writer; he dropped out of high school. Despite such lack of encouragement, Rodriguez persevered with his determination to be a writer, and in 1982, having finally earned his high-school diploma at age 21, he enrolled at New York's City College, from which he eventually graduated with a degree in English literature and film.

Rodriguez built his literary reputation slowly, at first by publishing short stories in journals and anthologies. In 1993, he was able to bring some of these stories together in a collection entitled *The Boy without a Flag*. In these hard-hitting and uncompromising snapshots of troubled Hispanic teenagers, Rodriguez angrily exposed the harsh realities of ghetto life. In one of the stories, a 13-year-old commits his first burglary, while in another a teenage drug addict who dreams of motherhood ends up having an abortion.

Bleak vision?

The Boy without a Flag was followed by two important and powerful novels. *Spidertown* (1994) is the story of a South Bronx teenage drug runner, Miguel, who after meeting a beautiful new girlfriend, longs to escape his blighted existence but continues to find himself trapped by his past. In the imaginative, disturbing, and yet bleakly humorous *Buddha Book* (2001), two high-school friends, Dinky and Jose, create and anonymously distribute a comic book in which they reveal the violent criminal underbelly of their lives.

Some commentators have criticized Rodriguez's work for its unremittingly negative images of Puerto Rican teenagers. The author's bleak vision, however, arises from his determination to avoid easy or comforting stereotypes, and is always countered by deep sympathy for his characters' predicament and his pride in his Puerto Rican American heritage.

Award-winning writing

Rodriguez has won a number of prizes for his fiction. In 1993, *The Boy Without a Flag* was a *New York Times'* Notable Book of the Year. In 1995, *Spidertown* won an American Book Award, while, in 2000, Rodriguez was the recipient of a New York Foundation for the Arts grant. His work has been published in a wide range of anthologies and literary magazines, including *Story, Best Stories from New Writers, Chattahoochie Review*, and *Alternative Fiction and Poetry*. Rodriguez has also served as a literary panel member on the New York State Council of the Arts. He has also opened a small publishing imprint of his own, named Art Bridge.

Further reading: Rodriguez, Abraham, Jr. *The Boy without a Flag*. Minneapolis, MN: Milkweed Editions, 1992.
www.nationalbook.org/arodriguezbio.html (short biography).

KEY DATES	
1961	Born in New York City.
1993	Publishes debut short-story collection, *The Boy without a Flag*.
1994	Publishes *Spidertown*.
1995	*Spidertown* wins an American Book Award.
2001	Publishes *The Buddha Book*.

RODRÍGUEZ, Albita
Musician

Widely known simply as "Albita," dynamic Cuban singer Albita Rodríguez appeals to traditional and contemporary audiences alike. She has popularized traditional Cuban music with a style that combines influences including son (a precursor to salsa), jazz, Cuban country music, and modern pop-music arrangements. Albita's lyrics address her own experiences in Cuba and also often recount the traditions and history of her homeland; she defected from Cuba in 1993.

Early life
Born in Havana, Cuba, in 1962, Rodríguez was the daughter of well-known musicians. She credits her parents as her biggest influence. Introduced by them to *punto guajaro*, a form of acoustic country music, Rodríguez began her professional career at age 15 performing with her parents. By the time she was 19, Rodríguez was widely known throughout Cuba as the youngest performer on the weekly television showcase *Palmas y Cañas*.

Commercial success
In 1988 Rodríguez released her first album, *Habrá Música Guajira,* followed by the single "Parranda, Laúd y Son," which reached No. 1 in several Latin American countries.

In the early 1990s, she was offered a major recording contract in Colombia, where she lived at the time. She released the albums *Si Se Da La Siembra* and *Cantaré* in 1991. In 1993 she moved to the United States, and settled in Florida. Miami's Cuban community was delighted at the musician's arrival, and her regular performances in the Centro Vasco restaurant attracted large crowds and successful musicians, including Madonna and Gloria and Emilio Estefan. She was signed by Emilio Estefan's Crescent Moon label, releasing her first single in the United States, "Que Manera de Quererte," in 1994.

▲ *Rodríguez's music has been acclaimed by fellow artists Gloria Estefan and Madonna, and several of her songs have appeared on film soundtracks.*

Rodríguez's first U.S. album, the critically acclaimed *No Se Parece a Nada* (1995), sold 100,000 copies. *Dicen Qué...* followed in 1996, *Una Mujer Cómo Yo* and *Cuba Dos Épocas* in 1997, and *Albita Rodríguez Y Su Grupo* in 1998. Subsequent albums include *Son* (2000), *Hecho A Mano* (2002), and the 2004 album *Albita Llegó*.

Awards and recognition
Rodríguez has received several awards for her work: In 1998 she received a Grammy nomination for best tropical Latin performance. She was also selected as one of *Newsweek*'s "100 personalities for the 21st Century," and performed the Cuban classic "Guantanamera" at President Bill Clinton's second inauguration in 1997. Rodríguez won a Latin Grammy award for best contemporary tropical album in 2004. In the following year, she starred as Evalina Montoya in the Broadway show *The Mambo Kings*.

See also: Estefan, Emilio; Estefan, Gloria

Further reading: Sweeney, Philip. *The Virgin Directory of World Music*. New York, NY: Henry Holt, 1992.
http://www.albitaonline.com (Rodríguez's official Web site).

KEY DATES	
1962	Born in Havana, Cuba.
1988	Releases first album, *Habrá Música Guajira*.
1993	Defects to the United States.
2004	Wins Latin Grammy for best tropical album.
2005	Appears in *The Mambo Kings* on Broadway.

RODRIGUEZ, Alex
Baseball Player

Alex Rodriguez was one of the best shortstops ever to play the game of baseball. He began his career in the mid-1990s, at a time when a whole new breed of hard-hitting shortstops, including Derek Jeter and Nomar Garciaparra, were emerging to redefine what had traditionally been a weak-hitting position. His early success with the Seattle Mariners brought Rodriguez celebrity and landed him the largest contract in sports history in 2001 when the Texas Rangers agreed to pay him $252 million over 10 years.

▼ *Alex Rodriguez believes that young players have a duty to pay tribute to great baseball stars such as Ernie Banks, Cal Ripken, and Ozzie Smith.*

The unprecedented contract placed extraordinary pressure on "A-Rod," as he is known to his fans, to produce a world championship, something he was unable to do with a pitching-poor Rangers club. Ultimately, the Rangers were unable to develop the rest of their club because of their contractual obligations to Rodriguez. In 2004 they traded him to the wealthiest team in baseball, the New York Yankees, in return for Alfonso Soriano. In order to facilitate the trade, Rodriguez agreed to switch positions and play third base so that Yankee captain Jeter could remain at shortstop.

Early life
Rodriguez comes from a humble background. He was born in New York City on July 27, 1975, to Dominican immigrant parents. His father, Victor, had been a professional baseball player in the Dominican Republic. He passed on to his son a love of the sport. Victor Rodriguez abandoned the family when Rodriguez was 10, after which he was brought up by his mother, Lourdes. Rodriguez joined the Hank Kline Boys and Girls Club in Miami, Florida, where he was influenced by director Eddie Rodriguez (*see box on page 53*).

Rodriguez attended Westminister Christian School in Miami, where he showed a special talent for baseball. Inspired by hero Cal Ripken of the Baltimore Orioles, and mentored by coach Rich Hoffman, Rodriguez was batting .450 by his junior year. In 1992, he went on to help Westminister win the national high-school championships.

Making a star
Rodriguez's talent brought him to the attention of the Seattle Mariners, who in 1993 picked him in the first round of the amateur draft. He debuted briefly with the Mariners in July of the following year and played for the Dominican Republic in the winter of 1994–1995. He broke into the major leagues for good in 1996, smashing 36 home runs at the age of 21. The right-handed-hitting Rodriguez led the American League in batting that year with a .358 average; he just missed winning the Most Valuable Player Award. Rodriguez became the youngest shortstop to play in an All-Star game, and was named Player of the Year by *Sporting News.*

During Rodriguez's five full seasons with the Mariners, he emerged as a hitting machine, swatting 184 home runs

INFLUENCES AND INSPIRATION

As the highest-paid baseball player in history, and a role model for many young Americans, particularly Latinos and Latinas, Alex Rodriguez has dedicated a lot of his time to helping the community and youth organizations that encouraged him to develop into a successful and productive sports star.

As a child, Rodriguez was a member of the Hank Kline Boys and Girls Club in Miami, a youth development organization. He was particularly influenced by its director, Eddie Rodriguez (no relation). Eddie was like a father to the young Rodriguez, especially after his real father, Victor, had left the family home. The baseball star said that Eddie Rodriguez taught him to believe in himself, "be positive, and stay grounded."

In 2002, Rodriguez paid tribute to his mentor by signing up with the actor Denzel Washington and basketball legend Shaquille O'Neal as national spokespersons for the club. In the first bilingual advertising campaign for the club, Rodriguez helped launch "Campaign 3 P.M.," which called for every U.S. child to be involved in safe, supervised, daily after-school activities, either at home, at a boys and girls club, or in some other high-quality community program.

and driving in 574 runs. His contract with the Mariners ended in 2000, and he decided to move on.

Making the news

After a brief contractual flirtation with the New York Mets, Rodriguez hit the headlines when he signed with the Rangers for the record sum of $252 million. The fee caused public outcry, and Rodriguez was widely denounced by critics for being overpaid. His fee also brought fears that the Rangers would not be able to pay for or attract other top players. Fans in Seattle resented the manner of Rodriguez's departure, and the passage of time did little to reduce their resentment: He was roundly booed whenever he returned there with visiting teams.

During Rodriguez's three years with Texas, he hit 52, 57, and 47 home runs, and drove in 135, 142, and 118 runs, respectively. As a result, he won the Most Valuable Player Award in 2003. In addition to his prowess with the bat, Rodriguez distinguished himself in the field, earning Gold Glove Awards in 2002 and 2003. Despite these impressive personal achievements, the Rangers finished at the bottom of the league in all three years.

A valued player

In 2004, Rodriguez joined the New York Yankees. In his first year, he was criticized for performing below expectations during the regular season, even though he still hit 36 home runs and drove in 106 runs. In 2005, Rodriguez's numbers improved dramatically when he swatted 48 home runs, drove in 130 runs, and hit .321. However, many blamed him for the failure of the Yankees to make the World Series, attributing their defeat to Rodriguez's poor hitting in the playoffs. During the 2005 campaign, Rodriguez hit his 400th career home run; he became the first player to reach that landmark before the age of 30.

Although raised mostly in South Florida, Rodriguez remains proud of his Dominican ancestry and created controversy when he expressed an interest in playing for the Dominican Republic, rather than the United States, in baseball's first World Classic, an international knockout tournament in March 2006.

KEY DATES	
1975	Born in New York on July 27.
1985	Father abandons family.
1992	Helps the Westminister Christian School in Miami win the national high-school championships.
1993	Drafted by the Seattle Mariners.
1996	Youngest shortstop to play in an All-Star Game; named *Sporting News* Player of the Year.
2000	Becomes best-paid player of all time; signs contract worth $252 million with the Texas Rangers.
2004	Joins the New York Yankees.

See also: Garciaparra, Nomar

Further reading: Stout, Glenn. *On the Field with Alex Rodriguez.* Boston, MA: Little, Brown, 2002.
http://www.juniorbaseball.com/wheniwasakid/Rodriquez_pg2.shtml (short interview).

RODRÍGUEZ, Arsenio
Guitarist, Bandleader

Arsenio Rodríguez was a prolific composer of *son*, a style of popular dance music that originated in the Oriente province of Cuba. He was a hugely influential and innovative bandleader, and is universally recognized as the individual most responsible for revolutionizing the way traditional Cuban *son* was played in the 1940s. Rodríguez is also recognized as one of the three "inventors" of the mambo, which became a worldwide musical craze in the 1950s. He was nicknamed "El ciego maravilloso" (The Blind Marvel), due to the blindness caused by a mule kick he received as a child.

Early life and influences
The African flavors that Rodríguez injected into much of his music reflect the fact that his grandfather was a slave brought to Cuba from the Congo during the 19th century. Born in Matanzas province in 1911, Rodríguez was christened Ignacio Arsenio Travieso Scull. He grew up listening to a range of musical styles, including Congolese spirituals, and learned to play a variety of instruments. He eventually chose the tres (a guitar with three sets of double strings). By the early 1930s Rodríguez had moved to Havana. He began playing music professionally, forming his first group, Sexteto Boston. Later, in 1937, Rodríguez briefly joined José Interian's group, Septeto Bellamar.

Creating a musical legacy
Although he was less of a commercial or popular success than his contemporaries Benny Moré, Pérez Prado, or Frank "Machito" Grillo, many people believe that Arsenio Rodríguez was the most important single figure in 20th-century Cuban music. Initially, due to the lack of more than a handful of quality recordings by his own group, Rodríguez's genius and wide-ranging influence on his contemporaries were known mostly through recordings of his compositions by other artists. During the 1930s and 1940s Rodríguez almost single-handedly reinvented Cuban *son* music through a series of daring innovations in instrumental format and rhythmic structure. Rodríguez's talent as a songwriter is evidenced by his many compositions that have become Latin music standards. Some of his most best-known works are "Pasó en Tampa," "Bruca Manigua," and "La Vida es un Sueño."

Rodríguez finally got a real chance to record his own compositions in 1937, when he acted as a musical adviser

▲ **Cuban bandleader Arsenio Rodríguez plays the tres guitar, an instrument that features three sets of double strings.**

to the famous Casino de la Playa band, which featured Miguelito Valdés on vocals. In his recordings with Casino de la Playa, Rodríguez helped bring Cuban dance music into the modern age by injecting it with a new rhythmic and lyrical African flavor that had previously been confined to the Afro-Cuban slums.

One example of this new approach was the song "Bruca Manigua." It was described as a "canto congo" (Congo chant) by Rodríguez and featured a distinctive African rhythm. "Bruca Manigua" was innovative in a lyrical sense as well. It was sung in neo-bozal language (the broken Spanish spoken by recently arrived Cuban slaves in the 19th century), and its lyrics described the plight of poor Afro-Cubans. The lyrics of the song translate roughly as, "I am a carabalí / Black man of a nation / Without liberty / I cannot live / White man finished off / My heart / So mistreated / They kill the body."

| INFLUENCES AND INSPIRATION |

As well as artistic challenges, Rodríguez also found social challenges to his musical innovations. As in the United States, there were many limitations to life as a black person in Cuba at the time. Rodríguez's success was aided in part by the new Cuban constitution of 1940 that granted blacks admission to most public places. During the 1940s the public gardens of the La Tropical brewery became Rodríguez's musical home. He played at La Tropical with his conjunto band twice a week. Rodríguez also performed live early each evening on radio station 1010.

The conjunto was massively popular among the black public but found it difficult to find a white audience. Rodríguez's band was not hired by white Cubans to play for their weekend balls in the casinos and nightclubs, partly because they were racially prejudiced but mostly because they were unable to dance to the African influenced rhythms that Rodríguez was playing. Later, in New York, Rodríguez would also find that, despite being a founding father of the mambo, his style was not diluted enough to capture a wider audience.

Bandleader and innovator

In the 1940s Rodríguez formed his own band and became a trailblazer in the development of the *son's* instrumentation and rhythmic structure. First, he introduced new instruments to the traditional *son* septet. These new instruments were taken from the world of jazz. In particular, Rodríguez added the piano, with its ripping, percussive solos that imitated (and eventually replaced) the tres guitar. He also added a second (and later a third and fourth) trumpet. Other instruments such as the conga drums and the *cencero* (cowbell) played a more improvisational role, simultaneously giving the new arrangement a loose *son* feel and a tight jazz feel. Rodríguez called his new band formation a *conjunto de son,* and it has since become the standard formation for nearly all salsa bands.

Rodríguez developed two new styles of *son*: the *son guaguancó* and the *son montuno*. The *son guaguancó* melded elements of the authentic Afro-Cuban rumba with the *son*, while the *son montuno* melded elements of the more staid *danzón* to the *son*. (*Danzón* is a type of ballroom dance music played by orchestral ensembles; it is the official music of Cuba.)

This second innovation, influenced by the musical arrangements of brothers Orestes and Israel "Cachao" López, who played with Rodríguez's rival bandleader Antonio Arcaño, eventually gave rise to the repeating figures played by the trumpets, called "diablos" by Rodríguez. It was this high-energy, brass-fueled style of *son montuno* that was eventually reinvented and popularized by Pérez Prado as the mambo.

Life in the United States

In the early 1950s Rodríguez immmigrated to Miami in the United States. He soon abandoned Miami because of racism, and eventually settled in the South Bronx, New York City, instead. Rodríguez never became a popular success in the United States, due in part to his refusal to dilute the heavily African sound of his *conjunto* in order to fit into the high-energy mambo mania of 1950s New York. He died in penniless obscurity in Los Angeles in 1972, just as the salsa music that he was largely responsible for inspiring enjoyed its greatest popular and commercial success in New York.

See also: Lopez, Israel "Cachao"; Machito; Prado, Pérez

Further reading: Sublette, Ned. *Cuba and Its Music: From the First Drums to the Mambo.* Chicago, Il: Chicago Review Press, 2004.
Website: http://www.milonga.co.uk/cuba/arsenio.html (Information about Argentine tango and Cuban *son* music).

KEY DATES

1911   Born Igancio Arsenio Travieso Scull in Matanzas, Cuba, on August 11 (although records are uncertain).

1935   Begins to play music professionally in Havana in a variety of *son* sextets and septets.

1937   Makes the first recordings of his songs, including "Bruca Manigua."

1940   Founds his own band and begins playing at La Tropical and on radio station 1010.

1952   Immigrates to the United States, eventually settling in the South Bronx, New York City.

1972   Dies in penniless obscurity in Los Angeles.

RODRIGUEZ, Arturo S.
Activist

Since 1993 Arturo S. Rodriguez has been president of the United Farm Workers (UFW), the powerful agricultural union that since the 1960s has campaigned for better pay and working conditions for California's largely Mexican and Filipino farmworkers. His wife, Linda Chávez Rodriguez (1951–2000), was the daughter of the union's founder, César Chávez, and was also an important activist in the UFW.

Early life

Born on June 23, 1949, in San Antonio, Texas, Rodriguez was the son of a sheet-metal worker and a school teacher. He was educated in Roman Catholic schools in his home town, graduating from La Salle High School in 1967. Rodriguez subsequently studied sociology at San Antonio's Catholic university, St. Mary's, where he completed his bachelor's degree in 1971. He went on to gain a master's degree in social work from the University of Michigan at Ann Arbor in 1973.

Activist

During his college years, Rodriguez became increasingly active in the UFW, helping to organize the nationwide boycotts of growers' produce that were a key part of the union's strategy at this time. He first met the UFW leader in 1973 and the following year met and married Chávez's daughter, Linda. Over the following years, the couple

▼ **In 1994, Arturo S. Rodriguez (right) led a march through California in honor of César Chávez, who had died the previous year.**

moved around the United States, helping to arrange boycotts, raising public consciousness about the farmworkers' plight, and encouraging California's workers to join the union. In 1981 Rodriguez was elected to the UFW national executive board, based in La Paz, California.

Revitalizing the UFW

During the 1980s, the UFW became a less powerful political entity as its membership fell dramatically and California's state government became less sympathetic to the union's goals. In 1993 Chávez died, and soon afterward Rodriguez was elected to serve as the UFW's new president. He immediately set out to revitalize the union, launching membership-recruitment drives. Rodriguez held high-profile events such as 1994's 343-mile (546km) Delano–Sacramento march in memory of Chávez and introduced the building of low-cost housing for workers.

As president of the UFW, Rodriguez has emphasized the continuity between his own and Chávez's presidencies. In the mid-1990s, for instance, he launched a new campaign focused on California's poorly paid strawberry workers that emulated Chávez's famous table-grape campaign of the 1960s. Rodriguez has also sought to modernize the union, developing UFW's Spanish-language radio station, Campesina, as a tool to educate migrant workers.

See also: Chávez, César; Labor Organizations

Further reading: Shrag, Peter. *California: America's High-stakes Experiment.* Berkeley, CA: University of California Press, 2006. www.ufw.org (Web site of the UFW including biography of Rodriguez).

RODRIGUEZ, Chi Chi
Golfer

Best remembered for his showmanship on the golf course, Juan "Chi Chi" Rodriguez was one of the first prominent Latin players on the Professional Golf Association (PGA) Tour. In 26 years on the tour, Rodriguez won only eight events and never won a major, but his playful demeanor brought him a loyal following. Rodriguez is also held in high regard for his generosity of spirit. He made more than $7 million in career earnings, and for the past 40 years he has donated money and time to numerous charitable organizations and people in need. Today, the Chi Chi Rodriguez Youth Foundation, located in Clearwater, Florida, helps troubled, abused, and disadvantaged children.

Early life
Born the fifth of six children in impoverished Rio Piedras, near San Juan, Puerto Rico, on October 23, 1935, as a child Rodriguez helped his father in the sugarcane fields. He also boxed in the streets for sodas until he was 15, and pitched in semiprofessional baseball against such future stars as Roberto Clemente and Orlando Cepeda. In fact, Rodriguez took his nickname from a baseball player named Chi Chi Flores. Rodriguez also worked as a caddie to local golfers from the age of eight.

▼ *Chi Chi Rodriguez was a popular figure on the PGA Tour. He now devotes much of his time to his charity.*

KEY DATES	
1935	Born in Rio Piedras, Puerto Rico, on October 23.
1960	Plays in his first PGA Tour event, the Buick Open.
1963	Wins the Denver Open, his first Tour victory.
1979	Cofounds the Chi Chi Rodriguez Youth Foundation in Clearwater, Florida.
1981	Ties for sixth at the U.S. Open, his best finish in a major golf event.

In the mid-1950s, Rodriguez volunteered for the U.S. Army for two years, during which time he won the base golf championship at Fort Sill, Oklahoma, in 1957. Soon afterward, Rodriguez returned home and was hired as the caddie master at the Dorado Beach Club, where he quickly found himself under the tutelage of Pete Cooper.

In 1960, Rodriguez played in his first PGA Tour event, the Buick Open, winning $450. He had other early successes, and was soon playing practice rounds with legendary golfers such as Sam Snead and Tommy Bolt, but Rodriguez did not earn his first tour victory until 1963 when he won the Denver Open. Despite his slight stature (a result of childhood bouts of rickets and tropical sprue), Rodriguez acquired a lively fan base because of his playful antics. Fans also appreciated the fact that, despite his size, Rodriguez was one of the longest drivers on the tour. He routinely hit the ball distances of 300 yards (275m).

Rodriguez was also likable for loftier reasons. When he won the Texas Open in 1967, he gave $5,000 of his $20,000 purse to victims of the tornadoes that had ravaged Illinois one week earlier. In 1979, Rodriguez cofounded the Chi Chi Rodriguez Youth Foundation, which teaches social skills and life management, as well as golf. Golf was incorporated into the program not only because it is Rodriguez's own sport, but also because it is a game in which successful players do not have to be strong to excel.

See also: Cepeda, Orlando; Clemente, Roberto

Further reading: Rodriguez, Chi Chi, John Anderson, and Peter Jacobsen. *Chi Chi's Golf Games You Gotta Play.* Champaign, Il: Human Kinetics Publishers, 2003.
http://www.chichi.org (Chi Chi's foundation's Web site).

RODRIGUEZ, Cleto
Medal of Honor Recipient

Cleto Rodriguez was born on April 26, 1923, in San Marcos, Texas. He lived there until he was nine. After his parents were both killed in an automobile accident, he stayed with relatives in San Antonio. Rodriguez attended Washington Irving and Ivanhoe schools. In 1944, he joined the U.S. Army. Private Rodriguez was assigned to Company B, 148th Infantry Division, and shipped to the Philippines after training to fight in World War II (1939–1945).

Engaged in combat

On February 9, 1945, Rodriguez's unit was pinned down under heavy enemy gunfire at Paco Rail Station during an attempt to take Manila, the capital of the Philippines. Rodriguez and another soldier, John C. Reece, took the initiative to split from the unit and advance under fire. Rodriguez was an expert shot with his automatic weapon. Reaching a house some 40 yards (36m) from the enemy, he and Reece began firing, killing more than 35 men. Rodriguez advanced farther into the enemy zone and

▼ *Cleto Rodriguez's bravery and effective soldiering earned him the Congressional Medal of Honor.*

KEY DATES	
1923	Born in San Marcos, Texas, on April 26.
1944	Enters military service.
1945	Earns the Congressional Medal of Honor during combat in the Philippines.
1990	Dies on December 7.

tossed grenades, killing seven more of the enemy, and destroying machine guns and heavy artillery. During the following two and a half hours, Rodriguez and Reece killed 82 of the enemy. As they regrouped, however, Reece was killed.

Without much rest, Rodriguez's platoon pressed forward and, two days later, Rodriguez was again in the middle of combat. This time alone, Rodriguez killed six more of the enemy and destroyed the 20-millimeter gun that was cutting his buddies down. For his valor, Rodriguez was awarded the Congressional Medal of Honor. He was only the fifth Mexican American soldier to receive the award.

The hero

Rodriguez came home to a hero's welcome, and married his girlfriend, Flora Muniz. Over the next two decades, they had four children. The stories of Rodriguez's bravery were told by the chest full of medals he displayed when in dress uniform. Otherwise, however, he was very modest about his exploits during the war. Rodriguez earned 21 medals during his years of service, including two Bronze Stars, a Silver Star, and a Purple Heart in addition to the Congressional Medal of Honor.

Rodriguez worked briefly for the Veteran's Administration, helping other former soldiers with benefit claims and services. He returned to military service in the 1950s with the U.S. Air Force and again with the Army into the 1970s. A group of Chicano artists memorialized his likeness in a mural on the walls of the Casiano Housing Projects in San Antonio. After Rodriguez's death in 1990, other memorials were established in his honor, and a local school was named for him.

Further reading: http://www.tsha.utexas.edu/handbook/online/articles/RR/frobv_print.html (biography).

RODRIGUEZ, Eloy
Biologist

Eloy Rodriguez studies plants, fungi, and insects in the quest to isolate valuable natural drugs. His most important discoveries include compounds that inhibit the growth of tumors and prevent malaria.

Early life
Rodriguez was born in 1947 in Edinburgh, Texas, to a family of Mexican origin. He first became interested in science while cleaning laboratories at his college, and he decided to switch from accountancy to zoology. In 1969, Rodriguez graduated from the University of Texas, Austin. Six years later he received his doctorate, and in 1976 he was appointed assistant professor of ecology and evolutionary biology at the University of California, Irvine. He made regular field trips to gather plants for analysis in the hope of finding new drugs.

A new approach
In 1980, a colleague observed some interesting behavior in wild chimpanzees, noting that the primates grimaced when they ate certain leaves. Rodriguez found that the leaves

▼ *Eloy Rodriguez is a biologist who is best known for his realization that apes eat certain plants to control diseases.*

contained substances that prevented the growth of parasites. Rodriguez realized that the apes were eating plants for their medicinal value rather than nutritional benefit. The breakthrough signaled the start of a new approach to pharmacy called zoopharmacognosy, which means "animal drug knowing." It examines the plants used by animals for any medicinal value. Using the technique, Rodriguez identified an antiviral compound named thiarubrin, which could help fight HIV.

Rodriguez also gained valuable insights from the indigenous peoples of rain forests in Africa and South America, where the knowledge of the medicinal value of certain plants extends as far back as 40,000 years. Local people do not have access to antimalarial drugs, and use native plants instead. Rodriguez hopes to develop inexpensive alternative drugs from these plants.

Community chemist
Rodriguez is also involved in promoting careers in science to young people. While at the University of California, he participated in Kids Investigating and Discovering Science (KIDS). KIDS continues to provide children from low-income Latino families with the opportunity to attend university-based science projects.

Rodriguez has also written more than 150 scientific articles and a book about his research. He is married to the writer Helena Maria Viramontes. They are both professors at Cornell University.

See also: Viramontes, Helena María

Further reading www.sacnas.org/beta/pdf/rodriguez_eloy_H.pdf (autobiography).

RODRIGUEZ, Ivan "Pudge"
Baseball Player

Ivan "Pudge" Rodriguez is considered one of the greatest all-round catchers in baseball history. His great fielding skills combined with a formidable presence at the plate to make Rodriguez a perennial All Star in the major leagues throughout the 1990s and into the 21st century.

Early life

Rodriguez was born in 1971 in Manati, Puerto Rico. After playing baseball for Lino Padron Rivera High School in Vega Baja, Rodriguez signed with the American League (AL) Texas Rangers in 1988 at age 16. He made his major league debut on June 20, 1991, the same day he married his wife, Maribel Rivera.

By the time Rodriguez debuted with the Rangers in 1991, he had established himself as an outstanding defensive catcher. His prowess behind the plate quickly earned him major league honors: He won 10 consecutive Gold Glove awards as catcher from 1992 to 2001, and another in 2004, giving him the most Gold Glove awards by a catcher in the history of baseball. Rodriguez's nearly flawless play behind the plate combined with a cannon of an arm that gave would-be base stealers huge problems.

An all-around game

Soon after the baseball world became aware of his superb defensive play, Rodriguez began to develop his offensive skills. After hitting a respectable .260 in his first full season with the Rangers, Rodriguez saw his batting average steadily increase each following year. Both his batting average and his power numbers rose to near historical levels for a catcher, culminating in the 1999 season, when he posted 35 home runs, 113 runs batted in, and 29

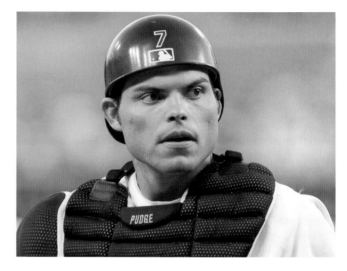

▲ *Pudge Rodriguez is one of the best catchers in baseball and a formidable all-around player.*

doubles to go along with a .332 average. That year, and for the third straight season, Rodriguez also threw out more than 50 percent of runners attempting to steal a base. His outstanding performance for the Rangers in 1999 won him the AL Most Valuable Player (MVP) award, the first time a catcher had won the award in the league since Thurman Munson in 1976.

Before the start of the 2003 season, Rodriguez joined the National League (NL) Florida Marlins as a free agent. That year, he played an important part in leading a young Marlins team to a World Series championship—his only one to date—and was named the MVP in the NL Championship Series. The following year, Rodriguez again became a free agent. He signed with the American League Detroit Tigers for the 2004 season, where his spectacular play continued. He was elected to the All Star team in both 2004 and 2005, giving him a total of 12 All Star appearances.

Pudge Rodriguez and Maribel Rivera have three children. They divide their time between homes in the United States and Puerto Rico.

KEY DATES	
1971	Born in Manati, Puerto Rico, on November 30.
1988	Signed by the Texas Rangers, aged 16.
1991	Makes major league debut with the Texas Rangers on June 20.
1999	Voted Most Valuable Player in the American League.
2001	Wins 10th consecutive Gold Glove Award.
2005	Named to 12th All-Star Game.

Further reading: Demarco, Tony. *Ivan Rodriguez (Latinos in Baseball).* Hockessin, DE: Mitchell Lane, 2000.
http://www.pudge.org/personallyPudge.htm (Rodriguez's official Web site).

RODRIGUEZ, Jennifer
Speedskater

Speedskater Jennifer Rodriguez has won two Olympic bronze medals and several world titles. Her achievements are especially impressive given that she did not start to skate on ice until she was 20.

Early life
Born in Miami, Florida, on June 8, 1976, Jennifer Rodriguez is the daughter of a Cuban father and a U.S. mother. She started roller skating aged four at a party held at a roller rink. By age five, Rodriguez had started to enter roller speedskating and figure-skating competitions. Rodriguez became the first competitor ever to win medals in both roller figure skating and speedskating at the World Championships. In 1993, she won a gold medal at the World Inline Roller Speedskating Championships.

▼ *Jennifer Rodriguez credits her husband, speedskater K. C. Boutiette, with being one of her greatest influences.*

Switching to ice
Soon afterward, Rodriguez met the three-time Olympic champion speedskater K. C. Boutiette. He had roller skated for years before switching successfully to ice. He persuaded Rodriguez that she could make the transition to ice and compete in the Winter Olympics. In 1996, she moved to Milwaukee, Wisconsin, to learn to ice skate. Through sheer determination, Rodriguez took fourth place in the all-round U.S. Championships a year later.

In 1998, Rodriguez qualified for the Olympic Games in Japan in four speedskating events: the 1,000 meters, the 1,500 meters, the 3,000 meters, and the 5,000 meters. She had hoped for a top-15 place in her best event, the 3,000 meters, but surprised everyone by taking fourth place.

Rodriguez slipped out of the world top-10 ranking in 1999, but became the U.S. All-round Champion in the same year. In 2001, Rodriguez won her first gold medal in the World Cup for the 1,000 meters. A year later, at the Olympic trials, Rodriguez became the first U.S. woman ever to qualify for a place on the Olympic team in five events. She won bronze medals in both the 1,000 meters and the 1,500 meters. Between 2003 and 2005, Rodriguez won 25 World Cup medals, including 13 golds. Based in Utah, Rodriguez is now married to Boutiette.

KEY DATES	
1976	Born in Miami, Florida, on June 8.
1993	Wins gold medal in the World Inline Speedskating Championships.
1996	Starts to skate on ice.
1998	Takes fourth place in the 3,000 meters at the Winter Olympics in Japan.
1999	Becomes U.S. All-round Champion.
2001	Wins gold medal at World Cup for 1,000 meters.
2002	Wins bronze medals at the Olympic Games in 1,000 meters and 1,500 meters.
2003	Wins 14 international medals, including five golds.
2005	Wins the U.S. Sprint Championships.

Further reading: http://www.usolympicteam.com/ 26_1030.htm (Web page on Rodriguez).

RODRIGUEZ, Johnny
Singer

Johnny Rodriguez was the first Mexican American to break into the national country music scene. He went on to earn seven major awards from the industry.

Early life

Rodriguez was born in 1951, and brought up in Sabinal, Texas, just west of San Antonio. There were eight other children in the Rodriguez household. Rodriguez's older brother, Andres, was a big country music fan, and bought Rodriguez a guitar when he was seven. Rodriguez took to music readily, and was exposed to different genres; his parents loved Mexican music, and his sisters and friends loved rock and roll. Rodriguez picked at his guitar to emulate all sounds and styles, and became a proficient player. By age 16, Rodriguez had formed a band, The Spocks, named after a character in the TV series *Star Trek.* Rodriguez was also an altar boy, a star football player, and an excellent student. However, when his father died, Rodriguez then went into a tailspin, dropped out of school, and landed in jail four times.

Although the Texas Ranger Division has a tarnished reputation among Chicanos, Rodriguez was saved by Ranger Joaquin Jackson. While Rodriguez was in jail, he happened to be strumming his guitar and singing when Jackson visited and was impressed with the young inmate's talent and good looks. In an attempt to rehabilitate Rodriguez, Jackson got him a job at a nearby country music amusement park in the early 1970s.

A star is born

A visiting recording executive from Nashville, Tennessee, encouraged Rodriguez to visit him and cut a record demo

▲ *Johnny Rodriguez began playing country music at age seven, after his brother gave him a guitar.*

or two. With a mere $14 in his pocket, and his guitar wrapped in a plastic bag, Rodriguez arrived in Nashville, and became the lead guitarist and singer in Hall's Storytellers. His first single, "Pass Me By (If You're Only Passing Through)," recorded for the Mercury label in 1973, became his first chart hit. Every song he recorded from then on made the charts. His debut album, *Introducing Johnny Rodriguez,* was number one in all major trade charts.

In 25 years in the country music business, Rodriguez cut 26 albums, and 45 of his singles charted, amounting to millions of sales. In the late 1970s, he had a string of 11 consecutive number one hit singles on the country charts. Rodriguez's popularity was so great that he was a featured performer at the inaugural balls of both presidents Jimmy Carter and George W. Bush.

Further reading: http://www.gatalent.com/Acts/Johnny_Rodriguez/johnny_rodriguez.html

KEY DATES	
1951	Born in Sabinal, Texas, on December 10.
1958	Teaches himself to play guitar, age seven.
1971	Flies to Nashville and fronts Hall's Storytellers.
1973	Releases first single, "Pass Me By (If You're Only Passing Through"; releases first album, *Introducing Johnny Rodriguez*; is nominated by the Country Music Association for "Male Vocalist of the Year."
2001	Plays at inauguration of President George W. Bush.

RODRIGUEZ, Josefa "Chipita"
Victim of Injustice

In the 1830s, shortly before Texas independence from Mexico, Pedro Rodriguez fled from the Mexican president and dictator, Antonio López de Santa Anna, north to Texas. He and his young daughter, Josefa "Chipita," settled on the banks of the Aransas River in San Patricio de Hibernia, near Corpus Christi. Life was tough for the small family, and Pedro Rodriguez died while defending his claim and siding with the Anglo-American insurrectionists.

Hard life

Left alone, Chipita was forced to make the best of meager resources, and she earned money by providing bed and board for travelers along the river or on El Camino Real, the road that ran through San Patricio. During her many years in San Patricio, Chipita gave birth to a son, but the father ran off, taking the child with him. Chipita also took in a mentally retarded boy, Juan Silvera, who assisted her with chores; some thought he was also her child.

By the 1860s, Chipita's cabin was well known to travelers and combatants in the Civil War (1861–1865). Cotton was a major export commodity, and was at that time being transported overland to Mexico, rather than to the port in Corpus Christi for shipment.

The murder of John Savage

It was during this time that John Savage stayed with Chipita. Savage was a wealthy horse trader who made money by buying and selling horses to Cotton Road travelers and to both the Union and Confederate armies during the Civil War. Facts surrounding the story are scarce, but it is understood that Savage was returning from a profitable sale in San Antonio and stopped for lodging at Chipita's cabin. He slept on the porch with a large amount of gold in one pocket and his gun on the other side; it was a very hot and humid night.

KEY DATES

1830s Moves to San Patricio, Texas, from Mexico with her father. After her father is killed, she survives by cooking, and taking in travelers.

1863 John Savage is murdered on August 23. Chipita is hanged from a tree in San Patricio County, Texas, on November 13.

A few days later, some slave girls found John Savage's body stuffed in a sack in the Aransas River not far from Chipita's cabin. His head had been split open with an axe.

Sheriff William B. Means assumed the murderer was someone Chipita may have known or boarded. When he went to question Chipita, he found the porch stained with blood. Chipita acknowledged that Savage had stayed with her a few nights previously, but insisted the blood was that of chickens Juan Silvera had slaughtered for her. Despite the weak evidence, Means arrested them both. Chipita was charged with first degree murder, and Juan with second degree murder for assisting her.

Trial

The trial of Juan Silvera and Chipita was a travesty. The sheriff's best friend was the foreman of the jury, several jury members were indicted or convicted felons, and the Corpus Christi newspaper, *El Ranchero*, opined that Mexicans should not have the same rights as Americans. Most fundamentally, the evidence of the blood on the porch was purely circumstantial. However, the sheriff did manage to make Silvera say that he had dragged the body to the river. Chipita refused to testify, except to say that she was not guilty. Significantly, though, gold belonging to Savage, worth approximately $600, was found upriver a week before the trial, which seemed to many observers to cast substantial doubt over the motive for the murder.

Verdict and aftermath

Both Chipita and Juan Silvera were convicted, but the jury recommended leniency. Judge Benjamin F. Neal, however, was unmoved, and sentenced Silvera to five years in the penitentiary. Chipita was given the death sentence. On the fateful day of November 13, 1863, Chipita was hanged by the neck at the end of a rope for hours. She was such a light and a small woman that her neck did not break. Legend has it that she was buried alive and that she now haunts the area.

Kate McCumber befriended Chipita while in jail awaiting trial. Later, she claimed it was Chipita's lost son who killed Savage and ran off with horse and gun. Josefa had refused to testify to protect him.

Further reading: http://www.tsha.utexas.edu/handbook/online/ articles/RR/fro50.html (Handbook of Texas Online).

RODRÍGUEZ, Luis J.
Writer

Luis J. Rodríguez transformed himself from a Los Angeles gang member into an internationally recognized author, publisher, speaker, and community activist. He is one of the most widely acclaimed Chicano writers in the United States, and has produced works of fiction, nonfiction, poetry, and children's literature, as well as a memoir and several audio books.

A troubled start

Rodríguez was born in El Paso, Texas, in 1954, and his family moved to Los Angeles, California, when he was two years old. He got off to a bad start in life, and was stealing, taking drugs, and getting involved in gangs while still in elementary school. He dropped out of school and became homeless at age 15, and was arrested numerous times before he was 18 for stealing, assaults, and even attempted murder. When Rodriguez turned 18, he faced a six-year prison sentence, was addicted to heroin, and had seen 25 of his friends killed in gang crimes in the barrio (Latino quarter) of Los Angeles.

Despite his criminal activities, Rodríguez also participated in some of the key events of the Chicano movement, such as the East Los Angeles Blowouts (1968) and the National Chicano Moratorium against the Vietnam War (August 29, 1970). Taking part in these actions, Rodriguez made new friends in the community, who encouraged him to get clean, give up the gang lifestyle, and go back and finish high school. Rodriguez felt a responsibility to these new friends and took their advice.

Further education

After finishing high school, Rodríguez attended California State University, Los Angeles, where he became active in the student organization Movimiento Estudiantíl Chicano de Aztlán (MEChA). Next, continuing his education in the evening at East Los Angeles Community College while working during the day, Rodríguez became a reporter and photographer for several Los Angeles newspapers, including the *Eastside Sun.* That same year, 1980, Rodríguez attended the Summer Program for Minority Journalists at the University of California, Berkeley, and began writing for the *San Bernadino Sun.* He also returned to his Chicano roots in East Los Angeles, editing and publishing *ChismeArte* magazine, which was based at the Self-Help Graphics visual arts center.

▲ *Luis Rodríguez was dragged into Los Angeles gang life as a youth, but participation in community activism inspired him to turn his life around and become an author.*

Writer, publisher, and activist

Later in the 1980s, Rodríguez worked for organizations that shared his sense of social justice, such as California Public Radio and the American Federation of State, County, and Municipal Employees (AFSCME). In 1985, Rodríguez moved to Chicago, Illinois, where he wrote for a leftist newspaper, freelanced for *The Nation* magazine, wrote for the archdiocese of Chicago, and worked at several radio stations as a writer and reporter. While in Chicago, Rodríguez became active in the spoken-word and poetry scene, eventually opening his own publishing house, Tía Chucha Press, in 1989. It was devoted to lesser-known artists. Rodríguez subsequently devoted himself to writing, publishing, and political activism.

Rodríguez has written more than a dozen books, including *Poems across the Pavement* (1991), *The Concrete River* (1991), *America Is Her Name* (1998), *Hearts and*

INFLUENCES AND INSPIRATION

Luis J. Rodríguez's story is one of inspiration that he hopes will motivate others to leave gang life and become productive, good, and healthy human beings. Rodríguez credits words in the form of music, poetry, journalism, and fiction, with saving his life. He entered English-only public school speaking only Spanish and struggled. It was a teacher at East Los Angeles Community College, Mr. Takagi (a Japanese American writer), who, recognizing Rodríguez's talent and determination, mentored him one-on-one for a semester, and fostered his writing skills. Now, Rodríguez advises other young people to find mentors, regardless of their ethnic background, and to write about what they know. The stories will resonate with others who share those experiences.

Hands: Creating Community in Violent Times (2001), *Sí, Se Puede! Yes, We Can* (2002), *The Republic of East L.A: Stories* (2002), and *Music of the Mill* (2005).

Main claim to fame
Rodríguez is best known for his 1993 international best-selling memoir, *Always Running: La Vida Loca, Gang Days in L.A.* The book is essentially an autobiographical warning to his son, Ramiro, not to follow in his father's footsteps. The work won a Carl Sandburg Literary Award, a *Chicago Sun-Times* Book Award, and was a *New York Times* Notable Book, with more than 250,000 copies sold. Despite that success, in 1999 the American Library Association (ALA) named *Always Running* one of the 100 most censored books in the United States. That is because, although it has always been popular with students and teachers, it is widely held to glorify violence. As a result, efforts have been made to remove it from public school libraries in Illinois, Michigan, Texas, and California.

In addition to book-length works, Rodríguez has written and reported for *US News & World Report,* the *Chicago Tribune,* the *Los Angeles Times,* and the *Utne Reader*. He has been interviewed and reviewed by some of the most prestigious radio and television programs and newspapers around the world.

Awarded career
Many awards have been bestowed on Rodríguez for his works. They include the Lila Wallace-Reader's Digest Writer's Award (1996), the Hispanic Heritage Award for Literature (1998), the Paterson Prize for Books for Young Adults (1999), and the Premio Fronterizo at the Border Book Festival in Las Cruces, New Mexico (2001). Greatly in demand on the lecture-tour circuit, Rodríguez has addressed audiences throughout the United States, as well as in numerous foreign countries, including Austria, Canada, El Salvador, England, France, Germany, Guatemala, Honduras, Italy, Mexico, the Netherlands, Nicaragua, and Puerto Rico.

KEY DATES	
1954	Born in El Paso, Texas.
1989	Starts Tía Chucha Press.
1993	Publishes *Always Running: La Vida Loca, Gang Days in L.A.*
2001	Receives Unsung Heroes of Compassion Award from the Dalai Lama for "Wisdom in Action"; opens Tía Chucha's Café Cultural with his wife and brother-in-law.
2002	Receives Sundance Institute Arts Writing Fellowship.

Beyond Rodríguez's prolific writings and numerous awards, he has maintained throughout his later life an unwavering commitment to the Chicano community and its youth. In 1994, he founded Youth Struggling for Survival and began working with the Mosaic Multicultural Foundation, helping youth through art and mentoring. Noting a lack of bookstores that carried the works of Latin authors, in 2001 Rodríguez, his wife, Trini, and their brother-in-law Enrique Sánchez opened Tía Chucha's Café Cultural, a bookstore, café, art gallery, and performance art space, in Sylmar, California. In 2004, they opened the companion Tía Chucha's Centro Cultural, which houses Tía Chucha Press, Dos Manos Records, and *Xispas* magazine.

Personal life
Luis Rodríguez currently works in southern California, where he lives with his wife. He has four children: Ramiro, who has served time in an Illinois state prison, and to whom *Always Running* is dedicated; Andrea, a schoolteacher and the first in the family to complete college; Ruben; and Luis. Rodríguez also has four grandchildren.

Further reading: Rodríguez, Luis. *Always Running: La Vida Loca, Gang Days in L.A.* New York, NY: Touchstone, 1994. http://www.luisjrodriguez.com (Rodríguez's official website).

RODRIGUEZ, Michelle
Actor

Michelle Rodriguez is a Puerto Rican Dominican actor who made her movie debut as a boxer, and then quickly established herself as a popular star.

Auspicious entry

Rodriguez was born in 1978 in Texas, and raised there and in the Dominican Republic, Puerto Rico, and New Jersey. As a child she was an avid movie fan, and her ambition was to become a writer, director, or actor. She first appeared on screen as an extra in Spike Lee's *Summer of Sam* (1999). Her breakthrough came in writer-director Karyn Kusama's *Girlfight* (2000), in which she played a frustrated, fiery Latina learning the art of boxing. Kusama cast the inexperienced Rodriguez after auditioning some 350 hopefuls.

Rodriguez made a convincing boxer in the gripping fight scenes. She also impressed in the domestic episodes, conveying her character's complex relationship with her volatile father. *Girlfight* was a sensation at the Sundance Film Festival, and won Rodriguez an Independent Spirit Award in 2001. *Rolling Stone* magazine wrote that she "smolders with the beauty and intensity of a born star."

Testy heroines

Rodriguez's *Girlfight* role established a trend for subsequent characters. She frequently played no-nonsense, smart-talking but sultry heroines who excel in their chosen field. After *Girlfight*, Rodriguez made two auto-themed movies. She played a taxi driver opposite Danny Glover in *3 A.M.* (2001), and joined a youthful ensemble for a blistering thriller about illegal street racing, *The Fast and the Furious* (2001), in which she played Vin Diesel's girlfriend. *The Fast and the Furious* was panned by critics but triumphed at the box office thanks to its music, high-speed stunts, and dazzling camerawork.

After appearing on stage in Eve Ensler's *The Vagina Monologues*, Rodriguez played a succession of dynamic characters. She joined Milla Jovovich for the sci-fi adventure *Resident Evil* (2002), a screen version of the zombie-infested computer game. Her next roles were as a skilled surfer opposite Kate Bosworth in *Blue Crush* (2002) and an elite Los Angeles police officer alongside Colin Farrell in *S.W.A.T.* (2003). Rodriguez went on to start her own production company, and later appeared in two horror fantasies: *BloodRayne* (2005) and *The Breed* (2006). She has also been seen in the popular ABC television series *Lost*.

Further reading: *Interview* magazine, September 2000.
http://archives.cnn.com/2000/SHOWBIZ/Movies/09/29/girlfight/ (profile).

▼ **Michelle Rodriguez has managed her acting career skillfully to avoid the typecasting that has hindered the progress of other Latina actors.**

KEY DATES	
1978	Born in Bexar County, Texas, on July 12.
1999	Makes screen debut as an extra in *Summer of Sam*.
2000	Wins rave notices for *Girlfight*.
2001	Wins Independent Spirit Award for her role in *Girlfight*.
2005	Stars in second season of ABC TV's *Lost*.

RODRÍGUEZ, Narciso
Fashion Designer

Cuban American Narciso Rodríguez is one of the most sought-after fashion designers in the United States. His sleek, polished, and exquisitely tailored designs have been worn by celebrities such as Oprah Winfrey, Claire Danes, and Salma Hayek.

"Unmacho"

Rodríguez was born in 1961 in Newark, New Jersey, where his father, Narciso, a retired dock worker, and his mother, Rawedia María, had settled after emigrating from Cuba five years previously. He was highly creative as a teenager, and his early ambition was to become an architect. When he later decided to become a fashion designer, he concealed his decision from his parents because he knew they would oppose a career that was widely regarded as "unmacho" (effeminate) in the Cuban American community.

After high school, Rodríguez won a place at the prestigious Parson's School of Design in New York, and with time his parents became reconciled to his choice of

▼ *Narciso Rodríguez is one of the leading fashion designers of the late-20th and early-21st centuries.*

career. After graduation, he worked in various New York fashion houses, including a position assisting Donna Karan, then chief designer at Anne Klein. In 1995, Rodríguez was simultaneously appointed design director at TSE in New York and at Cerruti in Paris, France.

Into the limelight

In 1996, Rodríguez attracted international attention when he designed a $40,000 wedding dress for Calvin Klein publicist Carolyn Bessette. Although her marriage to John F. Kennedy, Jr., was held in private, a single photograph of the couple, with the bride wearing the designer's simple, silk sheath dress, appeared in newspapers and magazines around the world. Rodríguez's sudden celebrity helped him launch his own fashion label in Milan, Italy, the following year. He won a cluster of industry awards, including Hispanic Designer of the Year.

Rodríguez then went to Madrid, Spain, to work as creative director for the fashion label Loewe, and it was only in 2001 that he returned to the United States and began to design clothes under his own name again. Rodríguez now found himself at the forefront of the U.S. fashion industry. His clothes have been featured regularly in *Vogue*, and in 2002 and 2003 he was named Womenswear Designer of the Year.

Rodríguez's designs are typically described as "minimalist": shape and silhouette (outline) are emphasized, materials are luxurious yet subtle, and colors are often restrained—whites, blacks, grays, and creams. In 2003 he launched For Her, a women's perfume line.

See also: Hayek, Salma

Further reading: www.narcisorodriguez.com (company Web site with biography and images of his work).

RODRIGUEZ, Paul
Actor, Director

One of the most bankable stars in Hollywood, Paul Rodriguez is a comedian, actor, writer, movie director, and producer.

Early life

The son of Mexican migrant farmworkers, Rodriguez was born in 1955 in Culiacan, Sinaloa, Mexico, and grew up in Los Angeles, California. He attended Dominguez High School, Long Beach City College, and California State University, Long Beach. He studied law, but his life changed when his drama teacher took him to the Comedy Store in Los Angeles. It was there soon afterward that he got his start in show business. He toured the comedy circuit, and eventually landed a job as the warm-up comic on Norman Lear's *Gloria*, a spin-off from the television series *All in the Family*. Lear was so impressed by Rodriguez that he developed the situation comedy *AKA Pablo* for him. Although *AKA Pablo* did not last long, the talk show, *El Show de Paul Rodriguez*, had a four-year run on the television station Univision.

Range of activities

In addition to making numerous comedy specials, during the 1980s Rodriguez branched out into movies. After appearing in *D.C. Cab* (1983), a movie that also featured Irene Cara, and *Born in East L.A.* (1987), he went on to appear alongside some of the biggest names in Hollywood: Lupe Ontiveros in *La Pastorela* (1991), Jimmy Smits in *Price*

▼ **Paul Rodriguez directed and played the lead role of Juan Lopez in the movie A Million to Juan,** *a romantic comedy about a Mexican immigrant.*

KEY DATES	
1955	Born in Culiacan, Sinaloa, Mexico, on January 19.
1983	Appears in his first movie, *D.C. Cab*.
1984	Stars in television show *AKA Pablo*.
1994	Scripts and stars in *A Million to Juan*.
2002	Appears in *Blood Work*, directed by and starring Clint Eastwood.

of Glory (2000), Whoopi Goldberg in *Rat Race* (2001), Will Smith in *Ali* (2001), and Clint Eastwood in *Blood Work* (2002).

Meanwhile, Rodriguez set up his own company, Paul Rodriguez Productions (PRP). One of its principal aims was to advance the careers of talented Latino and Latina actors and filmmakers. PRP's first movie, *A Million to Juan* (1994), was based on a story by Mark Twain. It was scripted by Rodriguez, who also appeared in it with Cheech Marin and Edward James Olmos. It cost only $165,000 to make and was released in only 200 U.S. theaters, but eventually grossed more than $13 million, mainly through video sales and foreign distribution revenues.

Off set

In his free time, Paul Rodriguez works extensively for charity, hosting comedy shows and golf tournaments for the National Hispanic Scholarship Fund (NHSF). He is also involved with organizations such as the National Association of Latino Elected Officials (NALEO), Project Literacy, and Comic Relief. For his efforts, Rodriguez has been honored by the National Council of La Raza (NCLR) with the Ruben Salazar Award for promoting positive portrayals of Latinos.

Rodriguez's son, Paul Rodriguez, Jr., is a leading professional skateboarder.

See also: Cara, Irene; Marin, Cheech; Olmos, Edward James; Ontiveros, Lupe; Smits, Jimmy

Further reading: "Comico o Dramatico: Paul Rodriguez Tries His Hand at Acting." *Semana*, June 8, 2001.
http://www.imdb.com/name/nm0735467 (Internet Movie Database [IMDb] Web site).

RODRÍGUEZ, Pellín
Singer

A renowned Puerto Rican salsa singer, Pellín Rodríguez was an original member and the leading vocalist of El Gran Combo de Puerto Rico, one of the most famous orchestras in Latino music.

Child performer

Pedro Rodríguez de Gracia was born in 1926 in Villa Palmeras, Puerto Rico. He came from a poor home, and after completing his primary education he was forced to work for a living.

Rodríguez was raised in a musical family. His mother, Tomasita de Gracia, had been a singer when young. Rodríguez began to perform in public at age 13. He formed the duet Rodríguez de Córdova with his older sister Alicia. The young Rodríguez was soon impressing audiences with his singing voice and dancing skills.

Rodríguez began singing in other local bands, but his professional career began in earnest when he joined the band Conjunto Moderno. In 1945, Rodríguez was invited to become a member of Rafael Elvira's band Orquesta Tropicana. In 1947 Rodríguez moved to New York, where

he performed with great Puerto Rican artists such as Noro Morales, Tito Puente, and José Fajardo. In 1953, Rodríguez married Elba López Pérez, with whom he had three sons, Pedro, Michael, and Tommy. In the mid-1950s, Rodríguez moved to Chicago, Illinois, hoping to form his own band. While in Chicago, Rodríguez frequently traveled back to New York to perform with Xavier Cugat, another Puerto Rican music legend.

International star

Rodríguez returned to Puerto Rico in 1960. Two years later, he joined the band El Gran Combo, becoming one of the leading singers of the group. The group was known for its choreographed dancing as well as its music. Rodríguez, Andy Montañez, and Mike Ramos were the lead dancers. El Gran Combo's first album, *Acángana*, became a number-one hit in New York, Panama, and Puerto Rico. With El Gran Combo, Rodríguez's fame spread throughout Latin America.

In 1973, after nearly a decade of performing with El Gran Combo, Rodríguez left the band to launch a solo career. He was one of the most talented salsa singers of the era, and was popularly nicknamed "El Caballo de Hierro" (The Iron Horse).

Rodríguez was also a celebrated bolero singer. Many of his songs have become Puerto Rican classics. In 1982, El Gran Combo re-formed for a brief comeback tour named El Gran Combo Del Ayer (The Big Combo of Yesterday). Rodríguez died in San Juan in 1984.

See also: Cugat, Xavier; Puente, Tito

Further reading: http://www.musicofpuertorico.com/en/pellin_rodriguez.html (biography).

▼ *Pellín Rodríguez (left) performs with El Gran Combo in 1982.*

RODRIGUEZ, Richard
Writer

Richard Rodriguez is a prolific author whose views on affirmative action, assimilation, and bilingual education have made him a controversial figure in the Hispanic American community.

Early life
One of four children, Rodriguez was born in 1944 in San Francisco, California, shortly after his parents, Leopoldo and Victoria Moran Rodriguez, had emigrated from Mexico. When he was still a young boy, the family moved to Sacramento, where he was educated at the Sacred Heart Catholic school from age six. Lessons there were in English, a language that Rodriguez scarcely spoke, and the enforced change from his mother tongue, Spanish, had a profound influence on his attitudes in later life.

After graduating from high school, Rodriguez majored in English at Stanford University, and then enrolled in Columbia University's religious studies program. He won a Fulbright fellowship that enabled him to study at the Warburg Institute in London, England. He later received a PhD in Renaissance literature from the University of California at Berkeley.

Controversial writings
Rodriguez entered the national spotlight in 1981 with the publication of *Hunger of Memory: The Education of Richard Rodriguez*, a collection of autobiographical essays. In the work, he describes how his bilingual upbringing—speaking Spanish at home and English at school—created a split between his private and public personas, and thus had a damaging effect on his sense of identity. From his own experience he concluded that bilingual education is detrimental to the individual because the individual never learns to become a fully integrated member of society.

▲ *The often provocative opinions of Richard Rodriguez have encouraged many Mexican Americans to revise their views on a range of political subjects.*

Rodriguez also opposes affirmative action, the formal effort to provide increased employment opportunities for women and ethnic minorities, to overcome past patterns of discrimination. In his view, people who benefit from affirmative action inevitably leave behind the very things that make them a minority. If affirmative action is to exist, then it should be based on class rather than gender, race or ethnicity. Of assimilation, Rodriguez took the view that it was inevitable when two cultures meet, but not necessarily desirable. His views were not universally welcomed by fellow Mexican Americans.

In addition to his writing, Rodriguez has worked as an editor for the Pacific News Service, and has appeared regularly as an essayist on *The NewsHour* with Jim Lehrer, a Public Broadcasting Service (PBS) television show.

See also: Bilingualism

Further reading: Rodriguez, Richard. *Hunger of Memory: The Education of Richard Rodriguez: An Autobiography*. Boston, MA: D. R. Godine, 1981.
http://www.pbs.org/now/arts/rodriguez.html (biography with links to interviews and online essays).

KEY DATES

1944   Born in San Francisco, California, on July 31.

1981   Publishes *Hunger of Memory*, a collection of autobiographical essays.

1992   Publishes *Days of Obligation: An Argument with My Mexican Father*.

1997   Receives George Foster Peabody Award for "outstanding achievement in broadcast and cable."

RODRÍGUEZ, Robert
Filmmaker

Robert Rodríguez is a Mexican American filmmaker who emerged in the 1990s. By the early 21st century, he had established himself as one of the leading names in North American cinema. Although principally a director, he has also written, edited, and produced several movies.

Early life
Rodríguez was born in 1968 in San Antonio, Texas. As a child, he loved to entertain his four brothers and five sisters by drawing comic books and making home movies. He eventually found work in both areas. For three years, Rodríguez drew a regular comic strip about his family life for the *Daily Texan* newspaper. His family relationships also inspired his first proper short film, *Bedhead* (1991), which he produced while studying film at the University of Texas at Austin.

Road to fame
On graduating, Rodríguez set his heart on making a full-length movie but lacked the financial backing needed to do so. Having been turned down by banks and other commercial lenders, he raised the money required for the project by volunteering to undergo medical experiments at a local hospital, where he spent one month being tested for a cholesterol-related drug. Throughout the period he was developing his script for *El Mariachi*, an explosive tale about a Mexican folk troubadour who is mistaken for a gunman. He eventually directed, edited, and produced the movie, which took two weeks to shoot and cost only $7,000. He cut costs in every way he could, using nonprofessional actors and even borrowing the camera. The critical acclaim *El Mariachi* received on its release in 1992 kickstarted Rodríguez's career. He later wrote *Rebel without a Crew*, a book about the making of the film.

Into the big time
After writing and directing the TV movie *Roadracers* (1994), which was completed in only 13 days, Rodríguez's next full-length screen feature, *Desperado* (1995), covered much the same ground as *El Mariachi*. Spanish star Antonio Banderas took the lead role as the mariachi (Mexican folk musician). Throughout his career, Rodríguez has made a point of using as many Hispanic actors and crew as possible. His rationale is straightforward: "I made *Desperado* because there really wasn't a Latin action hero,"

he told *Creative Screenwriting* in 1995. "I wanted my action movie to be just as strong as regular action movies, but with Latins in it."

At one stage, Rodríguez also looked set to direct Banderas in *Zorro*, but when the film was eventually contracted in 1998, Martin Campbell was chosen as director. Both *Desperado* and *El Mariachi* were compelling mixtures of humor, violence, sex, and action. Rodríguez's films commonly blend together such contrasting tones, none more so than his delirious road movie *From Dusk till Dawn* (1996), which was scripted by Quentin Tarantino, the acclaimed director of such movies as *Reservoir Dogs* and *Pulp Fiction*.

Children first
Rodríguez's next project was *The Faculty* (1998), a high-school fantasy in which the teachers are aliens. The movie established him as a director who coaxed strong performances from young actors. He enhanced his reputation with *Spy Kids* (2001), a PG-rated action

▼ *Robert Rodríguez began his career as a cartoonist before becoming one of the leading movie directors of the 1990s.*

71

adventure featuring juvenile performers and containing a host of James Bond-style gadgets. It followed the fortunes of a brother and sister whose parents, both master spies, are spirited away by an evil TV presenter. *Spy Kids*—set in South America, but shot in Austin, Texas—was a box-office smash, making more than $100 million in the United States alone, and it won an American Latino Media Arts (ALMA) award. A sequel, *Spy Kids 2: Island of Lost Dreams* (2002), was commissioned before the first movie was completed, and in the wake of its success came *Spy Kids 3D: Game Over* (2003).

Family affair

The Adventures of Sharkboy and Lavagirl in 3-D (2005) was another family affair. The movie was inspired by a suggestion made to Rodríguez by one of his sons, Racer, and starred his other children—Rocket, Rebel, Rogue, and Rhiannon—in supporting roles. Most of Rodríguez's films have also been produced by Elizabeth Avellan, his wife since 1990.

Old theme revisited

Rodríguez next returned to the mariachi theme, this time in the epic *Once upon a Time in Mexico* (2003), which again starred Antonio Banderas. By now Rodríguez had established a stock company of Hispanic actors, including Banderas, Salma Hayek, Cheech Marin, and Danny Trejo. Rodríguez followed up with the ultra-violent *Sin City* (2005), a faithful adaptation of the graphic novel series by Frank Miller that starred Mickey Rourke and Bruce Willis. Miller codirected the movie, but when the Directors Guild of America (DGA) refused to allow him to be credited for his work, Rodríguez left the guild in protest. It was a brave move, since some studios work only with DGA-registered talent.

In *Sin City*, Rodríguez made use of the latest digital technology. The actors performed scenes against a green screen, and the backgrounds and special effects were

KEY DATES	
1968	Born in San Antonio, Texas, on June 20.
1991	Produces first movie, *Bedhead*, a short, while still a student at the University of Texas at Austin.
1992	Release of *El Mariachi*, his low-budget debut feature.
1994	Directs *Roadracers*, a TV movie.
1995	Completes *Desperado*, starring Antonio Banderas.
1998	*The Faculty* is a box-office hit.
2001	*Spy Kids* gains popular acclaim; spawns two sequels.
2003	*Once upon a time In Mexico*.
2005	Codirects *Sin City* with author Frank Miller.

added later. The film won a technical award at the Cannes Film Festival, and quickly spawned a sequel, *Sin City 2* (2006). Rodríguez plans to make screen versions of all Miller's books.

Cooperative efforts

Rodríguez's directorial technique is highly flexible. While filming *Desperado*, it emerged that one scene needed a second camera crew. Rodríguez felt uncomfortable with that, and so when Antonio Banderas offered to direct it he had no hesitation in agreeing. Rodríguez also directed some of the scenes of *Pulp Fiction* in which Quentin Tarantino acted on screen.

See also: Hayek, Salma; Marin, Cheech

Further reading: Rodríguez, Robert. *Rebel without a Crew, or, How A 23-Year-Old Filmmaker with $7,000 Became a Hollywood Player*. New York, NY: Dutton, 1995. http://www.troublemakerstudios.com (Web site for Rodríguez's production company).

RODRÍGUEZ DE TIÓ, Lola
Poet

Lola Rodríguez de Tió was a renowned intellectual and poet. She is probably best known for writing the lyrics to the Puerto Rican national anthem "La Borinqueña."

Early life

Born in 1843 in the town of San Germán, Puerto Rico, Rodríguez was the daughter of Sebastián Rodríguez de Astudillo, an eminent lawyer, and Carmen Ponce de León. She began attending school in her hometown of Mayagüez, but was later home-schooled by her parents. Their domestic library helped Rodríguez develop a passion for reading history, religion, and travel books, and provided her with all the materials she needed to inspire her own poetry writing.

Becoming a writer

At age 20, Rodríguez married journalist and poet Bonocio Tió Segarra, with whom she shared patriotism and a passion for literature. Both Rodríguez de Tió and her husband were fiercely against Spain's colonization and tyranny of their island. They hosted many literary gatherings, which were attended by distinguished intellectuals in San Germán and Mayagüez. It was at one of these events that Rodríguez de Tió composed the acclaimed lyrics to the revolutionary version of Puerto Rico's national hymn "La Borinqueña."

In 1876, Rodríguez de Tió collected a series of poems in the anthology *Mis Cantares* (My Songs). A year later, she was forced to leave the island with her husband, banished for her political activities. They settled in Venezuela, where they lived for three and a half years. In 1880, after returning to Puerto Rico, Rodríguez de Tió

▲ *Lola Rodríguez de Tió was the first Puerto Rican poet to achieve a reputation throughout the Caribbean. She is best known for her lyrics to "La Borinqueña."*

composed "Mi Ofrenda" (My Offering), a poem in memory of her close friend, the poet José Gautier Benítez. In the following year, Rodríguez de Tió and her husband launched *La Almojábana*, a literary magazine.

During this period, Rodríguez de Tió became involved in the release of 16 political prisoners and patriots, among them Román Baldorioti de Castro and Ramón Marín. This led to a second exile for Rodríguez de Tió and her husband, this time on the island of Cuba. The couple organized literary gatherings there, and developed friendships with Manuel Sanguily and Enrique José Varona, among others. Rodríguez de Tió's next poetry anthology, *Mi Libro de Cuba* (My Book of Cuba), was published in 1893. Two years later, Rodríguez de Tío moved with her husband to New York. After the Spanish–American War (1898), the couple moved back to Cuba in 1899. Rodríguez de Tío died in 1924 in Havana.

KEY DATES

1843	Born in San Germán, Puerto Rico, on September 14.
1867	Composes the verses for the patriotic version of the national hymn "La Borinqueña."
1876	Publishes her first book, *Mis Cantares*.
1877	Exiled to Venezuela for more than three years.
1889	Exiled to Cuba.
1924	Dies in Cuba on November 10.

See also: Benítez, José Gautier

Further reading: http://www.prboriken.com/lola.htm (biography).

RODRÍGUEZ-DÍAZ, Angel
Artist

Angel Rodríguez-Díaz is a Latino artist working in the United States. He pursues issues of cultural identity, mainly through portraiture.

Early life

Rodríguez-Díaz was born in 1955 in Puerto Rico. He graduated in 1978 from the University of Puerto Rico with a BA in fine arts. He then moved to New York City to study for a master's in fine art at Hunter College, City University. He remained in the city after his graduation in 1982 and participated in several solo and group exhibitions. In 1994 he moved to San Antonio, Texas.

The question of identity is central to the work of Rodríguez-Díaz: As a citizen of Puerto Rico he is an American, but in the United States he is wrongly identified as a Mexican. These contradictions are expressed in his portrait painting, which seems to follow the tradition of his 18th-century compatriot José Campeche, although he does not acknowledge Campeche as a source of inspiration. As with Campeche, the detail and context of the portraits are more revealing than the portraits themselves. Rodríguez-Díaz places his sitters in surreal surroundings: *The Protagonist of an Endless Story* (1993), for example, is a portrait of Sandra Cisneros, a leading Chicana author, in a heroic posture against a blazing skyscape. The purchase of the painting by the Smithsonian American Art Museum in 1996 helped establish Rodríguez-Díaz's career. In 1998 he was appointed artist in residence at the ArtPace Foundation in San Antonio. There he produced *Splendid Little War*, an installation that celebrated the centenary of the end of the Spanish–American War (1898) and included a self-portrait on the facade of the ArtPace Building made out of 8,500 Christmas lights. More recently he has concealed his subjects under a variety of masks used by *luchadores* (Mexican wrestlers), as seen in the exhibition at the Rudolph Projects/ArtScan Gallery in Houston in 2005.

KEY DATES	
1955	Born in San Juan, Puerto Rico, on December 6.
1982	Completes masters degree in fine art.
1998	Appointed artist in residence at the ArtPace Foundation in San Antonio, Texas.

▲ **Blue Demon** *is one of several works by Rodríguez-Díaz to be inspired by the world of Mexican wrestling.*

Although portraiture in oil painting is his main medium, Rodríguez-Díaz also produced *Birth of a City*, a mural 54 feet (16.4m) in length, for the Development and Business Services Center in San Antonio in 2003. The work combines high technology with traditional painting methods: It depicts a night view of San Antonio made of a collage of small photographs digitally enlarged and transformed by overpainting.

See also: Campeche y Jordán, José; Cisneros, Sandra

Further reading: Riggs, Thomas (ed.). *St. James Guide to Hispanic Artists: Profiles of Latino and Latin American Artists.* Detroit, MI: St. James Press, 2002.

ROLAND, Gilbert
Actor

Gilbert Roland was a swashbuckling screen actor who appeared in more than 100 movies in a career that lasted 60 years.

Early life

One of six children, Roland was born Luis Antonio Damaso de Alonso in 1905 in Juárez, Chihuahua, Mexico. In 1911, he moved with his family to the United States to escape the Mexican Revolution. He was raised in El Paso, Texas, until 1920, when he moved to California. He found work in Hollywood as an extra in silent films. He took his stage name from the last names of two of his favorite silent screen stars: matinee idol John Gilbert and serial queen Ruth Roland.

Gilbert Roland secured his first major onscreen credit at age 19 for his role in *The Plastic Age* (1925). While filming, he befriended the star, Clara Bow (1905–1965), and for a time the two were lovers. His first leading role was in *Camille* (1926), in which he appeared opposite Norma Talmadge. Over the next three years, Roland played the romantic lead in seven further films, and by the end of the 1920s he was an established celebrity.

Unlike several stars of the silent screen, Roland made a successful transition to talkies. His appeal was based on his looks and athleticism, however, and when they

▼ *Gilbert Roland with Norma Talmadge in a scene from* Camille.

declined as he aged in the 1930s and 1940s, so too did his box-office appeal. By 1940, he had appeared in 35 movies.

Roland served in the U.S. Army during World War II (1939–1945), and afterward returned to acting at Monogram Studios, where he played the Cisco Kid, a role that had previously been acted by, among others, César Romero.

In 1949 Roland appeared in *We Were Strangers*, directed by John Huston, which gave his career a welcome boost. Now he was sought after for character roles. Movie historians Luis Reyes and Peter Rubie wrote: "Roland's screen characters were always dashing, romantic and sly. No matter how roguish a character he played … audiences knew he would always do the right thing by the last reel."

Later years

Although Roland continued to make occasional film appearances in the 1950s and 1960s, notably in John Ford's *Cheyenne Autumn* (1964), most of his later work was in television. He made special guest appearances in series such as *Wagon Train*, *The High Chaparral*, *Kung Fu*, *The Sacketts*, and *Hart to Hart*. His final movie roles were in *Caboblanco* (1980) and *Barbarosa* (1982). He died in 1994 at age 88.

See also: Romero, Cesar

Further reading: Reyes, Luis, and Peter Rubie. *Hispanics in Hollywood: A Celebration of 100 Years in Film and Television.* Hollywood, CA: Lone Eagle, 2000.
http://www.imdb.com/name/nm0738042 (International Movie Data Base [IMDb] Web site).

ROMAN, Phil
Animator

Award-winning animator Phil Roman has directed, produced, and animated some of the United States's most popular cartoon series, including *The Simpsons*.

Early life

Born in Fresno, California, on December 21, 1930, Roman was the son of Mexican immigrant grape workers Pedro and Ceceña Roman. Aged 13, Roman fell in love with animation after his mother took him to see the Disney movie *Bambi*. Roman convinced the editor of his school newspaper to allow him to publish a cartoon strip. He also took several art correspondence courses; he had a tutor named "Sparky," whose real name was Charles M. Schulz, the creator of the popular character Charlie Brown.

A love affair with art

After graduating in 1949, Roman worked in the local Warner Brothers Theater, where he saw every cartoon that was released. A colleague convinced Roman to move to Los Angeles to study animation. In 1949 he boarded a bus to the city; he had a letter of recommendation from the theater manager and just $60 in his pocket. He enrolled at the Hollywood Art Center.

Following the outbreak of the Korean War (1950–1953), Roman spent almost four years in the Air Force. Following his return, he rejoined the Art Center as a student under the terms of the GI Bill. One of his teachers, Ted Bonics, who had been a Disney animator, particularly influenced him. In May 1955 Disney hired Roman as an assistant animator on *Sleeping Beauty*, initially on a one-month trial basis. Roman worked there for almost two years, but after realizing that there were not many opportunities for career

▲ *Phil Roman has established educational scholarships to help young animators.*

advancement, he left to work for Imagination, Inc., a San Francisco-based company, where Roman picked up invaluable experience in every aspect of animation.

Roman soon established a reputation for being an excellent animator, a fact that made it easy for him to return to work in Hollywood at the end of the 1950s. Over the next decade he worked for several major companies, including Warner and MGM Animation. In the 1970s Roman successfully collaborated with Bill Melendez, with whom he worked first as an animator on CBS specials such as *He's Your Dog, Charlie Brown*, and then as a codirector on 16 specials, including *Bon Voyage, Charlie Brown*. He was nominated for 15 Emmy Awards, winning three.

In 1984 Roman established his own company, Film Roman, Inc. Its first production was the Emmy-winning *Garfield in the Rough*: Roman made nine more Garfield specials, all of which were nominated for Emmys. Building on the company's success, Roman produced the acclaimed series *The Simpsons*. Other hits included *King of the Hill* and *The Mask*. To raise money for its huge-scale projects, Film Roman went public in the late 1990s. Roman eventually resigned, although he maintained his shares in the company. In 1999, Roman started Phil Roman Entertainment, a small animation company that has produced such children's movies as *Bluebeard the Pirate*.

See also: Melendez, Bill

Further reading: http://www.philromanent.com (official site of Phil Roman Entertainment).

KEY DATES	
1930	Born in Fresno, California, on December 21.
1955	Begins working at Disney.
1957	Moves to Imagination, Inc.
1970	Begins collaborating with Bill Melendez, with whom he works until 1983.
1984	Founds Film Roman, Inc.
1999	Founds Phil Roman Entertainment.

ROMANO, Octavio
Publisher, Academic

Mexican-born publisher and professor of behavioral science Octavio Romano helped launch the literary careers of many important Chicano writers, including Rudolfo Anaya and Tomás Rivera.

Making a difference

Born in Mexico City on February 20, 1923, Octavio Ignacío Romano-Vizcarra was the youngest child of María and Manuel Romano. He spent his early life in Tecate, Mexico, before his family moved to National City, California. In 1943 Romano enlisted in the U.S. Army. He won several medals for bravery in World War II (1939–1945).

On his return to the United States at the end of the conflict, Romano attended college on the GI Bill. He graduated in 1952 with a BA in anthropology from the University of New Mexico, and went on to earn a master's and a PhD in anthropology from the University of California at Berkeley. From 1963, Romano was associate professor of behavioral science at the School of Public Health at Berkeley.

▼ *Octavio Romano was a man of many talents—a gifted publisher, writer, and teacher.*

In 1967, Romano founded Quinto Sol Publications, which later became Tonatiuh Quinto Sol, a groundbreaking publishing house for Mexican American authors. In addition to publishing the poetry and fiction of unpublished Chicano writers, the company was responsible for producing the influential Chicano magazine *El Grito* and *The Journal of Mexican American Thought*. In the first issue of *El Grito*, published between 1968 and 1974, Romano wrote an editorial that called for Mexican Americans to fight against stereotypical representations of their lives and culture in everyday life. Romano believed that only Mexican Americans could change the way Anglo Americans viewed them.

In 1967, Romano published *El Espejo* (*The Mirror*), the first anthology of modern Chicano literature. Romano also wrote a number of important essays, such as his influential "The Historical and Intellectual Presence of Mexican-Americans" (1969), in which he analyzed the cultural diversity of Chicano culture and created new categories to define the culture that are still in use today.

Romano retired from his academic position in 1989. He died of a stroke on February 26, 2005, at the age of 82, in Berkeley. He was survived by his wife, Olga, and two sons. Romano's legacy includes establishing Premio Quinto Sol, the first national award for Chicano literature.

See also: Anaya, Rudolfo; Rivera, Tomás

Further reading: Romano, Octavio (ed). *El Espejo. An Anthology of Chicano Writers.* Berkeley, CA: Tonatiuh Quinto Sol Publishers, 1967.
www.berkeleydailyplanet.com (obituary written by his wife).

ROMERO, Anthony D.
Attorney, Civil Rights Activist

In 2001 Anthony D. Romero became the first Hispanic American to head the American Civil Liberties Union (ACLU), one of the most important national nongovernmental organizations to safeguard U.S. citizens' individual rights and freedoms. As both a Hispanic and an openly gay man, Romero is widely seen as a leading spokesman for America's minority communities. Romero took up the directorship of the ACLU only a week before the terrorist attacks by Al Qaeda on New York and Washington, D.C., on September 11, 2001. He subsequently took a central—and sometimes controversial—role in the debate over how best to promote the United States's security while preserving its civil liberties.

Early life
Born in the Bronx, New York City, in 1965, Romero was the son of working-class Puerto Rican migrants Demetrio and Coralie Romero. In his native Puerto Rico, Demetrio Romero had been a laborer on a sugar plantation. In New York City, he worked first as a cleaner and later as a waiter in one of the city's hotels.

Romero and his family were eventually able to leave their apartment in a run-down Bronx housing project to settle in a working-class district of New Jersey. Romero learned about discrimination from an early age: His father, Demetrio, was repeatedly denied promotion because of racial discrimination, and he only managed to move up the career ladder after a union lawyer intervened on his behalf.

Romero's parents had little access to education. His mother, whom Romero describes as "the brains of the family," particularly encouraged her children to do well at school. Romero became the first member of his family to graduate from high school. He won a place at New Jersey's Princeton University, one of the United States's most prestigious colleges, no mean feat for a young man from a poor Hispanic background. Romero graduated from Princeton's Woodrow Wilson School of Public Policy and International Affairs in 1987, and went on to study law at Stanford University, from which he graduated in 1990.

A passion for civil rights
A qualified attorney with excellent academic credentials, Romero could have chosen to work for any large law firm. He decided to pursue a career in the field of civil rights, working for two of the most eminent New York–based

▲ **Anthony D. Romero claims that most civil rights organizations concentrate on one particular issue; in contrast, the ACLU is the "only organization that defends the civil liberties of all Americans."**

charitable organizations promoting international democracy and rights. Initially he joined the Rockefeller Foundation, where he specialized in civil rights advocacy. In 1992 he left to work for the Ford Foundation, where he served first as program officer for civil rights and racial justice, and later in the high-profile position of director of human rights and international cooperation. In the latter role, he was responsible for giving millions of dollars in grants to civil right groups around the world: In 2000 alone, the Ford Foundation donated $90 million to such groups.

Making a difference
Romero's passionate dedication to maintaining and fighting for civil rights, together with his strong leadership skills, won him many admirers. In early 2001, Romero was chosen to succeed Ira Glasser, executive director of another leading New York–based nongovernmental organization, the American Civil Liberties Union (ACLU). First founded in 1917, the ACLU has been instrumental in helping minority groups achieve equal rights; it instigated several important civil rights cases that opposed segregation and defended flag burning as a form of free expression. Romero took up his new post in 2001.

LEGACY

Anthony D. Romero began his tenure as president of the American Civil Liberties Union (ACLU) wanting to spark "a new dialogue about the bedrock values of American democracy." He said that his goal was to create a new generation of committed civil rights activists.

Romero's championship of American civil rights in the aftermath of the 2001 terrorist attacks brought him to the forefront of a national debate.

For many people, Romero became a figurehead for national dissent. He objected to some of the restraints brought in by President George W. Bush's administration post-9/11. The government pressed ahead with a radical program of counterterrorist legislation, such as the USA PATRIOT Act, which gave the government and law enforcement agencies greater powers but was considered by the ACLU to infringe the civil rights of

many U.S. citizens. Romero's effective leadership of the "Safe and Free" campaign helped challenge such legislation and highlighted rights abuses.

While Romero's stance has been commended as courageous by some supporters, critics have accused Romero and the ACLU of being unpatriotic and uncompromising. They claim that sometimes individual freedoms have to be sacrificed for the greater good of society.

"Safe and Free"

As director of the ACLU, Romero has continued to address the broad range of issues that have traditionally been the organization's preserve, including racial equality, privacy, freedom of speech, and religious freedom. He has, however, given special emphasis to minority rights. In the wake of 2005's Hurricane Katrina, Romero helped draw attention to the racial inequalities in New Orleans that led the city's African American population to suffer disproportionately from the effects of the disaster. In the field of lesbian and gay rights, Romero has promoted campaigns to extend marriage and parenting rights to same-sex couples.

Romero's overriding focus, however, has been to challenge what he and the ACLU consider to be the rapid erosion of civil rights in the post-9/11 United States. In particular, the organization has attacked the USA PATRIOT

Act (initially passed in October 2001 and renewed in March 2006), which introduced sweeping new powers for U.S. law-enforcement agencies to aid their struggle against terrorism. To publicize its case, the ACLU launched the "Safe and Free" campaign, calling for an end to the USA PATRIOT Act and other associated laws. It has also launched several lawsuits against the government that challenge the constitutionality of some of the act's provisions. Romero and other ACLU activists consider that much of the government's post-9/11 agenda has violated constitutional rights to privacy and dissent (the right to oppose official policies and ideas). In speeches and interviews, Romero has drawn particular attention to the discriminatory effects of the PATRIOT Act on U.S. minority and immigrant communities, some of whose members have faced oppression in the form of surveillance and unreasonable detention.

In addition to his work for the ACLU, Romero is active in several other civic groups, including the Center of Disability and Advocacy Rights, the New World Foundation, the Council on Foreign Relations, and Hispanics in Philanthropy. He was a Dinkelspiel Scholar at Stanford, a Cane Scholar at Princeton, and a National Hispanic Scholar at both colleges. In 2005 *Time* magazine listed Romero as one of the top 25 most influential Hispanics in America.

KEY DATES

1965   Born in the Bronx, New York City.

1987   Graduates from Woodrow Wilson School of Public Policy and International Affairs, Princeton University, New Jersey.

1990   Graduates from Stanford Law School.

2001   Appointed director of the American Civil Liberties Union (ACLU); terrorist action against the United States by Al Qaeda on September 11, 2001.

2003   Named public interest lawyer of the year.

2005   *Time* magazine lists him as one of the top 25 most influential Hispanic Americans.

See also: National Organizations

Further reading: Ta-Nehisi, Paul Coates. "The Champion of Civil Rights: Anthony Romero (The 25 Most Influential Hispanics)." *Time* (August 22, 2005).
www.aclu.org (Romero biography plus information about ACLU's campaigns).

ROMERO, Cesar
Actor

Cesar Romero was an actor known for playing Latin lovers in Hollywood movies in the 1930s and 1940s. He starred in such films and TV programs as *Springtime in the Rockies, The Captain from Castile,* and *The Cisco Kid* sequels during Hollywood's Golden Age. Later fans knew him in his role as the Joker in the 1960s' television series *Batman.* Romero appeared in more than 100 movies, received a Golden Globe nomination, and earned two stars on the Hollywood Walk of Fame during his 70-year career.

Early life
Cesar Julio Romero was born on February 15, 1907, in New York City. His parents, Cesar Julio Romero and Maria Mantilla, were wealthy Cubans who lost their fortune during the Great Depression of the 1930s. Romero studied at Collegiate and Riverdale County schools before leaving to become a ballroom dancer.

A Latin star
Romero began his stage career dancing in the Broadway show *Lady Do* (1927), and had a lead role in the stage comedy *Strictly Dishonorable* (1930). He went on to make his film debut three years later in *The Shadow Laughs* (1933), which was soon followed by *The Thin Man* (1934). Romero appeared in several subsequent movies, including giving a memorable performance in *The Devil Is a Woman* (1935) and starring with child actor Shirley Temple in the movie *Wee Willie Winkie* (1937).

A versatile performer, Romero appeared in comedies, musicals, romances, and Westerns. He became well known to audiences as the bandit the Cisco Kid in the popular film series of the same name. His other well-known performances include playing renowned Spanish explorer Hernán Cortés in *The Captain from Castile* (1947).

▲ *During his long career, Cesar Romero was known in many different guises—as the suave Latin lover in several early Hollywood movies, as the Joker in the cult series* **Batman,** *and in later life as the sophisticated Peter Stavros in* **Falcon Crest.**

Romero enjoyed a successful film career for several decades, with *Julia Misbehaves* (1948), *Around the World in Eighty Days* (1956), and the Rat Pack's cult movie *Ocean's Eleven* (1960). In 1962 Romero was nominated for the Best Comedy Picture Golden Globe for his performance in *If a Man Answers.*

From silver screen to small screen
Romero appeared in the TV series *Passport to Danger* (1954), and his guest appearances included *Rawhide, Zorro,* and *Bewitched.* Romero's best-known TV role, however, was playing the green-skinned, grinning villain the Joker in the ABC series *Batman* (1966 to 1968) and in the spin-off 1966 movie. Romero also appeared in the popular soap opera *Falcon Crest* (1985 to 1987).

Romero returned to the big screen in a string of popular Disney comedies, such as *The Computer Wore Tennis Shoes* (1969) and *The Strongest Man in the World* (1975). His last roles were in *Simple Justice* (1990) and *The Right Man* in 1993. Romero died on January 1, 1994, in Santa Monica, California.

KEY DATES	
1907	Born on February 15 in New York City.
1933	Makes film debut in *The Shadow Laughs.*
1962	Nominated for Best Comedy Picture Golden Globe.
1966	Plays the Joker in *Batman* for two years.
1994	Dies on January 1 in Santa Monica, California.

Further reading: Calistro, Paddy. *The Hollywood Archive: The Hidden History of Hollywood In the Golden Age.* New York, NY: Universe Publishing.
http://www.romerotributepage.com (tribute Web site).

ROMERO, Frank
Artist

Frank Romero is a contemporary artist whose work is intimately connected with Chicano life in California. Romero came to prominence as a first-generation Chicano artist when he cofounded the artists' collective Los Four, the first Chicano art group to gain recognition in the mainstream art market.

Early life
Romero was born in Los Angeles in 1941. A second-generation Mexican American, his father was from New Mexico and his mother from Texas. Romero grew up in the middle-class, multicultural neighborhood of Boyle Heights, Los Angeles. From an early age he became interested in art, and developed his interest throughout his school years. He studied art at the Otis Art Institute, and later at California State University, Los Angeles. During the 1960s and 1970s, Romero worked for the furniture designers Charles and Ray Eames. Between 1968 and 1969, he lived in New York, and traveled through Mexico with the artist Carlos Almaraz, whom he had met at college, where they saw the work of the Mexican muralists Diego Rivera, David Siqueiros, and José Clemente Orozco.

▼ **Frank Romero works on his vast mural** Going to the Olympics, *commissioned for the Los Angeles Olympic Games in 1984.*

KEY DATES

1941   Born in Los Angeles, California.

1974   Los Four Chicano artists collective exhibit in the Los Angeles County Museum of Art.

1984   Produces first public mural, *Going to the Olympics.*

1998   Presents his major solo exhibition, "Frank Romero: Urban Iconography," at California State University, Los Angeles.

Returning to Los Angeles in 1971, Romero became aware of the emerging Chicano civil rights movement. In 1973, with his friends Almaraz, Gilbert Luján, and Beto de La Rocha, he founded the artists' collective Los Four. Los Four presented a seminal exhibition at the University of California, Irvine, that moved in the following year to the Los Angeles County Museum of Art and thus became the first Chicano exhibition at a mainstream institution. The exhibition brought street graffiti into the art gallery, and was instrumental in defining Chicano art.

Later work
After Los Four dissolved in 1983, Romero established himself as a muralist, with work characterized by strong brushstrokes and vivid colors. In 1984, he was chosen to paint *Going to the Olympics*, a mural for the Olympic Games that celebrates the car culture of Los Angeles. His studio work deals with Chicano social issues, such as the trilogy *The Closing of Whittier Boulevard* (1984), *The Death of Ruben Salazar* (1986), and *The Arrest of the Paleteros* (1996).

Romero has been included not only in Hispanic and Chicano art exhibitions, but also in American art exhibitions, such as "Kaleidoscope: American Art at the End of the Century" (National Museum of American Art, Smithsonian Institute, Washington, D.C., 1996). His major solo exhibition "Frank Romero: Urban Iconography" (California State University, Los Angeles, 1998) surveyed his 30-year career.

See also: Almaraz, Carlos; Salazar, Ruben

Further reading: Serwer, Jacqueline. *American Kaleidoscope: Themes and Perspectives in Recent Art,* pp.84–91. Washington, DC: National Museum of American Art, 1996. http://www.aaa.si.edu/collections/oralhistories/transcripts/romero97.htm (Smithsonian Archives interview with Romero).

ROMERO, Trinidad
Businessman, Politician

Trinidad Romero was an early territorial and federal official from New Mexico, and one of the first Hispanics in the U.S. Congress. His family had been among the earliest settlers in New Mexico. When the Romeros arrived, the region was a Spanish territory; it was then a part of Mexico from 1821 to 1848, when it joined the United States. Romero was also one of the most successful New Mexicans to run freight on the Santa Fe Trail, a trade route that became a main line of the transcontinental railroad.

Early life

Romero was born to Miguel Romero and Josefa Delgado in Santa Fe County, New Mexico, on June 14, 1835. His mother, who was born in 1816 in Santa Fe, married his father in 1829, and had 10 children: five girls and five boys. Romero received a good private education. His mother epitomized business savvy, running a profitable creamery business from the family home, selling butter, cheese, and milk. Romero's family was also well connected politically. His paternal grandfather, José Romero, had been an officer in the Spanish army, and his father, Miguel, was appointed *alcalde* (mayor) by U.S. officials under General Stephen Watts Kearny. Romero's maternal grandfather was also a ranking military official in the Spanish army.

In 1851, Romero began a freight service that operated on the Santa Fe Trail, which ran from St. Louis, Missouri, to New Mexico. When the transcontinental railroad was built, Romero, his brother Eugenio, and their father started a mercantile company in addition to running sheep and cattle and operating a pharmacy. The Romeros made large profits in 1874 during the Red River War, when they

▲ *Trinidad Romero grew up in a wealthy and well-connected New Mexican family. He became a successful businessman, and held several public offices.*

contracted with the U.S. Cavalry to ferry supplies with six-mule wagons from Fort Union to other posts. The Romeros charged $10 per wagon per day for a total of $25,730. Cavalry officers praised the Romero operation as the most efficient in the area.

Politics

As a successful businessman, Romero became involved in politics, and led the Republican Party in San Miguel County, New Mexico. In 1863, he was elected to the Territorial House of Representatives (New Mexico did not become a state with an assembly until 1912). Romero was later appointed a probate judge in San Miguel County in 1869 and 1870. As a Republican, he was elected as a delegate to the 45th U.S. Congress in 1876. From 1889 to 1893, Romero served as U.S. marshal, appointed by President Benjamin Harrison. Trinidad Romero died a prosperous, respected private businessman in San Miguel County, New Mexico, on August 28, 1918.

KEY DATES	
1835	Born in Santa Fe, New Mexico (then part of Mexico), on June 14.
1863	Elected to New Mexico Territorial House of Representatives.
1869	Becomes probate judge in San Miguel County, New Mexico.
1876	Elected as a delegate to the United States Congress.
1889	Appointed a U.S. marshal by President Harrison.
1918	Dies in Las Vegas, New Mexico, on August 28.

Further reading: Miller, Darlis. *Soldiers and Settlers: Military Supply in the Southwest, 1861–1885.* Albuquerque, NM: University of New Mexico Press, 1989.
http://www.loc.gov/rr/hispanic/congress/romero.html (Hispanic Americans in Congress biography of Trinidad Romero).

ROMERO-BARCELÓ, Carlos

Politician, Lawyer, Economist

A politician, lawyer, and economist, Carlos Romero-Barceló was the first governor of Puerto Rico to hold a seat in the U.S. Congress.

Early life
Born in the city of San Juan on September 4, 1932, Carlos Antonio Romero-Barceló comes from a politically prominent family. His grandfather was Antonio Barceló, a former Union Party leader and the first president of the Puerto Rican Senate during the early part of the 20th century. Determined to pursue a career in politics, Romero-Barceló studied at Phillips Exeter Academy in Massachusetts, and received a BA degree in political science and economics from Yale University in 1953. After graduating from the University of Puerto Rico School of Law in 1956, he was admitted to the bar and began practicing law.

From law to politics
In 1968 Romero-Barceló stood for election as mayor of San Juan. After being elected to office, he served for two terms, improving and modernizing local government. An advocate of statehood for Puerto Rico, Romero-Barceló became president of an organization called Citizens for State 51 in 1965, a position he held for two years.

From 1974 to 1986, Romero-Barceló served as president of the New Progressive Party, a pro-statehood organization. In 1976 Romero-Barceló became the first elected Latino president of the National League of Cities and governor of Puerto Rico. Four years later he was elected for a second term as governor of the island, serving until 1985. During his two terms in office, Romero-Barceló dedicated his efforts to improving the country's infrastructure and its tourism industry, and

▲ **Throughout his political career, former governor of Puerto Rico Carlos Romero-Barceló was a leading advocate of Puerto Rican statehood.**

bringing tax relief to Puerto Rico's middle and working classes. His public image was affected, however, by the "Cerro Maravilla" incident. Following the 1978 assassination of two Puerto Rican pro-independence activists by the police at a communications facility, Romero-Barceló applauded the police's action. While some critics accused Romero-Barceló of complicity in the incident, he was never actually indicted on the charges in the case.

After his governorship, Romero-Barceló returned to his law practice in the private sector. In 1992 Romero Barceló was elected resident commissioner of Puerto Rico in Washington, D.C; he was reelected in 1996. During his time in office, he advocated Puerto Rican statehood and pushed for a referendum to clarify Puerto Rico's political status. Over the years, Romero-Barceló has been one of the most outspoken supporters of the statehood of Puerto Rico and an advocate for Puerto Rican rights.

KEY DATES	
1932	Born in San Juan, Puerto Rico, on September 4.
1968	Becomes mayor of the city of San Juan.
1976	Elected governor of Puerto Rico.
1989	Elected president of the New Progressive Party.
1992	Elected resident commissioner of Puerto Rico in Washington, D.C.

Further reading: http://www.loc.gov/rr/hispanic/congress/romerobarcelo.html (biography).

RONSTADT, Linda
Musician

An extremely versatile singer, Linda Ronstadt has sung everything from mariachi and folk to rock 'n' roll and opera. Best known for her country-rock ballads, she has sold more than 50 million albums, won several awards, including 11 Grammys, and collaborated with many leading performers, including Dolly Parton, Emmylou Harris, Rubén Blades, and Flaco Jimenez.

Early life
Linda Maria Ronstadt was born in 1946 in Tucson, Arizona, to a German Mexican father and a Dutch English mother. While a student at Arizona State University, she formed a duo with guitarist Bob Kimmel. They moved to Los Angeles, California, where they linked up with guitarist/songwriter Kenny Edwards. Their group, the Stone Poneys, had a major hit with "Different Drum," a single from its second album, *Evergreen—Vol. 2* (1967), but split up shortly afterward. Ronstadt then released a solo album, *Hand Sown, Home Grown* (1969), that maintained the Poneys' mild rock sound while introducing elements of country music. Most of Ronstadt's recordings in the 1970s were reworkings of country and rock songs. A series of hit singles, including several from her album *Heart Like a Wheel* (1974), accelerated her rise to stardom. Albums such as *Hasten Down the Wind* (1976) and *Living in the USA* (1978) consolidated her popularity.

Diversification
In the 1980s, Ronstadt began to explore different forms of music. She produced three albums of pre-rock-era ballads arranged by Nelson Riddle, then returned to country on the Grammy Award-winning *Trio* (1986), with Dolly Parton and Emmylou Harris. She also recorded *Canciones de Mi Padre* (Songs of My Father, 1987) and *Mas Canciones* (More

▲ *Linda Ronstadt has performed with many of the leading names in music. She says that working with such talent has "made my singing better."*

Songs, 1991), albums of traditional Mexican material. Ronstadt won another Grammy for her New Orleans-flavored *Cry Like a Rainstorm—Howl Like the Wind* (1989), which she made with Aaron Neville. Later albums included the Spanish-language *Frenesi* (1992) and *Winter Light* (1993). *Feels Like Home* (1995) marked a return to the style of her mid-1970s' hits.

In 1981 Ronstadt made her acting debut on Broadway in *The Pirates of Penzance*, a comic opera by Gilbert and Sullivan. A film of the production was released in 1983.

Private life
In the late 1970s, Linda Ronstadt had a long-term relationship with Jerry Brown, governor of California (1975–1983) and three-time candidate for the Democratic presidential nomination. In the 1980s, she was the companion of film director George Lucas. She has two adopted children, Carlos and Mary.

See also: Blades, Rubén; Jimenez, Flaco

Further reading: Amdur, Melissa. *Linda Ronstadt*. New York, NY: Chelsea House Publishers, 1993.
http://www.ronstadt-linda.com (unofficial tribute Web site).

KEY DATES	
1946	Born in Tucson, Arizona, on July 15.
1967	Has first hit single, "Different Drum," with the Stone Poneys, a folk-rock trio.
1974	*Heart Like a Wheel* reaches No. 1 on *Billboard* chart.
1983	Costars with Kevin Kline and Angela Lansbury in *The Pirates of Penzance*, a motion picture.

ROSADO DEL VALLE, Julio
Artist

Julio Rosado del Valle is recognized as one of the masters of 20th-century Puerto Rican painting. He came to prominence in the 1950s and 1960s as an abstract expressionist, but his long career and continued development make it difficult to categorize Rosado del Valle within a single artistic genre.

Early life
Born in 1922 in Cataño, Puerto Rico, Rosado del Valle was the son of a local barber. He developed an early talent for drawing at school, and after high school he went on to study fine art at the University of Puerto Rico, under the Spanish painter Cristóbal Ruíz. Rosado del Valle's first exhibition was in 1944 at the Escuela Superior at Bayamón, Puerto Rico.

Learning his craft
After studying at the progressive New School for Social Research, New York, between 1946 and 1947, Rosado del Valle became part of the generation of artists that profited from government grants to study abroad after World War II (1939–1945). He was able to study in Italy at the Academia de San Marco, Florence, from 1947 to 1948. He also studied in Paris, France.

Back in Puerto Rico
After traveling in Europe, Rosado del Valle returned to Puerto Rico. In 1950, he joined the División de Educación de la Comunidad. He founded the Centro de Arte Puertorriqueño with artists Lorenzo Homar, Rafael Tufiño, Félix Rodríguez Baéz, and José Antonio Torres Martinó. The center was established to promote Puerto Rican artists and also to serve as an educational center. It was an important institution in the development of Puerto Rican national art. From 1954 Rosado del Valle was artist-in-residence at the University of Puerto Rico, a position he held until 1982. Rosado del Valle was able to return to New York between 1957 and 1958, after he was awarded a Guggenheim Fellowship.

Work
In the 1940s, Rosado del Valle painted realistic landscapes of Cataño; in the 1950s, his work was reminiscent of both cubism, as seen in such portraits as *Niños con Lio de Roupa* (1950), and of abstract expressionism in landscapes

KEY DATES	
1922	Born in Cataño, Puerto Rico, on April 6.
1940s	Studies with Spanish painter Cristóbal Ruíz.
1946	Begins studies in the United States.
1950	Cofounds the Centro de Arte Puertorriqueño with Lorenzo Homar and other artists.
1954	Becomes artist-in-residence at the University of Puerto Rico.
1967	Represents Puerto Rico in the "Latin American Art Exhibition," held in Mexico City.
2002	Fire destroys hundreds of his paintings.
2004	Receives honorary degree from University of Puerto Rico.

such as *Paisaje* (1957) and *Pájaro I* (1960). In the 1960s, Rosado del Valle moved decisively into a personal abstract style. A decade later, he was producing murals that explored organic forms, as in *Murals of Marine Shapes*. Since the 1980s Rosado del Valle's work has become more expressionist, with vibrant colors and strong shapes.

Exhibitions
Rosado del Valle has had several solo exhibitions in Puerto Rico, including "Julio Rosado del Valle, 1980–1988" at the Museo de Arte Contemporánea de Puerto Rico, Santurce, in 1988, and "Julio Rosado del Valle: Pintura sobre Papel, 1999–2002" at the Instituto de Cultura Puertorriqueña, San Juan, from 2002 to 2003. His work has also been included in major surveys of Puerto Rican art in particular and of Latin American art in general. Although his work is widely distributed in museums and private collections in Puerto Rico and the United States, several hundred of his works were stored at a single warehouse in Carolina, which was destroyed, along with its enitre contents, in 1999. In 2004, Rosado del Valle received an honorary doctorate from the University of Puerto Rico.

See also: Homar, Lorenzo

Further reading: http://www.icp.gobierno.pr/apl/PDF/ rosadodelvalle.pdf (biography).

ROS-LEHTINEN, Ileana

Politician

In 1989, Ileana Ros-Lehtinen became the first Cuban American elected to the U.S. Congress. She had previously served as a Republican member of the U.S. House of Representatives, representing the 18th District of Florida. Throughout her career, Ros-Lehtinen's work has been driven by a commitment to human rights. As her career has developed, this commitment has taken an increasingly international focus.

Early years

Ileana Ros (later Ileana Ros-Lehtinen) was born on July 15, 1952, in Havana, Cuba. When she was aged seven, her parents fled President Fidel Castro's dictatorship, and brought her to Florida. She recalls that life was initially hard, and her family was forced to rely on food donations from various charities. The family settled in Miami-Dade, where Ros-Lehtinen attended local schools. From an early age, her ambition was to teach. Her father, who had first qualified as a teacher before switching to accountancy, encouraged her career plans.

In 1972, Ros-Lehtinen won a place at Florida International University (FIU) to major in higher education, with a minor in English literature. After graduation in 1975, she decided to continue to study for a master's degree in education while working. Ros-Lehtinen's first job was as a student teacher at Miami Killian Senior High School, but she chose to concentrate on elementary education and went on to teaching jobs at local schools. An opportunity then arose to purchase a private elementary school in Hialeah. Ros-Lehtinen bought it as a family business, working there both as a teacher and as the school's chief administrator.

Entry into politics

While running her school, Ros-Lehtinen began to help her friend Demetrio Perez, a Miami city commissioner, with his political campaigns. Developing a taste for politics, Ros-Lehtinen planned to run for a seat on the Miami-Dade School Board.

At the time, however, political changes were taking place in Florida. The creation of new single-member districts presented Ros-Lehtinen with an opportunity to run for a seat in the state legislature. In 1982, she became the first Latina elected to serve in the Florida House of Representatives. Four years later, she was elected to the Florida Senate.

LEGACY

Ileana Ros-Lehtinen was a fierce critic of President Fidel Castro's dictatorship in Cuba, and played an important role in the passage of the 1996 Cuban Liberty and Democratic Solidarity Act, also known as the Helms-Burton Act. The legislation strengthened the economic blockade against Cuba by imposing sanctions on non-U.S. companies that traded there. Although the act was welcomed by Ros-Lehtinen's Cuban American supporters, it attracted criticism from humanitarian groups who argued that the ruling would inflict poverty on ordinary Cubans.

In another example of her interest in international affairs, Ros-Lehtinen hosted an event at which key politicians and opinion-formers condemned Iran's practice of stoning prisoners to death. Although the practice still continues, it has begun to decline, partly as a result of international pressure. Ros-Lehtinen has also campaigned to improve human rights in countries including Lebanon, Iran, Saudi Arabia, and China.

As chair of a subcommittee on international operations and human rights, in 2001, Ros-Lehtinen held a hearing into atrocities committed by the Taliban in Afghanistan. She also protested sexual abuses by the military in Burma.

Ros-Lehtinen has been a staunch supporter of Israel's right to exist in peace, making several visits to Tel Aviv in the wake of the terrorist bombings. She presently heads the Subcommittee on the Middle East and Central Asia. In this high-profile role, she has helped secure funding for the war on terror, and for humanitarian aid for the women and children of Afghanistan.

KEY DATES

1952	Born in Havana, Cuba, on July 15.
1975	Earns a bachelor's degree in higher education.
1982	Elected to the Florida House of Representatives.
1986	Elected to the Florida Senate.
1989	Elected to the U.S. Congress for the first time.
2002	Reelected to the U.S. Congress.
2004	Reelected to the U.S. Congress.

One of Ros-Lehtinen's main goals was to improve standards of education in Florida. However, she was also motivated by international matters, such as opposition to Castro's dictatorship in Cuba. She started to aspire to office in the U.S. Congress.

Her chance came in 1989, when a special election was called following the death of a local congressman. Ros-Lehtinen's father organized her campaign, while her mother took charge of the campaign volunteers. Their joint effort succeeded, and Ros-Lehtinen won a hard-fought contest on August 29, 1989. She was the first Republican to win the 18th District since its creation in 1962, and her success was largely due to strong support from the local Cuban American community.

Ros-Lehtinen's campaign also had the support of her husband, Dexter Lehtinen, whom she had met in the Florida legislature. He later became U.S. Attorney for the Southern District of Florida.

Congresswoman

One of Ros-Lehtinen's first successes as a congresswoman was to increase access to higher education by introducing various tuition assistance plans. To help working families, Ros-Lehtinen created a tax credit for employers who provide child care for their employees. She also increased the rights of senior citizens in the workplace by creating the Senior Citizens Freedom to Work Act (2000).

Ros-Lehtinen was also concerned about the local environment, and won $25 million in federal funding to clean up the Miami River, making it more attractive to cruise liners, and more accessible by freight ships. Ros-Lehtinen has also been closely involved with the Everglades cleanup project. It aims to provide flood protection by creating marshland, and provides a habitat for animals such as the endangered Florida panther. She has also ensured that Stiltsville in Biscayne Bay has been placed on the National Register of Historic Places.

▲ *Ileana Ros-Lehtinen is one of a growing number of influential Latinas in U.S. politics.*

To boost the local economy, Ros-Lehtinen worked for the expansion of Miami International Airport. She has also helped to provide more affordable housing in Monroe County by winning funding for projects such as Housing Opportunities for People with AIDS.

Work for the gay community

Ros-Lehtinen also opposed discrimination against gay people. Her initiatives included a hate crimes bill, legislation to protect sexual minorities in federal jobs, and a bill—known in the press as "Don't Ask, Don't Tell"—that protected the rights of homosexuals in the military. However, Ros-Lehtinen voted against allowing gay couples to adopt children.

After taking the oath of office in 1989, Ros-Lehtinen was assigned to committees on international relations and government reform. She became the first Latina to chair a congressional subcommittee; her principal interests in the field of international relations were Africa, economic policy and world trade, and human rights.

Ros-Lehtinen won reelection to Congress comfortably in 2002 and 2004. Although based mainly in Washington, D.C., she retains a home in her South Florida constituency. She has two daughters, a stepson, and a stepdaughter.

Further reading: http://www.house.gov/ros-lehtinen
(Ros-Lehtinen's official Web site).

ROSSELLÓ, Pedro
Politician

Pedro Juan Rosselló, physician and politician, was the sixth elected governor of Puerto Rico, holding office from 1993 to 2001. A pediatric surgeon, university professor, and former director of health for the city of San Juan, Rosselló also served as president of the United States Council of State Governments, as chair of both the Democratic and Southern Governors' associations, and as president of the New Progressive Party of Puerto Rico, or Partido Nuevo Progresista (PNP).

Early life

Rosselló, the son of Juan Rosselló and Iris González, was born on April 5, 1944, in San Juan, Puerto Rico. During his youth, Rosselló was a talented tennis player, winning various Puerto Rican men's singles championships and being nationally ranked by the U.S. Tennis Association. Rosselló received his high school education at Academia del Perpetuo Socorro, graduating in 1962. In 1966, Rosselló obtained a bachelor's degree in science from the University of Notre Dame. He received distinctions for best student and best athlete in the same year that he graduated magna cum laude (with great distinction).

Rosselló, whose father was a psychiatrist, continued his studies in medicine at Yale University, completing a degree in 1970. He married Irma Margarita "Maga" Nevares on August 9, 1969; they had three sons.

▼ *A scholar and a politician, Pedro Rosselló is a pediatric surgeon and former governor of Puerto Rico.*

KEY DATES	
1944	Born in San Juan, Puerto Rico, on April 5.
1970	Completes his studies in medicine.
1991	Becomes president of the PNP.
1993	Becomes governor of Puerto Rico.
1997	Serves second term as governor of Puerto Rico.
2005	Serves in the senate of Puerto Rico.

Rosselló then attended Harvard University to specialize in pediatric surgery. In 1981, he earned a master's degree in public health at the University of Puerto Rico, and later obtained a degree in education from the Interamerican University of Puerto Rico. By the mid-1980s, Rosselló was a medical professor and a prominent pediatric surgeon.

In 1991, Rosselló became president of the PNP, a position he held until 1999. He was elected governor of Puerto Rico in 1992, and was subsequently reelected in the 1996 elections. During his tenure as governor, a health-care reform bill was approved, the industrial infrastructure was modernized, and an anticrime campaign known as *"Mano dura contra el crimen"* ("Strong hand against crime") was launched. As a strong supporter of statehood for the island, Rosselló focused on two campaigns for Puerto Rican statehood in 1993 and 1998, in which referendums were held on the island's political status and relationship with the United States. On both consultations, the commonwealth prevailed over statehood.

In 1999, Rosselló started negotiations with President Bill Clinton to resolve the ongoing controversy over the use of the Puerto Rican island of Vieques by the U.S. Navy for bomb tests and exercises. Rosselló's second term was blighted by accusations of corruption. Some members of his administration were convicted, but he himself was never implicated. Rosselló unsuccessfully ran for governor in the 2005 elections, but was able to hold a seat in the senate of Puerto Rico.

Further reading: Who's Who in American Politics. 16th ed., 1887–1998. New Providence, NJ : Marquis Who's Who, 1997. http://www.state.gov/s/p/of/proc/tr/11082.htm (list of key dates in political career).

ROYBAL, Edward
Congressman

E dward Ross Roybal was a trailblazing politician who fought for Mexican Americans to have their issues addressed by public officials and for more Latinos to serve in elected offices. Roybal also worked hard to increase Mexican Americans' participation in the U.S. democratic process.

Early life

Born in Albuquerque, New Mexico, on February 10, 1916, Edward Roybal moved with his parents to Los Angeles in 1928. After graduating from Roosevelt High School, Roybal served in the Civilian Conservation Corps (CCC). He attended UCLA, where he studied business administration, and Southwestern University, where he studied law.

The move to hold public office

From 1942 to 1944 Roybal was a public health educator at the California Tuberculosis Association, before serving in World War II (1939–1945). After the war he returned to work for the Tuberculosis Association for four years.

In 1947 Roybal made an unsuccessful bid to sit on the Los Angeles City Council. Two years later, Roybal got help from Fred Ross and the Community Service Organization (CSO), the activist organization that he had helped create. Roybal won by an overwhelming majority of 20,000 to 12,000. He was the first Chicano to hold a seat on the council since 1881; he was reelected, and served until 1962.

In 1959, along with Bert Corona and Eduardo Quevedo, Roybal founded the California branch of MAPA (Mexican American Political Association). The organization

▲ *During his time in Congress, Roybal promoted labor, health, and education issues in particular.*

supported Mexican American candidates for political office, educated voters, and lobbied on issues of importance to the community. In 1962 Roybal became the first Mexican American to be elected to the U.S. House of Representatives from California, representing the 30th Congressional district. He was an outspoken advocate for Latino education, authoring the first bill to provide schools with a bilingual education program assistance in 1967. Roybal stepped down after three decades in office in order that his daughter, Lucille Roybal-Allard, could be elected to represent part of his former district. Before his death in 2005, Royal consulted on gerontology at California State University Los Angeles.

See also: Corona, Bert; Roybal-Allard, Lucille

Further reading: Underwood, Katherine. "Pioneering Minority Representation: Edward Roybal and the Los Angeles City Council, 1949–1962." *Pacific Historical Review.* August 1, 1997. http://www.loc.gov/rr/hispanic/congress/roybal.html (Hispanic Americans in Congress Web site).

KEY DATES	
1916	Born in Albuquerque, New Mexico, on February 10.
1949	Elected to Los Angeles City Council.
1959	Elected president of California's Mexican American Political Association (MAPA).
1962	Elected to United States Congress.
1967	Authors the first bill to provide schools with bilingual education program assistance.
1992	Daughter Lucille Roybal-Allard elected to Congress.
2005	Dies in Pasadena, California, on October 24 .

ROYBAL-ALLARD, Lucille
Politician

Lucille Roybal-Allard was the first Mexican American woman to be elected to the U.S. Congress, and became the longest serving Chicana member. Roybal-Allard has taken up strong positions on immigration, education, women's rights, health care, housing, employment, and the environment. The name Roybal has been synonymous with public service and politics in Los Angeles, California, for more than half a century. Throughout her career, Roybal-Allard has never lost an election.

Childhood challenges

Lucille Roybal-Allard was born in 1941 in Los Angeles. She was the daughter of Lucille Beserra Roybal and Representative Edward R. Roybal. Growing up in Boyle Heights, Roybal-Allard was teased for speaking Spanish and forced to speak only English at school. As a congresswoman, she would repeatedly support bilingual education because of those childhood experiences and the halting Spanish that she speaks today as a result.

A political family

In 1962, Roybal-Allard's father became the first Mexican American to be elected from California to the U.S. House of Representatives. Edward Roybal sat in the House for three decades, stepping down in 1992 so that his daughter could represent part of his former district. Before that, in 1949, Edward R. Roybal was elected a city councilman in Los Angeles, the first Mexican American to hold that seat since 1881. People went to the Roybal house for assistance, not to City Hall. As a child, Roybal-Allard overheard many political conversations, and her parents discussed with her contemporary issues and the importance of helping others.

Early career

Roybal-Allard received a degree in speech therapy from California State University, Los Angeles, in 1965. After graduation, she was a homemaker and department-store clerk, and worked at the United Way, the National Association of Hispanic Certified Public Accountants, and the Alcoholism Council of East Los Angeles. Surprisingly, it was not until a childhood friend approached Roybal-Allard about running for political office (not her politically connected family) that she ever gave it any thought. As a teenager, she had wanted to work in show business.

An influential political career

In 1987 Roybal-Allard was elected to the California State Assembly representing the 56th District, a largely Hispanic and liberal neighborhood. She campaigned for the environment, preventing both a prison and a toxic-waste incinerator from being built in her district. She was reelected until 1992 by overwhelming majorities, testifying to the popularity of her policies and effective work in the Assembly. In 1991, Roybal-Allard was selected to serve as chair of the Ways and Means Subcommittee on health. While in the Assembly and on the Ways and Means Committee, she earned a reputation for carrying bills on social justice, such as domestic violence prevention, farmworker safety, consumer protection, education, and the environment. In 1990 and 1991, the California League of Conservation Voters awarded Roybal-Allard the highest ranking of any legislator.

Roybal-Allard was first elected to the United States House of Representatives in 1992, the year her father decided to retire. Had they both run in neighboring districts, they could have been the first father-daughter Congress members in U.S. history. During her first year in Congress, Roybal-Allard was named first vice president of the freshman class in the House.

Roybal-Allard has broken ground in many other ways. In 1998 and 1999, she was elected chair of the California Democratic Congressional Delegation, the first woman and the first Latina to hold the position. She also became the first woman chair of the Congressional Hispanic Caucus in 1999. When Roybal-Allard later became a

KEY DATES

1941	Born on June 12 in Los Angeles, California.
1965	Earns a bachelor's degree from California State University, Los Angeles.
1987	Elected to the California State Assembly.
1992	First elected to the United States House of Representatives.
2001	Appointed to the Democratic Homeland Security Task Force.
2005	Receives Edward R. Roybal Public Service Award from Mexican American Bar Association of Los Angeles.

Roybal-Allard is influenced by the diverse Los Angeles community in which her politically active parents raised her, and which she represents. However, Roybal-Allard understands that her work for her community can have wider effects. By representing her own district, Roybal-Allard can also help to shape policies for Hispanics and other Americans across the United States. In 1992 she said: "In 20 years, Latinos will become the majority population in states such as California, New York, Texas, Illinois, and Florida. We must invest today to ensure that our children will be prepared to lead these states into prosperity. In the 106th Congress, the Caucus will focus on education, economic development, and access to health care. All of these issues are critical to the well-being of the Latino community, and to the nation as a whole. Latino issues are American issues"

▲ *Lucille Roybal-Allard has followed in her father's political footsteps to become a representative. She is popular as a tireless advocate of social rights.*

member of the powerful House Appropriations Committee, she was again the first Latina to do so. She also serves on two important subcommittees: the Subcommittee on Homeland Security, formed after 9/11, and the subcommittee on Labor, Health and Human Services, and Education.

Some of Roybal-Allard's legislation and votes have been controversial, including voting against the authorization to use United States armed forces against Iraq in 2002. She also led a coalition of Congress members to prevent the airing of hard liquor advertisements on national television due to their prevalence and destructive effects on many minority communities. Roybal-Allard also took a progressive stand on undocumented workers, calling for literacy and citizenship classes to turn them into lawful, productive United States residents. Owing to her consistently liberal voting record, Americans for Democratic Action (ADA) continually gives her high marks, while organizations such as the American Conservative Union give her few or no points. In 2000, the League of United Latin American Citizens (LULAC) recognized Roybal-Allard's years of tireless political service when it gave her their Presidente de LULAC award.

Recent developments

Lucille Roybal-Allard still lives in Los Angeles with her husband, Edward T. Allard III, and commutes back and forth to Washington, D.C. The couple have four children (Ricardo, Lisa, Angela, and Guy Mark) and four grandchildren. Roybal-Allard's colleague, California Representative Xavier Becerra, said of her impact and legacy: "It won't be long before people begin to say that Ed Roybal is the father of Lucille instead of referring to Lucille as the daughter of Ed Roybal."

See also: Roybal, Edward

Further reading: Telgen, Diane, and Jim Kamp (eds.). *Notable Hispanic American Women.* Detroit, MI: Gale Research, 1993.
http://www.house.gov/roybal-allard (House of Representatives webpage for Lucille Roybal-Allard).
http://www.hispanicmagazine.com/1999/julaug/Features/stepping.html (*Hispanic* magazine article).

RUBIO, Eurípides
Medal of Honor Recipient

More than 2,000 Puerto Rican names are engraved on the San Juan War Memorial, the monument in the island capital that honors the men who gave up their lives in wars in defense of the United States. Among them is the name of Eurípides Rubio, Jr., one of four Puerto Ricans to be awarded the Congressional Medal of Honor (the others were Fernando Luis García, Carlos James Lozada, and Héctor Santiago Colón).

Rubio was awarded the United States's highest military decoration for an act of outstanding courage performed at the height of the Vietnam War (1964–1975). Rubio braved enemy fire to help his men, an action that resulted in his own death.

Many commentators believe that Rubio's death underscores the important role that Latinos in general, and Puerto Ricans in particular, have played, and continue to play, in U.S. military actions. During the Vietnam War, more than 168,000 Hispanics saw service, of whom about 48,000 were Puerto Ricans: Of that number, 270 Puerto Ricans were killed and more than 3,000 wounded in action.

From Puerto Rico to Vietnam
Rubio was born in the seaport city of Ponce, Puerto Rico, on March 1, 1938. After school, he enlisted in the U.S. Army, eventually rising to the rank of captain in the 1st Battalion of the 28th Infantry.

In 1965, the United States began to deploy troops in Vietnam on a massive scale, providing support to the government of South Vietnam in its ongoing struggle against the communists of North Vietnam. Contrary to the expectations of President Lyndon B. Johnson's administration (1963–1969) and its military advisers, who had predicted a swift victory, U.S. troops found themselves caught up in a prolonged and bloody conflict. Rubio was sent to Vietnam in July 1966.

Bravery
On November 8, 1966, Rubio, a communications officer serving in Tay Ninh Province, became involved in one of the many short, fierce battles that were to become characteristic of the war. Under heavy enemy attack from mortar rounds, rifle grenades, and rapid machine-gun fire, Rubio left the relative safety of his post to help other soldiers. Seriously wounded in two places while helping with the evacuation of wounded personnel, Rubio was then hit a third time, but he ignored his injuries to help keep beleaguered U.S. troops supplied with ammunition.

Selfless concern for his men
Despite the seriousness of his injuries, Rubio took over command of a rifle company whose commander had been evacuated from the field. As he rallied the men, he noticed that one of the smoke grenades that the army used to mark enemy positions had fallen too close to friendly lines. If it remained where it was, he realized, there was a danger that any U.S. airstrikes might target U.S. troops rather than the Viet Cong.

Disregarding his own safety, Rubio went to reposition the grenade, but he was immediately struck by enemy gunfire. Undeterred, he managed to scoop up the grenade, run toward enemy lines, and throw it close to a Viet Cong position, before finally succumbing to his wounds.

Enduring memorial
Rubio's actions enabled U.S. forces to target the enemy position accurately, and helped save the lives of other U.S. troops. Rubio was buried in Bayamon, Puerto Rico, and was posthumously awarded the Medal of Honor for his "conspicuous gallantry and intrepidity in action" and his "selfless concern for his men." His courage became a model for other Puerto Ricans in the U.S. Army.

Further reading: Capps, Walter. *The Vietnam Reader.* London, England: Routledge, 1992.
www.army.mil/cmh-pg/mohviet2.htm (Medal of Honor Web site, including citation).

KEY DATES

1938   Born in Ponce, Puerto Rico, on March 1.

1965   United States begins to send troops to Vietnam on a massive scale; Rubio arrives there on July 10, 1966, as captain, 1st Battalion, 28th Infantry.

1966   Fatally wounded while delivering ammunition and helping wounded soldiers in Tay Ninh Province on November 8; buried in Bayamon, Puerto Rico.

1975   Vietnam War ends: Some 168,000 Hispanics served there, more than 48,000 of whom were Puerto Rican; 270 died, including Rubio, and 3,000 were wounded.

RUIZ, John
Boxer

Despite his comparatively limited boxing abilities, John Ruiz used determination and will to become the first Latino heavyweight champion in history. Ruiz's boxing style, where he would grab his opponents and then hit them relentlessly from the clinch, was unpopular in the boxing world, which favors hard-punching heavyweights, but Ruiz still managed to fight his way to a career record of won 42, lost 6, drawn 1.

Early life

Ruiz was born in 1972 in Methuen, Massachusetts. His Puerto Rican parents named him for former U.S. president John F. Kennedy. Despite this patriotic gesture, they moved John and his siblings to Puerto Rico shortly after his birth. When John was six years old, his parents divorced. His father stayed in Puerto Rico, while his mother moved the children back to Massachusetts. John struggled with the new culture when he first returned the United States, especially since he only spoke Spanish.

By age 14, John had found comfort in a local gym, Somerville Boxing Club, run by a trainer named Norman Stone. Stone became a father figure to Ruiz, who hardly saw his biological father. Under Stone's influence, Ruiz was soon waking up at 5:00 A.M. to run before school; he then trained in the gym after his daily studies.

Professional career

With Stone, who had mortgaged his home multiple times to pay for Ruiz's boxing, Ruiz moved up the amateur boxing ranks and debuted professionally on August 20, 1992, beating Kevin Parker. Over the next two years, Ruiz

▲ *A determined fighter, Ruiz (right) was criticized for his lack of style, but still won two world titles.*

beat 17 opponents to earn his first title fight against the International Boxing Organization champion, Danell Nicholson. Ruiz lost by judges' decision.

Ruiz fought with success over the next few years, still determined to become the first Latino heavyweight boxing champion. His mission suffered a significant setback on March 15, 1996, when David Tua knocked him out in only 19 seconds. Critics considered the crushing defeat proof that Ruiz was not a quality contender.

Ruiz continued to fight his opponents and critics, too. On March 3, 2001, he knocked out the World Boxing Association (WBA) champion Evander Holyfield in the fourth round. With that, he became the first Latino world heavyweight champion. Ruiz defended the title twice, then, on March 1, 2003, lost it to Roy Jones, Jr. However, in 2004, Jones, Jr., a former light heavyweight, decided to return to that division, and Ruiz regained the WBA title by default.

Ruiz successfully defended his second title three times. Although he lost one of the bouts, the victor, James Toney, was subsequently disqualified after testing positive for steroids. In December 17, 2005, however, Ruiz finally lost the title again to Nikolai Valuev, a 7-foot (2.13m) tall Russian known as "the Beast from the East."

Further reading: www.johnquietmanruiz.com (Ruiz's Web site) www.maxboxing.com (boxing website with records and fight analysis).

KEY DATES

1972   Born in Methuen, Massachusetts, on January 4.

1992   Makes professional boxing debut on August 20, defeating Kevin Parker.

1996   Knocked out in the first 19 seconds of his title-fight with David Tua.

2001   Becomes the first Hispanic heavyweight champion by outscoring Evander Holyfield for the World Boxing Association (WBA) title on March 3.

2005   Loses his WBA title for the second time, to Russian fighter Nikolai Valuev.

RUIZ DE BURTON, María Amparo
Writer

Widely regarded as the first Mexican American author in the United States to write novels in English, María Amparo Ruiz de Burton used her work as a means to criticize the U.S. government's appropriation of Mexican land in the second half of the 19th century.

Early life
Born in 1832 to an aristocratic Mexican family in Loreto, Baja California, Mexico, Ruiz de Burton witnessed how the U.S. occupation of the Baja during the U.S.–Mexico War (1845–1848) led to the expropriation of a vast tract of land owned by her grandfather, Don José Manuel Ruiz.

Although the loss of the family estates left her in poverty, by the end of the military conflict in 1848 Ruiz de Burton had managed to recover from her misfortune. In the following year, she married Captain Henry Stanton Burton from Connecticut, and the couple moved, with her mother, to Alta California. There Ruiz de Burton obtained U.S. citizenship, and gradually found her way into a privileged social circle of Mexican and U.S. landowners.

▼ *The novels of María Ruiz de Burton describe some of the injustices endured by Mexican Americans.*

KEY DATES

1832	Born in Loreto, Baja California, Mexico.
1845	The beginning of the Mexican-American War represents the loss of family property.
1849	Marries Captain Henry Stanton Burton and moves to Alta California.
1869	Captain Burton dies of malaria fever. Ruiz de Burton returns to California to claim her property but is denied.
1872	Publishes *Who Would Have Thought It?*
1885	Finishes her second novel, *The Squatter and the Don.*
1895	Dies destitute in Chicago.

In 1869, Captain Burton died of malarial fever. His property did not pass to his widow, because she was a Mexican migrant, but was instead considered public domain, and made available for resettlement under the California Land Act of 1851. Ruiz de Burton tried to fight the ruling in the courts, but her legal challenge was unsuccessful, and she was again destitute. She began writing to console herself, and embarked on a series of novels based on her 10 years in the United States.

Into print
In 1872, Ruiz de Burton published anonymously her debut novel, *Who Would Have Thought It?*, a scathing criticism of Yankee hypocrisy, Anglocentrism, and racism toward Mexican landowners who settled in New England during the Civil War and Reconstruction. In Ruiz de Burton's second novel, *The Squatter and the Don* (1885), the story revolves around a plot to take control over the wealth of a defenseless Mexican in California. Like the protagonist of *The Squatter and the Don,* Ruiz de Burton never recovered her family's land. She died in 1895 in Chicago, Illinois, while still trying to obtain rights over her inheritance.

Further reading: Oden, Frederick Bryant. "The Maid of Monterrey: The Life of María Amparo Ruiz de Burton, 1832–1895." M.A. thesis. University of San Diego, 1992. http://www-rohan.sdsu.edu/dept/mas/chicanohistory/ chapter05/c05s07.html (San Diego Mexican and Chicano History Web site).

SÁENZ, Ben
Writer

Award-winning author Ben Sáenz has written poetry, novels, and children's books. His work explores Mexican and U.S. culture and identity. Sáenz has said that he writes "about decent people who have a lot of flaws … ordinary people who find themselves in painful situations but who want to be good."

Early life
Born in 1954 in his grandmother's house in the farming village of Picacho, New Mexico, Benjamin Alire Sáenz was one of the seven children of Mexican immigrant parents. His parents spoke Spanish at home, and Sáenz learned English from watching cartoons on television and from his brothers and sisters. A passionate reader, Sáenz loved comic books, especially those featuring superheroes such as Batman and Spiderman.

Sáenz began writing at an early age. He was also a talented artist. As a teenager, he became influenced by the left-wing Catholic activism of priests and the *Catholic Worker* newspaper.

The church and activism
After graduating from high school in Las Cruces, New Mexico, Sáenz entered St. Thomas Seminary in Denver, Colorado, after which he went to Belgium to continue his studies at the University of Louvain. As part of his training for the priesthood, Sáenz worked in other European countries and in East Africa. Traveling led Sáenz to become interested in the idea of cultural identity. He commented: "Identities, I learned very quickly, are always a matter of perspective. They're not permanent. They only make sense in context."

Ordained at the age of 26, Sáenz realized that he was not suited to the priesthood; he left holy orders in 1984.

Going back to college
In 1985, Sáenz decided to go back to studying writing, first attending the University of Texas at El Paso, where he earned a master's degree, and then the University of Iowa. In 1988, he went to Stanford University as a Wallace E. Stegner fellow in poetry, and pursued a doctorate in American literature.

Acclaimed writer
In 1991, Sáenz published his first collection of poetry, *Calendar of Dust*; it won the American Book Award. In 1992, he was awarded a Lannan Literary Fellowship, and published the short-story collection *Flowers for the Broken*.

In 1995, Sáenz published his first novel, *Carry Me Like Water*. The book examines race, gender, and class through such characters as the deaf-mute Diego, scrabbling to make ends meet in El Paso, Texas, and his rich sister, who lives in California and tries to cover up her Mexican heritage. *Carry Me Like Water* won that year's Southwest Book Award.

In 1997, Sáenz published his second novel, again to critical acclaim. *The House of Forgetting* concerns the abusive relationship between a respected Chicago professor and a Chicana whom he abducted as a child.

Sáenz has also written several popular children's books. The Texas Institute of Letters named *Grandma Fina's Wonderful Umbrella* (*La Abuelita Fina y Sus Sombrillas Maravillosas*) the Best Children's Book of 1999.

In 2002, Sáenz's third book of poems, *Elegies in Blue*, was nominated for the *Los Angeles Times* Book Prize. He published the collection *Dreaming the End of the War* in 2006. Sáenz also teaches creative writing at the University of Texas at El Paso.

KEY DATES

1954	Born in Picacho, New Mexico.
1980	Ordained as a priest.
1984	Leaves priesthood.
1985	Studies writing at the University of Texas at El Paso.
1988	Becomes Wallace E. Stegner fellow in poetry at Stanford University.
1991	Publishes first poetry collection, *Calendar of Dust*; wins American Book Award.
1994	Publishes first novel, *Carry Me Like Water*.
2006	Publishes *Dreaming the End of the War*.

Further reading: Sáenz, Ben. *Carry Me Like Water*. New York, NY: Hyperion, 1995.
http://www.loc.gov/today/cyberlc/feature_wdesc.php?rec=3631 (interview and live reading).

SÁENZ, José de la Luz
Teacher, Activist

José de la Luz Sáenz was a key figure in the early Mexican American civil rights movement of the 1920s and 1930s. He was a founding member of two important civil rights organizations and the author of a wealth of political and personal writings, including a powerful diary in which he recounted his experiences as a soldier during World War I (1914–1918).

Early life
José de la Luz Sáenz was born on May 17, 1888, in Realitos, a small town in southern Texas. He was one of the eight children of Rosalío Sáenz and Cristina Hernández. Growing up, Sáenz heard stories of his Mexican ancestry from his father, from whom he inherited a strong feeling of pride in his heritage.

In 1900, the family moved to Alice, Texas, where Sáenz graduated from the local high school in 1908. After high school, Sáenz went on to take a degree in business studies in San Antonio, and later trained as a teacher. Teaching would remain his vocation for the rest of his life. During his career as an educator in southern Texas, Sáenz became a passionate opponent of segregated schooling. At the time, white and black Americans were strictly separated in many areas of life, including the classroom.

Committed to his country
In 1917, Sáenz married María Petra Esparza; they had nine children. Sáenz's quiet new family life would not last long, however. World War I was being fought, and in 1918 Luz Sáenz volunteered as a soldier. He served in the 360th Regiment Infantry of the 90th Division from Texas, which was stationed first in France and later advanced into Germany. While in Europe, Sáenz kept a detailed diary. He described his hope that, given the "rhetoric of democracy" that was widely uttered by politicians during the war, Mexican Americans who had served their country would return from the horrors of war in a better position to fight for their right to be treated as full and equal citizens.

Sáenz eventually published the diary in 1933 under the title *Los México-Americanos en la Gran Guerra y su Contingente en pro de la Democracia, la Humanidad, y la Justicia* (Mexican Americans in the Great War and the Resulting Impact on Democracy, Humanity, and Justice). It is a moving testimony to the 200,000 Latinos—the majority of whom were Mexican Americans—who served in the war.

KEY DATES	
1888	Born in Realitos, Texas, on May 17.
1918	Fights in World War I and writes his diary.
1921	Is a founding member of the Order of Sons of America.
1929	Is a founding member of the League of United Latin American Citizens (LULAC).
1933	Publishes World War I diary.
1953	Dies in San Antonio, Texas, on April 12.

Disillusionment
Sáenz shared the disillusionment of many former Mexican American soldiers who came home to find that that they and their families were now subject to, if anything, even deeper discrimination than they had endured before the war. Their display of solidarity and their suffering on behalf of the United States had apparently been for nothing. In common with many other ex-servicemen, Sáenz channeled his anger into the developing civil rights movement. In 1921, he helped form the San Antonio-based Order of Sons of America, one of the first statewide Mexican American civil rights organizations in Texas. The Order was fiercely patriotic, and used peaceful means to lobby for desegregation in Texas schools and other public services.

Struggle
In 1929, Sáenz became a founding member of the League of United Latin American Citizens (LULAC), the first nationwide Mexican American civil rights organization. Through the 1930s, he served as president of its McAllen chapter. While bringing up his large family, he continued to publish articles and essays on civil rights themes.

José de la Luz Sáenz died on April 12, 1953, and was buried in San Antonio. An important collection of his papers is held as part of the Benson Latin American Collection at the University of Texas at Austin.

Further reading: Zamora, Emilio. "José de la Luz Sáenz," *El Mesteño.* Vol. 3, Issue 31 (April 2000). www.lib.utexas.edu/taro/utlac/00072/lac-00072.html (Short biography.)

SALAS, Floyd
Boxer, Writer

Floyd Salas has enjoyed success in three very different careers: boxing, writing, and teaching. He has received several awards for his work.

Early life

Born in Walsenburg, Colorado, on January 24, 1931, Floyd Sánchez Salas was the son of Edward and Anita Salas. His mother's family came to the Southwest with the Spanish explorer Juan de Oñate in the 1580s, while his father's family had immigrated from Spain to Florida in the 17th century before moving to Colorado. When he was eight, Salas moved with his family to California. Salas's father had a number of successul businesses and Salas moved several times during his childhood, changing schools six times in four years.

When Salas was 12, his mother died after a long illness. Deeply upset by her death, Salas went almost overnight from an A student to being arrested on a number of occasions for fighting. He was eventually sent to a juvenile detention center and later ended up in the Santa Rita Prison Farm after spitting in a cab driver's face following a traffic accident. While incarcerated, Salas closely observed prison life and later used some of his observations and experiences to good effect in his first novel, *Tattoo the Wicked Cross* (1967).

Boxing and writing

Salas channeled his energy into a more formal path when he took up boxing. His older brother Albert was a talented boxer who spotted Floyd's potential *(see box on page 98)* and encouraged the young Salas to pursue a career in the sport. In 1956 Salas's cousin, who was on the boxing team at the University of California at Berkeley, urged Salas to meet with the boxing coach there. The coach was so impressed by Salas's talent that he offered him the first boxing scholarship ever awarded by the university.

As well as being a talented boxer, Salas was a good student. He had decided as a child that he wanted to be a writer and had written stories from an early age. In 1958 Salas was awarded a scholarship; he was sent to study in Mexico City at El Centro Mexicano de Escritores, an institute funded by the Rockefeller Foundation. In 1963 Salas earned a BA from San Francisco State University. Two years later he was awarded an MA.

▲ *Floyd Salas often writes about his own life in his books. He also tours the country, speaking on drug abuse and the importance of education.*

Fighting his corner

After graduating, Salas taught and became heavily involved in college politics, and actively lobbied for more ethnic students to be accepted into the university. On one occasion Salas argued with the author Saul Bellow, who later won the Nobel Prize for literature, for the admittance of more underprivileged students to San Francisco State. Bellow later included the episode in his 1970 novel *Mr. Sammler's Planet.*

Salas taught first at his alma mater, San Francisco State University, before taking up the position of state coordinator of poetry in schools between 1973 and 1976. In 1975 he was appointed to the University of California at Berkeley as an assistant boxing coach. In addition to teaching English and creative writing at school, Salas taught creative writing at Folsom State Prison and later at San Quentin Prison. In 1977 he was awarded a Lynch fellowship at Berkeley and also a creative writing fellowship from the National Endowment for the Arts the following year.

INFLUENCES AND INSPIRATION

By his own admission, Floyd Salas considers that his sense of moral purpose and responsibility comes from his parents and siblings, through both positive and negative examples of how they lived their lives.

Salas credits his brother Albert with influencing his decision to become a boxer. Albert was an amateur boxing champion who turned professional. He spotted Salas's potential and encouraged the young Salas to take up boxing as a career.

Salas credits his oldest brother, Eddy, as having the greatest influence on his decision to become a writer. His brother, Salas says, combined their father's intellect with their mother's sensitivity and soul. However, Eddy committed suicide at age 30, despite having a seemingly successful life. Floyd, who was nine at the time, was devastated, as was Albert, who turned to drugs after Eddy's death. Albert was jailed on a number of occasions for his drug use and also for dealing. He also committed suicide and several of his 10 children became drug users.

Success

As well as teaching and boxing, Salas wrote fiction. His first novel, *Tattoo the Wicked Cross,* published in 1967, told the story of 15-year-old protagonist Aaron D'Aragon, who is sent to a prison farm and loses his innocence. He becomes a killer as a result of his prison experiences. Salas maintained that the book was not autobiographical. It was well received, unlike his second short novella, *What Now My Love* (1970), which told the story of three hippies on a drug trip. Like his protagonists, Salas spent much of the 1970s following, as Salas himself puts it, "the hippy trail from San Francisco to Marrakesh [Morocco]." While traveling, Salas wrote his next novel, *Lay My Body on the Line* (1978); the book is about Salas's own experience of the 1960s student struggles in the San Francisco Bay area. Both books received mixed reviews, although Salas's literary reputation continued to grow. During the 1970s he published both poetry and prose in a number of anthologies, including *Chicano Voices.*

Problems

A long period of literary silence followed in the 1980s as Salas dealt with many personal problems. *Stories and Poems from Close to Home,* a collection of poetry by well-known and unknown poets, edited by Salas, appeared in 1986, but he did not publish any original new work of his own. Salas continued to teach, and in 1980 was appointed lecturer in creative writing at Berkeley. Between 1984 and 1991, he also taught a poetry-writing seminar at San Quentin Prison.

Salas started to publish again in the 1990s. His 1992 memoir, *Buffalo Nickel,* was reviewed by the *Los Angeles Times* as "one of the most remarkable memoirs of the decade." In the book, Salas talks honestly about his dysfunctional family and his own battle to overcome drug addiction. After that book, Salas published another novel and a collection of poetry. *Color of My Living Heart,* which also appeared in 1996, collected many of Salas's own poems together for the first time. The book's theme was love. *State of Emergency,* a follow-up to *Lay My Body,* was also set in the 1960s. It was awarded the 1997 PEN Oakland Literary Censorship Award.

Honors

Salas has received several awards for his work, including the Jackson Award (1964), the Saxton Fellowship (1965), and the California Arts Council Literary Fellowship (1993). He is an inspirational speaker who lectures around the country on such issues as drug abuse and rehabilitation. Salas has been married three times and has two children.

KEY DATES

1931	Born in Walsenburg, Colorado, on January 24.
1939	Moves to California.
1943	Death of his mother, Anita Salas.
1958	Awarded first boxing scholarship at University of California at Berkeley.
1967	Publishes first novel, *Tattoo the Wicked Cross.*
1975	Appointed assistant boxing coach at Berkeley.
1996	Publishes *Color of My Living Heart,* his first book of poetry, and *State of Emergency.*

Further reading: Salas, Floyd. *Buffalo Nickel.* Houston, TX: Arte Público Press, 1992.
www.floydsalas.com (Salas's own Web site).

SALAZAR, Alberto
Athlete

Alberto Salazar is best known for dominating the New York City Marathon between 1980 and 1982, but he also set national records on the track and represented the United States at the 1984 Los Angeles Olympics.

Alberto Salazar was born in Havana, Cuba, on August 7, 1958. His family moved to the United States and finally settled in Wayland, Massachusetts, where Salazar started to compete on the running track at high school. It soon became clear that Salazar was an outstandingly promising athlete, and he won a scholarship to the University of Oregon in 1976. In his first year, Salazar helped the university take National Collegiate Athletic Association (NCAA) cross-country honors. A year later, in 1978, Salazar beat the fastest American marathon runner, Bill Rodgers, in a 7.1-mile (11.4km) road race.

New York domination
In 1980, Salazar ran for the first time in the New York City Marathon. He won the race in 2 hours, 9 minutes, and 41 seconds, which was then the fastest-ever debut marathon and the second-fastest ever by an American athlete. A year later, Salazar won his second New York City marathon. His time of 2 hours, 8 minutes, and 13 seconds broke the world record set by Australian athlete Derek Clayton 12 years earlier, although the course was later found to be short. In 1982, Salazar won at New York for a third consecutive year, in 2 hours, 9 minutes, and 29 seconds.

Salazar also ran in a fiercely contested Boston Marathon in 1982. The last mile of the race was an all-out sprint between Salazar and Dick Beardsley. Salazar crossed the line first in 2 hours, 8 minutes, and 51 seconds, and then collapsed from dehydration.

▲ *Alberto Salazar set a remarkable record, winning the New York City marathon in three consecutive years, 1980–1982.*

Declining form
At the trials for the 1984 Los Angeles Olympics, Pete Pfitzinger became the first U.S. athlete to beat Salazar in a marathon. Both won places on the team; at the games, Salazar finished a disappointing 15th. His poor form stemmed from before the 1983 World Championships in Helsinki, Finland, where he placed last after a cold, which later developed into bronchitis and asthma. Salazar made a comeback in 1994, winning the 55.9-mile (90km) Comrades Marathon in South Africa. Soon afterward, a serious injury cut short his new ultramarathon career.

Alberto Salazar later worked as a consultant for Nike. He also coaches the Nike Oregon Project, a program aimed at the development of promising young distance runners. In 2001, he was inducted into the National Long Distance Running Hall of Fame.

KEY DATES	
1958	Born in Havana, Cuba, on August 7.
1980	Wins his first New York City Marathon.
1981	Wins a second New York City Marathon, in world-record time of 2:08:13.
1982	Wins his third consecutive New York City Marathon; beats Dick Beardsley in a legendary Boston Marathon.
1984	Places a disappointing 15th in Los Angeles Olympics, following serious illness.

Further reading: Brant, John. *Duel in the Sun: Alberto Salazar, Dick Beardsley, and America's Greatest Marathon.* Emmaus, PA: Rodale Press, Inc., 2006.
www.runningtimes.com/issues/02apr/boston82.htm (profiles Salazar and Beardsley following their epic encounter).

SALAZAR, Rubén
Journalist

Rubén Salazar was an important Chicano journalist who was killed while reporting on an anti-Vietnam war protest in the United States. Hailed as a martyr of the Chicano movement, Salazar helped pave the way for other Chicanos to work in journalism.

Early life
Born in Ciudad Juárez, Mexico, on March 3, 1928, Rubén Salazar was the son of Salvador Salazar and Luz Chavez. He moved to Texas as a boy. After high school, Salazar joined the U.S. Army in the 1950s. Following the end of his tour of duty, Salazar earned a BA in journalism from the University of Texas at El Paso (UTEP) in 1954.

Journalism
In 1955 Salazar began his first job as a cub reporter at the *El Paso Herald-Post*. Salazar also wrote for other California-based papers and was eventually hired by the *Los Angeles Times* in 1959. After six years, Salazar became the paper's foreign correspondent, serving in Vietnam and Mexico City. He was kidnapped in Panama and held by antigovernment forces. By 1969 he was back in the United

KEY DATES	
1928	Born in Ciudad Juárez, Mexico, on March 3.
1955	Hired as cub reporter for *El Paso Herald-Post*.
1959	Hired by the *Los Angeles Times*; becomes foreign correspondent six years later.
1969	Becomes news director of KMEX in Los Angeles.
1970	Dies in Los Angeles on August 29.
1971	Posthumously awarded Robert F. Kennedy Journalism Award.

States, reporting on the Chicano civil rights movement. In 1969 Salazar became news director at KMEX, a Spanish-language television station in Los Angeles, California; he continued to write a column on Chicano affairs for the *Los Angeles Times*. Salazar used both jobs to speak out on key Chicano issues, including police brutality. His work made him the focus of investigations by the police and the FBI.

On August 29, 1970, Salazar and KMEX covered the Chicano moratorium, the largest Mexican American anti-Vietnam War protest, involving about 30,000 people. The crowd eventually settled in Laguna Park to listen to speeches. After a minor skirmish broke out at a local liquor store, it spilled over into the park and police rushed in to intervene. In the resulting stampede, more than 60 people were injured and about $1 million of property was damaged. After covering the protest, Salazar went to relax in the Silver Dollar bar. He was killed when a 10-inch tear-gas projectile, fired by Deputy Thomas Wilson into the bar, hit him in the head. An inquiry into Salazar's death determined that the policeman had acted in good faith. The Chicano community viewed Salazar's death as suspicious, however, and as an example of police injustice and racism. After his death, Salazar received many posthumous honors: Laguna Park was renamed Rubén Salazar Park, and in 1971 Salazar was awarded the Robert F. Kennedy Journalism Award.

▼ *Rubén Salazar became a martyr of the Chicano movement following his death in August 1969.*

Further reading: García, Mario T. *Border Correspondent: Rubén Salazar, Selected Writings 1955–1970*. Berkeley, CA: University of California, 1995.
http://www.democracynow.org/article.pl?sid=05/02/24/155226 (looks at Salazar's legacy).

SALINAS, Luis Omar
Poet

Luis Omar Salinas is widely regarded by his contemporaries as a founding father of Chicano poetry. Salinas's upbringing on the Texas–Mexico border has influenced his work, which deals with the harshness and cruelty of life.

Early life
Born in 1937 in Robstown, close to the Mexican border in Texas, Salinas moved to Mexico at the age of four with his father following the death of his mother. Aged nine, he went to live with his aunt and uncle in California, first in San Francisco and later in Fresno. In 1956, Salinas attended Bakersfield City College to study drama but dropped out before graduating. Salinas moved to Los Angeles two years later to live with his father in East Los Angeles and attend California State College. He was forced to give up studying after suffering a mental breakdown. In 1963, however, he began studying again, this time at California State College, Fresno.

▼ *Luis Omar Salinas is regarded by many critics as the most important poet of the Chicano movement. His work features prominently in Chicano studies.*

KEY DATES	
1937	Born in Robstown, Texas, on June 27.
1941	Mother dies of tuberculosis.
1970	Publishes first book of poetry, *Crazy Gypsy*.
1982	Publishes *Darkness under Trees/Walking behind the Spanish*.
2005	Publishes *Elegy for Desire*.

A Chicano poet
In 1970, Salinas published his first book of poetry, *Crazy Gypsy*. A popular and critical success, the book established Salinas as a leading poet of both the Chicano movement and the Fresno school of poets, which also included Gary Soto and Ernesto Trejo. Salinas's poems dealt with alienation, loneliness, and death. His work, written in English, synthesizes both Anglo and Hispanic culture. Salinas started to give readings across the country, and became part of the emerging Chicano literary scene, but he did not publish anything further until 1976, when some of his poems appeared in an anthology.

Salas's second book of poetry, *Afternoon of the Unreal*, appeared in 1980 and won the Stanley Kunitz Poetry Prize and the Earl Lyon Award. His next book, *Prelude to Darkness*, was published the following year. In 1982, he published *Darkness under the Trees/Walking behind the Spanish*. Considered by many critics to be among his finest works, the book is split into two parts, the second part paying homage to the Spanish Civil War and its war poets.

After winning the prestigious General Electric Foundation Award for Young Writers in 1985, Salinas published *The Sadness of Days: New and Selected Poems* in 1987. His 1990 collection, *Follower of Dusk*, won the Flume Award. After that, Salinas did not publish any new collections until 2005, when *Elegy for Desire* (*Camino del Sol*) appeared.

See also: Soto, Gary

Further reading: Salinas, Luis Omar. *Elegy for Desire* (*Camino del Sol*). Tucson, AZ: University of Arizona Press, 2005. www.thehypertexts.com/Luis_Omar_Salinas_Poetry_Picture_Bio.htm (brief biography).

SALINAS, María Elena
Journalist

Named as one of the top 100 most influential Hispanic Americans, and sometimes referred to as the "Spanish-language Barbara Walters," María Elena Salinas is a leading journalist. She describes herself as politically American and culturally Mexican.

Early life
Born in Los Angeles, California, in 1955, Salinas spent her early childhood in Mexico. The Salinas family moved back to the United States when Salinas was eight years old. Salinas's father was an intellectual: He spoke six languages and had a doctorate in philosophy. Her mother, whom Salinas often describes as her role model, was a seamstress who worked hard to give her family opportunities, and always emphasized the importance of a good education. Salinas's good looks led her to enter beauty pageants in her teens, but she had her sights set on working in the media.

▼ *An experienced journalist, María Salinas also promotes educational opportunities for Hispanics.*

KEY DATES

1955	Born in Los Angeles, California.
1981	Becomes a reporter for KMEX-34 in Los Angeles.
1988	Coanchors on Noticiero Univision national newscast and becomes a national star.
2002	Salinas's coverage of Hurricane Mitch in Honduras wins Univision an Emmy award.

Broadcasting career
After graduating, Salinas took a job broadcasting on a local radio station. In 1981, she became a reporter for KMEX-34 television, the Los Angeles affiliate of the Spanish International Network (SIN), which later became Univision. During the seven years that she worked at KMEX, Salinas gained valuable experience, reporting on everything from community affairs to music.

In 1988, Salinas was offered the chance to coanchor the Univision television program *Noticiero Univision,* a weekday national newscast. Broadcast in the United States and throughout most of Latin America, *Noticiero Univision* quickly became one of the most popular Spanish-language news programs, and turned Salinas and coanchor, Jorge Ramos, into national stars.

During a long career that followed with Univision, Salinas has reported on major international events and interviewed many of the world's political leaders. She has interviewed every U.S. president since Jimmy Carter and many Latin American leaders, including Augusto Pinochet of Chile. Known for her professional approach and attention to detail, Salinas has won many awards and honors for her work.

Salinas also writes for Spanish- and English-language newspapers, and broadcasts on Radio Unica. She is a dedicated activist, campaigning particularly on matters of benefit to the Hispanic American community. Salinas was a founding member and former president of the National Association of Hispanic Journalists, and has dedicated time to improving education for the Latin community, and encouraging young Hispanic Americans to stay in school.

See also: Ramos, Jorge

Further reading: http://www.mariaesalinas.com (official site).

SALINAS, Porfirio
Artist

Days before the Mexican Revolution broke out in 1910, Porfirio Salinas was born in Bastrop, Texas, to Porfirio G. Salinas and Clara G. Chavez. The times were hard, and the Mexican American family moved to San Antonio, where the young Porfirio could attend school and his father could find more suitable and lucrative employment. Porfirio attended school only until the third grade. By then he was following around Jose Arpa, director of the San Antonio Art School, who sketched in the streets and in the fields surrounding San Antonio. Porfirio loved drawing as well, and began to teach himself to become an artist, partly by watching Arpa work.

The bluebonnets

Robert Woods, a local landscape artist, hired Porfirio to paint bluebonnets (a variety of flower) on his landscape paintings because he hated the task and the flower. Porfirio grew adept at painting bluebonnets in fields for landscapes, or just as part of the scenery, and Woods paid him $5 every time he filled in the flowers. Salinas grew in confidence and soon began to create his own paintings, making a theme of the bluebonnets and Texas hill country landscapes.

It was Salinas's striking flower paintings that attracted the attention of local luminaries, such as Sam Rayburn and Lyndon B. Johnson, who both rose to national prominence in politics, and were collectors of art. As president of the United States, Johnson claimed Porfirio Salinas as his favorite painter.

Military duty

Older than most draftees, Porfirio was called for military service from 1943 until 1945. He was assigned to San Antonio for the duration of World War II. His commander for assignments at Fort Sam Houston, Colonel Telesphor

▲ *Porfirio Salinas at work in his home studio in San Antonio, where he produced most of his paintings.*

Gottchalk, commissioned Salinas to paint murals in the officers' lounge and other landscapes. Porfirio was considered such a valuable asset to the military that he was allowed to live at home throughout his military service. The arrangement was perfect for Porfirio because he had married Maria Bonillas, from Guadalajara, Mexico, just before he was inducted into the military.

El Aguila Azteca Award

The most prestigious award Mexico gives to non-Mexicans is the Premio Aguila Azteca. President Adolfo Lopez Mateos received a Salinas bluebonnet painting as a gift from President Lyndon B. Johnson. The Mexican president grew so fond of the artwork that he also became a collector, made friends with Porfirio and Maria Salinas, and presented the painter with the nation's highest award.

Further reading: Goddard, Ruth. *Porfirio Salinas.* Austin, TX: Rockhouse Press, 1975.
http://www.tsha.utexas.edu/handbook/online/articles/SS/fsa11.html (Handbook of Texas Online).

KEY DATES	
1910	Born on November 6, in Bastrop, Texas.
1942	Marries Maria Bonillas on February 15.
1967	Publishes *Bluebonnets and Cactus: An Album of Southwestern Paintings by Porfirio Salinas.*
1973	Dies on April 18 in San Antonio; city of Bastrop inaugurates an annual Salinas Festival in his honor.

SAMANIEGO, Mariano
Entrepreneur

Mariano Samaniego belonged to a group of Mexican businessmen and entrepreneurs who left a legacy of influence and achievements in Tucson and the rest of southern Arizona. Samaniego served in city, county, and state governments for nearly three decades. At one time, he was the only member of the Arizona territorial legislature with a Spanish name.

Background

Following the Gadsden Purchase in 1853, when the United States bought Mexican territory that is now southern Arizona and part of southern New Mexico, many Mexicans migrated north. Tucson, in southern Arizona, was a magnet for many of them. The family of Mariano Samaniego, along with many other men and women, came there from the northern Mexican states of Sonora and Chihuahua.

The future in the north

Mariano Samaniego was born in 1844 in Bavispe, Sonora, Mexico, to Bartolo and Ysabel Samaniego. On being widowed in the early 1850s, Mariano's mother moved to Mesilla, New Mexico, where she ran a grocery store. With a keen sense of the importance of an education, she sent her son to St. Louis University, Missouri, where Mariano received a degree in 1862. Mariano's formal education allowed him to move between the Mexican and Anglo-American worlds. It also gave him the ability to project the future of the region, and to make well-informed financial investments on the basis of his knowledge.

After college, Mariano Samaniego moved to Tucson, where members of his family were now established. He launched his business career hauling supplies to military posts in Arizona, New Mexico, and Texas. Even before the first train rolled into Tucson, Samaniego, foreseeing the demise of the stage-freighting business, started investing in other ventures. He founded ranches in the well-watered foothills north of Tucson. He also invested in real estate within the city limits. He subsequently invested in an irrigation company and a saddlery shop, as well as in stage lines to towns that did not have railroad connections.

Other distinctions

Samaniego achieved several other important distinctions. In 1886, he was appointed to the first University of Arizona Board of Regents, one of several roles he took in support of public education in Arizona. Subsequently, he was elected president of the Arizona Pioneers' Historical Society. Don Mariano, as he was known, was Tucson's most popular political figure.

Further reading: Sheridan, T. E. *Los Tucsonenses: The Mexican Community in Tucson, 1854–1941.* Tucson, AZ: The University of Arizona Press, 1986.

▼ *Mariano Samaniego (pictured here with his wife, Delores Aguirre de Samaniego) was a businessman and politician in Arizona, New Mexico, and Texas.*

KEY DATES	
1844	Born in Sonora, Mexico.
1850	Family moves to Mesilla, New Mexico.
1880	Elected to the first Arizona Territory Legislature.
1886	Appointed to the first University of Arizona Board of Regents.
1905	Dies on October 2.

SAMORA, Julián
Sociologist, Writer, Activist

Julián Samora was a pioneering and influential scholar in the field of sociology, the systematic study of human interaction within society. In 1953 Samora became the first Mexican American to receive a doctorate in the discipline. He went on to carry out groundbreaking studies of Mexican Americans, especially in relation to immigration, education, and public health. As a respected academic, he also played an active role in the Chicano civil rights movement that flourished in the mid-1960s.

Early life
Born on March 1, 1920, in Pagosa Springs, Colorado, Samora grew up in a harsh climate of discrimination toward the Mexican community. It made him determined to bring about change.

After completing high school in 1938, Samora won a scholarship to study at Adams State College in Alamosa, Colorado. He graduated with a degree in history and political science four years later. Further scholarships enabled Samora to gain a master's degree from Colorado State University, Fort Collins, in 1947 and a doctorate in sociology and anthropology from Washington University in St. Louis in 1953.

▼ *Julián Samora wrote several highly influential books about Mexican Americans, including* **Los Mojados: The Wetback Story** *(1971).*

KEY DATES

1920   Born in Pagosa Springs, Colorado, on March 1.

1959   Begins work as a professor at the University of Notre Dame, South Bend, Indiana.

1966   Publishes *La Raza: Forgotten Americans and Mexican Americans.*

1971   Establishes the Mexican American graduate studies program at Notre Dame; publishes *Los Mojados*.

1996   Dies in Albuquerque, New Mexico, on February 2.

An influential teacher and writer
Samora began his career as a university teacher and researcher while he was still studying. By 1959, he had a tenured associate professorship at the University of Notre Dame, Indiana, where he quickly rose to become head of the department of sociology and anthropology. In 1971, he set up the university's Mexican American graduate studies program, a pioneering project that helped extend Chicano access to postgraduate education. Often working in collaboration with students on the program, Samora wrote several influential books, including *Los Mojados: The Wetback Story* (1971), an important study of illegal Mexican immigration to the United States, and *Minority Leadership in a Bicultural Community* (1973). Samora taught until his retirement in 1985.

Activist
Samora was also active in the Chicano civil rights movement. In the 1960s, he played a major role in the compilation of a key survey of Mexican Americans for the Ford Foundation. In 1968, his recommendations resulted in the creation of the Southwest Council of La Raza (SWCLR). The SWCLR was the predecessor of the National Council of La Raza, the largest U.S. Latino civil rights organization. Samora also helped establish the Mexican American Legal Defense and Education Fund (MALDEF). Julián Samora died in 1996.

Further reading: Ohles, Frederik, Shirley M. Ohles, and John G. Ramsay. *Biographical Dictionary of Modern American Educators.* Westport, CT: Greenwood Press, 1997.
www.jsri.msu.edu/museum (short biography).

SÁNCHEZ, David
Jazz Musician

David Sánchez is widely acclaimed as being among the United States's most talented tenor saxophonists and bandleaders. In his music, he blends contemporary jazz with the traditional Afro-Latin sounds of his native Puerto Rico. He has won praise for both the technical precision and the impassioned lyricism of his playing.

Musical Influences
Sánchez was born on September 3, 1968, in Hato Rey, a suburb of San Juan, Puerto Rico. From an early age he was exposed to the island's rich folk music traditions; he started playing the conga drums at the age of eight. His musical talent won him a place at San Juan's prestigious Escuela Libre de Musica (Free School of Music), where he received a classical training. At the school, Sánchez learned to play a range of instruments, but soon specialized in the saxophone. He fell in love with jazz after hearing the album *Kind of Blue* (1959) by the African American trumpeter Miles Davis.

In 1986, Sánchez initially enrolled to study psychology at the Universidad de Puerto Rico in Rio Píedras. However, two years later he won a scholarship to study in the music

▼ *A talented saxophonist, Sánchez fuses Puerto Rican folk music with Latin jazz and classical influences*

department of Rutgers University in New Jersey, and was soon immersed in New York City's thriving jazz scene, playing alongside such established "Nuyorican" (New York-Puerto Rican) Latin-jazz musicians as the trumpeter Charlie Sepúlveda and pianist Eddie Palmieri. Sánchez's rising reputation brought him to the attention of the renowned African American trumpeter Dizzy Gillespie, who in 1990 invited him to tour with his United Nations Orchestra.

Acclaimed recording career
In 1994, Sánchez recorded his first solo album, *The Departure,* and during the following decade produced a succession of albums fusing jazz and Puerto Rican folk: *Sketches of Dreams* (1995), *Street Scenes* (1996), *Obsesión* (1998), *Melaza* (2000), and *Travesía* (2002). With 2004's album *Coral,* Sánchez added a new classical dimension to his work, setting the lush Latin jazz of his band against complex string arrangements provided by the Prague Philharmonic Orchestra.

Sánchez's pioneering work has won him numerous awards, including four Grammy nominations and a 2005 Latin Grammy for Best Instrumental Album for *Coral*. In 2005, Sánchez was commissioned by Chamber Music America to create a full-scale work for jazz sextet. For 2005–2006, Sánchez was artist-in-residence at the School of Music at Georgia State University.

See also: Palmieri, Eddie

Further reading: Holston, Mark. "A Daring Saxophonist in Tune with His Art." *Americas.* Vol. 57, Issue 2 (March–April 2005), p. 58ff.
http://www.davidsanchezmusic.com (Sánchez's official Web site).

SANCHEZ, George Isidore
Educator

George Isidore Sanchez was a college professor whose work as an administrator helped increase educational opportunities for his fellow Mexican Americans.

Early life

Sanchez was born in 1906 in Albuquerque, New Mexico, to Telesfor and Juliana Sanchez. On completing high school, Sanchez took a job as a teacher in Yrriarri, near Albuquerque. By 1930, he had been promoted to principal and administrator of Bernallio County, New Mexico, while completing a bachelor's degree in education and Spanish at the University of New Mexico. Sanchez then went on to complete a master's in educational psychology and Spanish at the University of Texas, Austin, and a doctorate in education at the University of California, Berkeley. In 1931 he became director of the Division of Information and Statistics at the New Mexico State Department of

▼ *George Sanchez was a college professor at the University of Texas, Austin.*

Education. From 1935 until 1938, he worked in Venezuela, then, from 1938 until 1940, he worked at the University of New Mexico. It was at this time that Sanchez began his struggle to achieve educational equality for Mexican Americans. It was a struggle that came at a price. A group of influential people who were opposed to his efforts pressured the university to let him go. At the same time, Sanchez accepted a position with the University of Texas, Austin. He remained there until his retirement.

Professorship

In 1940, Sanchez began his work at Austin as professor of Latin American studies. He also became president-elect of the League of Latin American Citizens (LULAC), and published *The Forgotten People,* his classic work about Mexican Americans in Taos, New Mexico. Sanchez continued his educational and political work on behalf of Mexican Americans, focusing on issues such as school funding, standardized testing, and segregation. By working through organizations such as LULAC and the courts, Sanchez drew attention to the privations faced by Mexican American schoolchildren in the Southwest.

While at Austin, Sanchez served as chairman of the Department of History and Philosophy of Education, and as director of the Center for International Affairs. He was a consultant to numerous educational, social, and political organizations, and remained a prolific writer throughout his career.

Further reading: Paredes, Americo. *Humanidades: Essays in Honor of George I. Sanchez.* Los Angeles, CA: Chicano Studies Center Publications/UCLA, 1977.
http://www.tsha.utexas.edu/handbook/online/articles/SS/fsa20.html (Handbook of Texas Online).

KEY DATES	
1906	Born in Albuquerque, New Mexico, on October 4.
1940	Appointed professor of Latin American studies at the University of Texas, Austin.
1972	Dies on April 5.
1984	Rueben E. Hinojosa endows the George I. Sanchez Centennial Professorship in Liberal Arts at the University of Texas, Austin.

SÁNCHEZ, Loretta and Linda
Politicians

Linda and Loretta Sánchez are the first sisters to serve simultaneously in the U.S. Congress. Both are Democratic representatives from California.

Early life

The daughters of Mexican immigrants, Loretta and Linda Sánchez were born in 1960 and 1969 respectively. The girls attended local schools in Anaheim, California. Their mother was a bilingual-education aide, who worked hard to improve opportunities for children with non-English-speaking parents. She inspired her daughters.

Loretta Sánchez

Loretta Sánchez studied economics at Chapman University in Orange County, before obtaining her MBA from the American University in Washington, D.C., in 1984. She ran her own successful consulting business before entering politics.

In 1994, Sánchez ran unsuccessfully on the Republican ticket for Anaheim City Council under her married name, Brixey. Two years later, having switched to become a Democrat, she decided to use her Spanish maiden name to stand in the election for the old 46th District. She narrowly won a bitter contest on the strength of Hispanic and working-class support. From 2002 onward she represented the newly created 47th District, which included the area where she was born. In 2006, Sánchez was serving her fifth term. A member of several committees, including the House Armed Services Committee and the House

▲ *Linda (left) and Loretta Sánchez both drew inspiration from their mother, who fought for the rights of the children of immigrants.*

Committee on Homeland Security, Sánchez also belongs to the Hispanic Caucus and the Congressional Human Rights Caucus.

Linda Sánchez

Linda Sánchez studied Spanish literature at the University of California, Berkeley, before pursuing a doctorate in law at the University of California, Los Angeles. As an attorney, Sánchez specialized in labor relations and worked for several trade unions, including the International Brotherhood of Electrical Workers (IBEW). Sánchez also served as executive secretary-treasurer for the Orange County Central Labor Council.

In 2003, she was sworn into office to represent the new 39th District of California. Sánchez is the first Latina to serve on the House of Representatives' Judiciary Committee, which deals with criminal judicial reform. Sánchez also sits on the Subcommittee on Immigration, Border Control, and Claims.

Further reading: www.house.gov/sánchez (Loretta Sánchez's biography).
http://www.lindasanchez.house.gov (Linda Sánchez's biography).

KEY DATES

1960   Loretta Sánchez born on January 7.

1969   Linda Sánchez born on January 28.

1994   Loretta Sánchez makes unsuccessful bid for Anaheim City Council as Republican candidate.

1997   Loretta Sánchez, now a Democrat, begins service in House of Representatives representing 46th District.

2000   Loretta Sánchez again elected to 46th District.

2002   Loretta Sánchez elected to 47th District.

2003   Linda Sánchez sworn into office to represent the 37th District.

SÁNCHEZ, Luis Rafael
Writer

Considered by many to be Puerto Rico's finest writer, Luis Rafael Sánchez achieved great international success with the English translation of his first novel, *Macho Camacho's Beat*, which appeared in 1981. He is a leading literary figure in Puerto Rico, and has worked as a distinguished academic, critic, and radio and stage actor. Sánchez's opinions and views on the literary and political culture of Puerto Rico continue to be eagerly sought across the island.

Early life
Born in the small town of Humanaco, southeast of Puerto Rico's capital, San Juan, in 1936, Sánchez received his early education in local schools. His family moved to San Juan, where he continued school. As a teenager, Sánchez realized that he wanted to, as he put it, "reorder my outlook on reality, and with that desire came the need to write." After majoring in theater studies at the University of Puerto Rico, Sánchez won a fellowship that allowed him to study theater and creative writing at Columbia University in New York. He later returned to the United States, where he completed a master's degree in Spanish literature at New York University in 1963.

A writer of repute
Back in Puerto Rico, Sánchez taught Spanish at the University of Puerto Rico. His debut play, *La Espera* (*The Waiting*), written as an undergraduate assignment, was well received, as was his first major play, *La Farsa del Amor Compradito* (*The Farce of Purchased Love*, 1960). He wrote several more plays during the 1960s, including *La Passion Según Antígona Pérez* (*Passion According to Antígona Pérez*). He also published a collection of short stories, *En Cuerpo de Camisa* (*In the Body of a Shirt*) in 1966.

In 1973, following the completion of his doctorate at the University of Madrid, Spain, Sánchez returned to his native island, where he became a professor of literature at the University of Puerto Rico. In 1980, Sánchez achieved international success when his novel *La Guaracha del Macho Camacho*, first published in 1976, appeared in an English translation, *Macho Camacho's Beat*. It was a major critical and popular success in the United States, and did much to extend Sánchez's reputation beyond Spanish-speaking countries. The book established Sánchez as a leading Latin American writer, and the novel was praised for its distinctive tone and clever use of a narrative built around the latest hit song that everyone on the island is listening to. In the wake of the book's success, Sánchez was awarded several grants and fellowships that allowed him to study and write outside Puerto Rico. He was a visiting professor at the City College of New York in 1988, and at Johns Hopkins University in Baltimore, Maryland, in 1989.

With the 1988 publication of *La Importancia de Llamarse Daniel Santos* (*The Importance of Being Daniel Santos*), Sánchez reconfirmed his position as Puerto Rico's leading writer. As with his earlier work, the book looks at the position of Puerto Rico as a colonial satellite of its more powerful neighbor, the United States. Sánchez argued that Puerto Rico needs to hold on to its identity.

In 1995, Sánchez proposed in the satirical essay "Minga y Petraca al Nuevo Senado" ("Minga and Petraca for the New Senate") that two popular drag comedians be elected to public office. The essay's publication prompted a media debate in Puerto Rico about the level of corruption and the disintegration of local politics. Events took another turn when the two comedians carried out a mock campaign rally on the steps of the Senate, which was broadcast.

Sánchez writes about Puerto Rico's mixed cultural identity. His work features homosexuals, mulattoes, blacks, and women. Although he champions these people, he says that he refuses to act as their spokesperson.

KEY DATES	
1936	Born in Humanaco, Puerto Rico, on November 17.
1955	Attends University of Puerto Rico.
1960	Writes major play, *La Farsa del Amor Compradito*.
1976	Publishes first novel, *La Guaracha del Macho Camacho*.
1981	Achieves international success.
1988	Publishes *La Importancia de Llamarse Daniel Santos*.

Further reading: Sánchez, Luis Rafael. *Macho Camacho's Beat.* New York, NY: Pantheon, 1981.
http://www.centerforbookculture.org/context/no6/rabassa.html (review and short article).

SANCHEZ, Poncho
Musician

Poncho Sanchez is one of the most popular and respected musicians working in Latin jazz today. He acknowledges various musical influences, ranging from the soul singer Ray Charles and the South African trumpeter Hugh Masekela to Latino legends Tito Puente, Tito Rodriguez, and the vibraphonist Cal Tjader.

Early life
Born in 1951 in Laredo, Texas, Sanchez grew up with six sisters and four brothers. He spent his early years in Texas, and the later part of his childhood in Norwalk, California, to which the family moved when his father took over a dry-cleaning business in the city.

Sanchez was immersed in music from an early age. His mother, who was from the north of Mexico, listened to *"musica norteña,"* his father liked mariachi music, and his sisters and brothers listened to a mixture of doo-wop, rhythm and blues, and the mambo and cha-cha music played by Los Angeles DJ Chico Cesno.

Sanchez bought his first guitar while he was still at school from a neighbor, Benny Rodriguez. Although he initially dreamed of playing guitar in a rhythm and blues band, he ended up singing lead with a high-school band instead. Sanchez always knew that he was not a natural singer, however. He also played the timbales and learned to play the conga, often playing along to records by Cal Tjader and Tito Puente.

Musical career
Sanchez went to study at Cerritos College in Norwalk, and worked in an aluminum foundry between gigs with local bands. His big break came in 1975, when Tjader invited him to play the congas with him on stage. The crowd loved Sanchez, and Tjader asked him to stay for a few more

▲ *Mexican American conga player Poncho Sanchez became a legend of Latino music in the 1970s.*

numbers. Although Sanchez did not expect to hear from Tjader again, he was invited to play with the band at the Coconut Grove at the Ambassador Hotel in Los Angeles on New Year's Eve, 1975. Sanchez played with Tjader's band for more than seven years, traveling the world. In 1980 he formed his own band, performing with it between tours with Tjader. He also recorded two albums.

Shortly before his death in 1982, Tjader introduced Sanchez to Carl Jefferson, the head of Concord Records, and recommended that Jefferson sign Sanchez. Since then, Sanchez has released more than 18 records with Concord, including the Grammy-nominated album *Bien Sabroso!* (1984) and the Grammy-winning *Latin Soul* (1999).

Sanchez has played with some of the world's most popular jazz and Latin musicians, including Puente, Freddie Hubbard, Dianne Reeves, and Mongo Santamaria. Sanchez's life has been the focus of a documentary entitled *Keeper of the Flame*, and he has published several books, including *Poncho Sanchez' Conga Cookbook* (2002).

See also: Puente, Tito

Further reading: http://www.ponchosanchez.com (official Web site with biography and discography).

KEY DATES	
1951	Born in Laredo, Texas, on October 30.
1975	Plays with vibraphonist Cal Tjader.
1980	Forms his first group.
1982	Signs with Concord records.
1999	Receives a Grammy award for *Latin Soul*.

SÁNCHEZ, Ricardo
Poet

The poet Ricardo Sánchez lived an eventful life, tragically cut short by his death at the age of 54 from cancer. Considered by many commentators to be one of the precursors of the Chicano literary tradition, Sánchez was a strong critic of U.S. society, which he saw as racist and materialistic. He believed that literature was an important tool to help Chicanos achieve equality with the Anglo-American community.

Early life

Born in El Paso, Texas, on March 29, 1941, Sánchez was the youngest of the 13 children of Pedro Lucero and Adelina Gallegos Sánchez. Raised in the tough El Paso neighborhood known as Barrio del Diablo (Devil's Neighborhood), Sánchez grew up influenced by the Pachuco gang culture. In later life, he criticized his early education for being stifled by racist teachers who did not encourage his literary aspirations. After school, Sánchez enlisted in the U.S. Army, and gained entry into officer cadet school. However, his life changed following the early deaths of two of his brothers. He fell into bad company, and committed armed robbery. Convicted, he served time in Soledad Prison in California, but was paroled in 1963. Following another armed robbery conviction, he served time again in Ramsey Prison Farm Number One in Texas; he was paroled in 1969.

Creating something good

Following his release, Sánchez earned a high-school equivalency certificate, and decided to continue with his studies. He also concentrated on writing poetry. In 1971 he published his first book, *Canto y Grito Mi Liberacíon*, through Míctla Publications, the publishing house that he

▲ *After serving time in prison for armed robbery, the poet Ricardo Sánchez educated Latino youths against the glorification of lifestyles that might lead to prison.*

founded to publish Chicano writers who could not find a publisher. Two years later, Anchor Books republished the work, bringing Sánchez to national attention as a poet. The collection contained poems that were conceived when he was in prison and written on his release. Blending English and Spanish, the work mixes poetry and prose to praise the Chicano people.

In 1974, the success of his poetry and the completion of a PhD resulted in Sánchez being offered a number of positions as a professor and writer-in-residence in schools across the United States.

In 1985, Sánchez published his last book of poetry. He wrote a column for the *San Antonio Express-News* (1985–1988), after which he wrote for the *El Paso Herald-Post* (1988–1991). He wrote about prejudice and also considered how people might reach their full potential in life. In 1990, Sánchez joined Washington State University as an associate professor. He was offered full tenure just before his death in September 1995.

KEY DATES	
1941	Born in El Paso, Texas, on March 29.
1960s	Incarcerated in California state prisons.
1973	Anchor Books republishes his first collection of poetry, *Canto y Grito Mi Liberacíon,* originally published in 1971 by Míctla Books.
1985	Publishes last book, *Selected Poems.*
1995	Dies of cancer in El Paso on September 3.

Further reading: López, Miguel R. *Chicano Timepiece: The Poetry and Politics of Ricardo Sánchez.* College Station, TX: Texas A&M University Press, 2006.
www.dr-ricardo-sanchez.com (Sánchez's Web site).

SANCHEZ, Ricardo S.
U.S. Army General

Lieutenant General Ricardo S. Sanchez was in 2006 the highest-ranking Hispanic American serving in the U.S. Army. He came to national and international prominence as commander of the U.S.-led ground forces involved in the occupation of Iraq following the end of the Second Persian Gulf War in May 2003. His outstanding career, however, was overshadowed by the torture and abuse of Iraqi prisoners at the Abu Ghraib Prison in 2003–2004, which took place under his command.

From Texas to the Gulf

Mexican American Sanchez was born in 1953 in Rio Grande City, Texas, a town close to the U.S. border with Mexico. Sanchez was raised by his mother, Maria, who supported her six children by working as a nurse's aide. The family was very poor, and lived in a house without electricity or plumbing. Nevertheless, Maria Sanchez instilled in her children the importance of education, hard work, self-discipline, and strong ethics, and Sanchez himself has frequently paid tribute to his mother's example and teachings.

During high school, Sanchez enrolled in the Reserve Officer Training Corps (ROTC), and after graduation won an ROTC scholarship to study at the University of Texas at Austin. Soon after, Sanchez transferred to Texas A&I University in Kingsville, where he graduated in 1973 with a bachelor's degree in mathematics and history. Later that same year, Sanchez joined the regular army as a second lieutenant, and later attended the Naval Postgraduate School, in Monterey, California, where he received his master's degree.

During the following years, Sanchez received rapid promotion, and was stationed in bases across the United States, as well as in Korea, Panama, and West Germany. In 1991, Sanchez served as a battalion commander in the First Persian Gulf War, taking part in the U.S.-led international operation to liberate Iraqi-occupied Kuwait. During the engagement, Sanchez won recognition not only for his strong leadership but also for his concern for the welfare of his troops.

Three-star general

After the First Persian Gulf War, Sanchez was promoted to brigadier general (one-star general), becoming the ninth Hispanic American to reach the rank of general in the U.S.

▲ **Lieutenant General Ricardo Sanchez is the highest-ranking Hispanic-American in the United States Army. His successful career was blighted in 2004 after allegations of involvement in the torture of POWs.**

Army. In that capacity, Sanchez served as deputy chief of staff, and later as director of operations, of the Miami-based U.S. Southern Command (USSOUTHCOM), which runs all U.S. military operations in Central and South America and the Caribbean. In 2001, Sanchez was promoted to major general (two-star general) in command of the 1st Armored Division, part of the prestigious V Corps (Fifth Corps) based in Wiesbaden, Germany.

Two years later, on June 14, 2003, Sanchez was promoted to lieutenant general (three-star general) in command of the whole of V Corps. Headquartered in Heidelberg, Germany, V Corps comprised some 41,000 servicemen and women. At the same time, Sanchez was also given command of the U.S.-led multinational Combined Joint Task Force-7, charged with the occupation of Iraq in the aftermath of the Second Persian Gulf War. Sanchez now faced the daunting task of overseeing 120,000 U.S. troops, in addition to thousands of troops from 29 other coalition countries.

The coalition troops led by Sanchez faced not only an ongoing struggle with Iraqi insurgents but also the job of assisting in the reconstruction of the war-torn country.

INFLUENCES AND INSPIRATION

In interviews through his career, Ricardo S. Sanchez has stressed how important his upbringing has been in enabling him to succeed. He pays special tribute to his mother, whose own life of self-sacrifice and duty, as well as her commitment to values such as patriotism, hard work, and ethical behavior, prepared him well for his life as a soldier. Sanchez explicitly identifies such values as Mexican or Hispanic. In one interview with *Hispanic* magazine he said: "When I became a soldier, the ethics and the value system of the military profession fitted almost perfectly with my own heritage. It made it very easy for me to adapt to the military value system."

Sanchez has also spoken of how the ingrained poverty of the community in which he grew up inspired him to achieve. Most local people in Rio Grande City made their living cotton picking, and he recalls how once, when he was 13 and complaining about school, his mother sent him to work for a day in the fields. A 14-hour day of backbreaking labor taught Sanchez the value of a good education. Such lessons drove Sanchez to succeed throughout his career.

Sanchez's immediate priority, however, was to track down the fugitive leaders of the former regime. High-profile operations led to the killings, in July 2003, of the two sons of former Iraqi president Saddam Hussein, and, in December, to the capture of the former president himself. Throughout this time, Sanchez received widespread praise for his handling of what was a extremely challenging situation. At the end of 2003, *Hispanic* magazine named him "Hispanic of the Year."

The Abu Ghraib Scandal

During 2004, however, the situation in Iraq deteriorated. Increasingly, Iraqi rebels engaged coalition troops in fierce battles, resulting in the loss of many lives, including those of U.S. soldiers. Sanchez's problems deepened in April 2004, when the United States media broke a story about the abuse of Iraqi prisoners of war (POWs) held by U.S. military personnel in Abu Ghraib Prison, a few miles outside the Iraqi capital, Baghdad. The resulting scandal threatened to jeopardize U.S. operations in Iraq, alienating international support for the occupation, and exposing troops to violent reprisals. Many commentators argued that, as the overall military commander in Iraq, Sanchez had ultimately to be held responsible for the abuse; some, moreover, accused him of failing to act to stop the torture or even of sanctioning its use. In April 2005, however, an official investigation into the affair cleared Sanchez of any wrongdoing, although subsequently a memorandum came to light in which Sanchez clearly authorized interrogation techniques that went far beyond usual U.S. Army guidelines. Some civil liberties organizations pressed for the events to be reinvestigated. They also urged that charges be brought against Sanchez and other military personnel and politicians who were thought to have been concealing direct involvement with the atrocities.

Post-Iraq

By the time the inquiry findings became public, Sanchez had already left his position as commander of Combined Joint Task Force-7. Commentators speculated that his departure from Iraq in July 2004—together with the fact that he had not been promoted to a four-star general as widely expected—was a direct consequence of the Abu Ghraib scandal, although this was officially denied.

Sanchez later returned to serve as commanding general of V Corps, stationed in Heidelberg with his wife and family. An elementary school in his hometown, Rio Grande City, is named in his honor.

Further reading: Holsten, Mark. "Soldier of Fortune." *Hispanic,* Vol. 16, No. 12 (December 1, 2003).

www.vcorps.army.mil/leaders/default.htm (official U.S. Army biography).

KEY DATES	
1953	Born in Rio Grande City, Texas.
1973	Joins the U.S. Army.
1991	Serves as a battalion commander in the First Persian Gulf War.
2001	Promoted to major general and given command of the 1st Armored Division, stationed in Germany.
2003	Promoted to lieutenant general. Appointed commander of the United States-led occupation of Iraq.
2004	Relinquishes command of Multi-National Forces (Iraq) in the wake of the Abu Ghraib scandal.

SANCHEZ, Roger
DJ, Musician

Roger Sanchez is one of the leading house music disc jockeys working today. Widely regarded as a "superstar DJ," he has made a significant contribution to dance music as both a remixer and producer. He has won several awards, including a Grammy for best remixed recording.

From Queens to the international stage

Born in Queens, New York City, on June 1, 1967, Sanchez was the son of Dominican immigrants. A talented breakdancer and graffiti artist, Sanchez started DJing at friends' parties when he was 13. He attended Manhattan's School of Art and Design, and went on to study architecture at the Pratt Institute, New York City. Sanchez began DJing at New York's Tunnel nightclub, and eventually dropped out of his studies to concentrate on music. Sanchez's first ventures included running the popular club, Ego Trip, and selling tapes of his mixing. He claimed: "A great DJ can take a record and give it an entirely new sound or vibe by the way they deal with the beats or chord progressions."

▼ **As a student Roger Sanchez was torn between his love of music and studying architecture: He said in the end music touched him more deeply.**

KEY DATES	
1967	Born in New York City on June 1.
1990	Releases hit "Luv Dancin."
1994	Releases hit "Another Star."
1998	Three mixes in the Top 30 during week of March 21.
2003	Wins Grammy for best remixed recording.

Sanchez's underground success brought him to the attention of leading house-music label Strictly Rhythm, which released Sanchez's "Luv Dancin" in 1990; the song was recorded under Sanchez's pseudonym Underground Solution, and became a huge underground hit. In 1991, Sanchez started remixing; his early work included remixes for Michael Jackson and Diana Ross. In 1994, Sanchez had his second major club hit with "Another Star."

Sanchez's subsequent releases encompass his DJ compilations, remix work, and solo recordings. They include "Livin 4 the Underground" (1995, as Roger S), "Release Yo Self " (1995, as Transatlantic Soul), and "Back" (1997, as the S-Men, a dance-music group he formed with Junior Vasquez and DJ Sneaks). The following year, Sanchez released his remix collection, *S-Man Classics*, and had three remixes in the *Billboard* Top-30 chart in one week in March. Sanchez's later releases include *House Music Movement* (1998) and his debut album as a solo artist, *First Contact* (2001), which featured "Another Chance," a No. 1 hit in the United Kingdom.

Global popularity

Sanchez's Release Yourself project encompasses compilation albums, nightclub residencies throughout the world, and a radio program that has more than a million weekly listeners worldwide, and which was acclaimed as the Outstanding Radio Show at the 2005 House Music Awards. Sanchez continues to remix leading artists such as Basement Jaxx and Kylie Minogue, and his remix of No Doubt's "Hella Good" earned him a Grammy (2003).

Further reading: Story, Rosalyn M. *All Music Guide to Electronica: The Definitive Guide to Electronic Music.* San Francisco, CA: Backbeat Books, 2001.
http://www.rogersanchez.com (Sanchez's official Web site).

SÁNCHEZ VILELLA, Roberto
Politician

The 20th-century Puerto Rican politician and administrator Roberto Sánchez Vilella was an important ally of the island's first elected governor, Luis Muñoz Marín, who is often held to be the father of modern Puerto Rico. Sánchez Vilella subsequently succeeded Muñoz Marín as governor, but is generally considered to have been much less successful than his charismatic predecessor.

Early life
The son of a prosperous merchant, Roberto Sánchez Vilella was born on February 19, 1913, in the seaport of Mayagüez, western Puerto Rico. He was raised and educated in the Santurce district of the capital, San Juan, but, like many wealthy young Puerto Rican men at the time, he went on to study on the U.S. mainland, graduating in 1934 with a degree in engineering from Ohio State University. After returning to Puerto Rico, he worked briefly as a professor at the University of Puerto Rico, but soon devoted himself to a career in politics.

A man of ideas
In 1938, Sánchez Vilella became a member of the newly founded Partido Popular Democratico (PPD or Popular Democratic Party). The PPD and its leader, Luis Muñoz Marín, rapidly came to dominate Puerto Rican politics; they introduced a wide-ranging package of reforms, including

▼ **Roberto Sánchez Vilella is pictured here with his wife, Jeannette Ramos Buonomo, in Washington, D.C., in October 1967.**

KEY DATES

1913   Born in Mayagüez, Puerto Rico, on February 19.

1938   Becomes a member of the newly founded Partido Popular Democratico (PPD).

1965   Begins term as the second elected governor of Puerto Rico.

1997   Dies in San Juan, Puerto Rico, on March 24.

the establishment of Puerto Rico as a self-ruling commonwealth within the United States (1952). Villela rose from being in charge of reforming the capital's public transportation system to secretary of state, and was widely seen as the governor's right-hand man.

In 1964, Muñoz retired as governor, and chose Sánchez Vilella to stand as the PPD candidate in the election to replace him. After a comfortable win, Sánchez Vilella entered office in 1965 promising "new ideas, new faces, a new style." In fact, Sánchez Vilella introduced few new reforms, although he did consolidate Puerto Rico's status as a commonwealth. In 1967, he held a plebiscite on the issue in which 60.5 percent of Puerto Rican voters declared themselves in favor of the status quo.

Although many commentators recognize Sánchez Vilella's ability as an administrator, they claim he was less able as a political leader: The PPD began to fall apart, as rivalries broke out among its different factions. Eventually, Sánchez Vilella even lost the support of Muñoz Marín, and in the gubernatorial elections of 1968 he was not chosen to stand as the party candidate. He promptly left the PPD, and founded his own party, the Partido del Pueblo (People's Party). He thus split the traditional PPD vote, and brought to power a new governor, Luis A. Ferré, leader of the New Progressive Party. After several attempts to return to politics, Sánchez Vilella eventually returned to teaching at the University of Puerto Rico. He died in 1997.

See also: Ferré, Luis A.; Muñoz Marín, Luis

Further reading: Pico, Fernando. *History of Puerto Rico: A Panorama of Its People.* Princeton, NJ: Markus Wiener Publishers, 2005.
www.britannica.com/eb/article-9114880?tocId=9114880 (article on Sanchez Vilella).

SANDOVAL, Arturo
Musician

Cuban-born musician Arturo Sandoval is an award-winning artist. He is regarded by many music commentators as one of the best trumpeters of his generation. Sandoval was part of the influential Cuban-band Irakere, along with Jesús "Chuco" Valdés and Paquito D'Rivera.

Early life

Sandoval came from humble beginnings. He was born in Artemisia, Cuba, on November 6, 1949, and lived most of his life in Havana. Sandoval was interested in music from an early age. Aged 12, he began studying the classical trumpet, playing in a local band. He idolized the musician Dizzy Gillespie, who influenced the way in which Sandoval played the trumpet. Sandoval wanted to become a professional musician, but his parents discouraged his dream, fearing that he would always struggle. Sandoval was eventually accepted into the National Music Institute in Havana, studying there from 1963.

The emergence of Irakere

In 1966 Sandoval helped found the informal group Orquestra Juvenil de Música Moderna with other musicians. Its members were incorporated into the official Orquestra Cubana de Música Moderna (OCMM), when it was created in 1967 by the Consejo Nacional de Cultura. It became the training ground for young musicians in Cuba.

In 1973 a group of musicians from the OCMM formed the group Irakere (*see box on page 117*). Sandoval subsequently joined the group after completing his compulsory military service. Irakere was very successful in incorporating jazz into the Cuban sound, and Sandoval became one of its main stars. During Sandoval's first visit to the United States in 1978, Irakere played at the Newport Jazz Festival and at Carnegie Hall. The group also won a Grammy award.

In 1977 Sandoval met his idol Gillespie, who was touring Cuba with his United Nations (UN) Orchestra for the first time. Impressed by Sandoval's talent, Gillespie took the young man under his wing and the two men became friends. Gillespie provided Sandoval with support, especially following his defection to the United States.

▼ *Trumpeter Arturo Sandoval has influenced many people, including the actor Andy Garcia, who produced a film about the musician's life in 2000.*

INFLUENCES AND INSPIRATION

Arturo Sandoval's brilliant technique and eclectic repertoire have often led critics to overlook his deep commitment to music education and also to the history of the music that he plays.

A supremely talented musician, Sandoval emerged as a star in Irakere, the group that pianist Jesús "Chuco" Valdés and saxophonist and composer Paquito D'Rivera helped create. Combining jazz, rock, Latin percussion, funk, and classical music, Irakere's sound was extremely innovative for the time. The band astounded U.S. audiences when it performed at the Newport Jazz Festival in 1978.

One of Sandoval's biggest influences was the trumpeter Dizzy Gillespie. Sandoval was greatly influenced by Gillespie's playing. Gillespie was equally impressed when he met the musician in the 1970s. Gillespie offered Sandoval a position in his band and later helped him defect to the United States.

From Cuba to the United States

The creation of the Jazz Plaza Festival in 1979, after a 20-year period of cultural isolation in Cuba, provided Cuban musicians with more direct contact with the international figures of jazz and Latin music. Sandoval became one of the three directors of the Plaza Festival and strengthened his association with the great names of the jazz world. Following his success with Irakere, Sandoval was able to pursue his individual career and form his own group in 1981. He began to appear regularly at jazz festivals in Europe, the United States, and Japan; he played with Gillespie on several occasions, and recorded *To a Finland Station* (1982) and *Arturo Sandoval and His Group with Dizzy Gillespie* (1985) with him.

In 1987 Sandoval joined Gillespie's UN Orchestra. In 1990 he fled to the U.S. Embassy in Rome during a European tour and, helped by Gillespie, acquired political asylum in the United States. Sandoval settled in Miami,

Florida, with his wife and son. He taught at the music school at Florida International University. He subsequently obtained U.S. citizenship in 1998.

Living in America

Sandoval signed with GRP records, and in 1991 he released his first album in the United States, *Flight for Freedom*. This was followed by yearly releases that received critical acclaim, including *I Remember Clifford* (1992), a tribute to the American jazz trumpeter Clifford Brown, *Dream Come True* (1993), the Grammy-winning *Danzón* (1994), *Latin Train* (1995), and *Swingin* (1996).

Since living in the United States, Sandoval has developed his style into a more eclectic format, broadening his repertoire both in recording and performing into a variety of musical genres, including jazz, bebop, traditional Cuban, and classical music. He has appeared with such orchestras as the National Symphony Orchestra, the Los Angeles Philharmonic Orchestra, the Pittsburgh Symphony Orchestra, and the National Symphony Orchestra of Washington, D.C. He also composed a *Concerto for Trumpet*, which he recorded with the London Symphony Orchestra (1994).

Sandoval has also played in several films, including *The Mambo Kings* (1992), based on a novel by Oscar Hijuelos. In 2000 he won an Emmy for the soundtrack of the film based on his own life story: *For Love or Country: The Arturo Sandoval Story*. Sandoval is associated with three scholarships, including Arturo Sandoval's Dizzy Gillespie Trumpet Scholar Award.

See also: D'Rivera, Paquito; Garcia, Andy; Hijuelos, Oscar

Further reading: Acosta, Leonardo. *Cubano Be, Cubano Bop: One Hundred Years of Jazz in Cuba*. Washington, D.C.: Smithsonian Books, 2003.
http://www.arturosandoval.com (Sandoval's Web site).

KEY DATES	
1949	Born in Artemisia, Cuba, on November 6.
1961	Begins to study the classical guitar.
1964	Starts to study music at the Conservatory in Havana.
1973	Joins Irakere.
1977	Meets Dizzy Gillespie about this time.
1978	First performs in the United States.
1981	Forms own group.
1990	Defects to the United States.
1994	Wins Grammy for *Danzón*.
2000	Wins Emmy for soundtrack for movie *For Love or Country: The Arturo Sandoval Story*, produced by Andy Garcia.

SANDOVAL, Hope
Musician

Hope Sandoval is a singer-songwriter with the alternative rock bands Mazzy Star and Hope Sandoval & The Warm Inventions. Her laconic vocals combine country, blues, and folk influences. Her best-known release is the 1994 single "Fade into You," which was recorded with the band Mazzy Star.

Early life

Sandoval was born in 1966 in East Los Angeles, California, to Mexican American parents. She formed her first band in 1986 with a friend, Sylvia Gomez. It was a folk duo called Going Home, in which Sandoval sang vocals and Gomez played guitar. Gomez gave a tape of their music to Kendra Smith of Dream Syndicate. Smith passed it on to David Roback, a fellow member of the alternative psychedelic band. Roback subsequently produced some recordings for Going Home that were never released, but which cemented a lasting friendship between him and Sandoval.

▼ **Hope Sandoval's singing and songwriting talents have brought her a number of chart successes.**

KEY DATES

1966   Born in Los Angeles, California.

1990   "Blue Flower" reaches number 29 on U.S. rock chart.

1994   Mazzy Star's album *So Tonight That I Might See* enters the U.S. Top 40 album chart.

1996   Releases the album *Among My Swan*.

2001   Releases *Bavarian Fruit Bread* with Hope Sandoval & The Warm Inventions.

Going Home continued to perform live in California, and when Smith left Roback's subsequent band, Opal, during a tour, Roback asked Sandoval to step in. After the tour, Sandoval and Roback continued working together, and renamed themselves Mazzy Star. The remaining members of Opal left and, although Mazzy Star often featured additional musicians, the partnership between Sandoval and Roback formed the creative core of the band. Sandoval wrote most of Mazzy Star's lyrics. A reluctant live performer, she has always claimed to prefer studio work.

Mainstream success

Mazzy Star's debut, *She Hangs Brightly,* was released in 1990. The single "Blue Flower" reached number 29 in the U.S. rock chart. Mazzy Star's 1993 album, *So Tonight That I Might See,* was initially a modest success. However, the success of the single "Fade into You" in 1994 propelled *So Tonight That I Might See* onto the U.S. Top 40 album chart. "Fade into You" has since appeared on many film soundtracks, including *Starship Troopers* and *Swept Away*.

Mazzy Star's last album was *Among My Swan* (1996). Although they did not officially disband Mazzy Star, both Sandoval and Roback began pursuing individual projects. Sandoval formed the folk-pop band Hope Sandoval & The Warm Inventions with Colm O'Ciosoig from the British group My Bloody Valentine, and they recorded *Bavarian Fruit Bread* in 2001. Sandoval has also collaborated with Bert Jansch, Bernard Butler, Suede, The Jesus and Mary Chain, and The Chemical Brothers.

Further reading: Story, Rosalyn M. *Back to the Miracle Factory: Rock Etc. 1990s.* New York, NY: Forge Books, 2002.
http://www.hopesandoval.com (official Web site).

SANTALIZ AVILA, Pedro
Writer, Director

Puerto Rican-born writer and director Pedro Santaliz Avila has written more than 60 plays. He is the founder of the New York-based theater company Nuevo Teatro Pobre de América.

Early life
Born in Isabela, Puerto Rico, on May 28, 1938, Santaliz Avila was raised in Río Piedras, near the University of Puerto Rico. He studied at the university's Teatro Infantil (Children's Theater). At age six, Santaliz Avila acted in a play by the renowned Spanish writer Federico García Lorca, performing with some of Puerto Rico's leading actors. After graduating from high school, Santaliz Avila studied for a BA at the university, where he specialized in literature, languages, and drama.

A passionate interest in drama
As a student, Santaliz Avila became involved in the drama companies Comedia Universitaria (University Comedy) and Teatro Rodante (Traveling Theater). After graduating, he traveled to Hungary in 1962, where he began writing a novel. He became more interested in drama after moving to Poland, where he was influenced by the theater director Jerzy Grotowski (1933–1999).

Nuevo Teatro Pobre de America
In 1964, Santaliz Avila moved to New York, where he founded the company Nuevo Teatro Pobre de América (New Poor Theater of America) in the following year. The actors in the company were encouraged by Santaliz Avila to improvise. He put on plays by Latino authors, as well as established works of world drama, including *Saint Joan* by George Bernard Shaw. In addition to directing, Santaliz Avila acted in several of his productions.

Perhaps the most important characteristic of the Nuevo Teatro Pobre de América was that it provided drama for the community, offering educational workshops to the public. Like fellow actor and theater founder Miriam Colón, Santaliz Avila believed that drama should be accessible to the masses. To that end, he put on many outdoor productions in the streets and in public spaces, such as Central Park.

A man of diverse talents
During the 1960s, Santaliz Avila also participated in poetry and music events produced in Central Park by Joseph Papp. He presented his play *El Castillo Interior de Medea Camuñas* during Papp's Latin American Festival in New York. In 1965, he also took part in the New York Shakespeare Festival in Delacorte.

In 1969, Santaliz Avila went to France, where he was a member of the theater company L'Autre Théâtre (The Other Theater). Following his return to the United States, he resumed work at the Nuevo Teatro Pobre de América. In 1975, he returned to his native Puerto Rico, where he again worked in community theater.

Social comment
Santaliz Avila's writing reflects his concern with social issues. For example, *El Castillo Interior de Medea Camuñas*—an adaptation of a 5th-century-B.C. play by the Greek dramatist Euripides—deals with domestic violence against women in Puerto Rican culture. His other work includes *El Cartero Del Rey* and *Concupiscencias*. In 1991, Santaliz Avila published *Teatro*, a highly influential study of drama in performance.

See also: Colón, Miriam

Further reading: Santaliz Avila, Pedro. *Teatro.* San Juan, Puerto Rico: Instituto de Cultura Puertorriqueña,1992.
http://fordfound.org/elibrary/documents/0146/028.cfm (Ford Foundation Page for Hispanic Theater in United States and Puerto Rico).

KEY DATES

1938   Born in Isabela, Puerto Rico, on May 28.

1962   Goes to Hungary, where he writes a novel; goes to Poland, where he is influenced by the Polish theater director and educator Jerzy Grotowski.

1965   Creates the Nuevo Teatro Pobre de América in New York; participates in the New York Shakespeare Festival, Delacorte.

1969   Works as an actor in France's "L'Autre Théatre"

1975   Returns to Puerto Rico to continue work begun with Nuevo Teatro Pobre de América.

1991   Publishes *Teatro*.

SANTANA, Carlos
Musician

One of the outstanding musicians to emerge from the 1960s' psychedelic scene, Carlos Santana pioneered a unique fusion of rock, Latin, Afro-Cuban, and other global music influences for more than four decades.

Early life

Carlos Santana was born in 1947 in Autlán de Navarro, Jalisco, Mexico. His father, José, was an accomplished mariachi (Mexican folk) violinist who introduced Santana to Mexican music and taught him to play the violin. At age eight, Santana moved with his family to the border town of Tijuana, where he was exposed to the music of blues legends B. B. King, John Lee Hooker, and T-Bone Walker. Almost immediately, Santana stopped playing violin, and switched to guitar. He later said: "Once I got that electric sound, there was no turning back. I knew I wasn't going to be an accountant or an English teacher." A few years later, he began playing in clubs and bars with local bands. When his family moved to San Francisco, California, in the early 1960s, he stayed behind to remain immersed in Tijuana's music scene. Joining his family two years later when he turned 14, Santana performed with Bay Area bands while finishing high school.

Own band

In 1966, Santana helped organize the Santana Blues Band, which was originally founded as a collective of Hispanic and white musicians. The group's name, later shortened to

KEY DATES

1947   Born in Autlán de Navarro, Jalisco, Mexico, on July 20.

1966   Founds the Santana Blues Band, a name that is later changed to Santana.

1969   Records his first album, *Santana*, and gives a legendary performance at the Woodstock Music and Art Festival.

1972   Becomes a devotee of Shri Chinmoy, who gives him the name "Devadip."

1988   Wins a Grammy Award for Best Instrumental Performance on *Blues for Salvador*.

1999   Releases *Supernatural* to great commercial and critical success.

Santana, bore Carlos's last name primarily because of music union regulations that required them to appoint a nominal leader. On June 16, 1968, promoter Bill Graham gave the band its debut at the historic Filmore West, where many famed San Francisco acts got their start. In September of that year, Santana recorded for the first time on *The Live Adventures of Mike Bloomfield and Al Kooper* while playing at the Filmore.

Soon afterward, Santana signed with Columbia Records and released a self-titled album with his own group. Most of the tracks were instrumentals that employed Latin rhythms with a rock edge. On a tour to promote *Santana*, the group lit up the famous Woodstock Festival in August 1969. The band's set was one of the surprise hits of the three-day event; its eight-minute instrumental "Soul Sacrifice" was included in the festival's soundtrack album, and featured in the movie *Woodstock* (1970). In the same year, *Santana* reached number four on the U.S. album charts, and the hit single "Evil Ways" peaked at number nine on the *Billboard* Hot 100.

Further acclaim

In 1970, the Santana band gained commercial success with its second album, *Abraxas*, which reached number one on the album charts and sold more than four million copies. The blend of Latin, Afro-Cuban, and rock music—increasingly featuring nontraditional percussive instruments, such as the congas, alongside Santana's virtuoso guitar—won widespread popularity. The band's cover of "Black Magic Woman" put a new, Latin-inspired twist on the Fleetwood Mac song, reaching number four in the singles chart. Santana's fresh interpretation of Tito Puente's "Oye Como Va" reached number 13.

The Santana band's rapid rise put tremendous pressure on its members. Creative differences became more pronounced when band member Gregg Rolie—influenced by progressive rock—wanted to play longer, classically inspired instrumentals, emphasizing keyboards. Santana himself, on the other hand, wanted to compose shorter, percussion-heavy songs in the African tradition. The increasingly fragmented group held together for two years but finally disbanded in 1972, after releasing two more albums. Although another band named Santana was later formed under licence by the original members, it had no permanent lineup: Musicians came and went, there were

Despite his Mexican heritage, Carlos Santana has no doubt about the primary source of his musical inspiration. He has said: "Blues was my first love. It was the first thing where I said 'Oh man, this is the stuff.' It just sounded so raw and honest, gut-bucket honest." As soon as he first heard the blues on the radio in Tijuana, Mexico, he gave up playing the violin—until then his main instrument—and took up the guitar. Xavier Batiz, a local musician, awakened a sense of real-life magic in the young Santana, who later recalled: "He dressed like Little Richard, played like B. B. King, with a little Ray Charles in there. He had a beautiful tone on his guitar. My mom took me to the park to hear Batiz's band, the TJs, and the sound of the electric guitars, amps and everything. For me it was like watching a flying saucer for the first time. I started following him like a guided missile."

numerous guest appearances, and the group's playing style abandoned its roots and shifted toward jazz-rock fusion.

Spirituality

In the early 1970s, Santana became a devotee of the Indian guru Shri Chinmoy, who bestowed on him the name "Devadip," meaning "the eye, the lamp, and the light of God." Baptized with a new name, Santana was initiated into a community of talented, spiritually inclined musicians. He teamed up with John McLaughlin, the legendary guitarist of The Mahavishnu Orchestra and a fellow devotee of Shri Chinmoy, to produce *Love, Devotion, Surrender* (1973), an album that reached the Top 20 and went gold. Santana next collaborated on *Illuminations* with Turiya Alice Coltrane, the widow of jazz great John Coltrane. *Illuminations* spent two months in the Top 100. Although Santana later broke with Shri Chinmoy, he continued to view music as a spiritual path with the power to unify people.

In the 1970s and 1980s, Santana continued his musical odyssey, exploring jazz, blues, and world music with numerous artists, including Willie Nelson, Herbie Hancock, Wayne Shorter, Pharoah Sanders, Ismael Lo, Salif Keita, and Ali Akbar Khan. In 1988, Santana won a Grammy Award for Best Instrumental Performance on *Blues for Salvador*. During the 1990s, Santana took a break from recording, but returned in 1999 with *Supernatural*, an album true to his Latin roots that included a diverse mix of young guest artists such as Dave Matthews, Lauryn Hill, and Wycleaf Jean. The first single from the album, "Smooth," a salsa-inspired hit featuring Rob Thomas's throaty vocals and Santana's high-pitched guitar riffs, spent 12 weeks at number one on the *Billboard* Top 100. *Supernatural* sold 15 million copies in the United States alone, and gained Santana a new generation of fans.

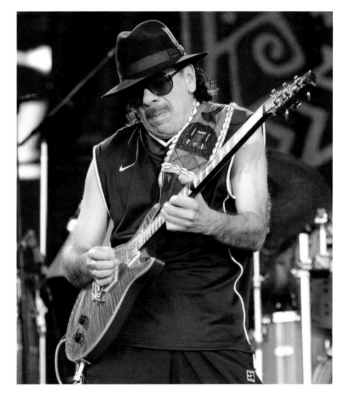

▲ *Guitar legend Carlos Santana performs live on stage during his 2002 world tour to promote the album* **Shaman.**

See also: Puente, Tito

Further reading: Leng, Simon. *Soul Sacrifice: The Story of Santana*. London, England: Omnibus Press, 2000. http://www.findarticles.com/p/articles/mi_m0GER/is_2000_Summer/ai_63500762 (interview with Carlos Santana).

SANTAYANA, George
Writer, Philosopher

A major figure in the history of American letters, George Santayana was a poet, novelist, cultural critic, and preeminent philosopher. Although he spent 40 years of his life in the United States, and wrote in English, he was a Spaniard who never took U.S. citizenship.

Early life

Jorge Agustín Nicolás Ruiz de Santayana y Borrás was born in 1863 in Madrid, Spain. His father, Agustín Santayana, was a lawyer and diplomat who had served as a colonial administrator in the Philippines. There he met Josefina Borrás, whom he married in 1861. With three children from a previous marriage, Josefina moved to Boston, Massachusetts, in 1869. George remained with his father in Spain until 1872, when they both joined the family in Boston.

In the United States, Santayana adopted the forename George, the English equivalent of Jorge, and learned English at his siblings' kindergarten before enrolling at the Boston Latin School. In 1882, he entered Harvard

▼ *This photograph of George Santayana was taken in 1944 in Rome, Italy, where he spent the last years of his life.*

University, receiving a BA in 1886 and a PhD in 1889. In the same year he became a faculty member at Harvard, where he remained until 1912. Among the students he lectured in philosophy were T. S. Eliot, Robert Frost, and Wallace Stevens: The work of all three poets shows the influence of their teacher.

In 1912, Santayana, tired of academic life and financially secure thanks to a small inheritance, took early retirement at age 48. He left the United States, never to return, and moved to Europe. He lived at various times in England, France, and Italy, and wrote prolifically until his death in Rome in 1952.

Legacy

Of Santayana's numerous philosophical books, the most important is generally thought to have been *The Life of Reason* (1905–1906). The five-volume work contains his most famous maxim: "Those who cannot remember the past are condemned to repeat it." Santayana also published many books of poetry, as well as a novel, *The Last Puritan* (1935), which was nominated for a Pulitzer Prize and became an international best seller. His autobiography, *Persons and Places* (1944), is regarded as a masterpiece of the genre.

Further reading: McCormick, John. *George Santayana: A Biography*. New Brunswick, NJ: Transaction Publishers, 2003. http://plato.stanford.edu/entries/santayana/ (Stanford Encyclopedia of Philosophy online).

SANTEIRO, Luis
Playwright, Children's TV Writer

Cuban-born Luis Santeiro is an Emmy Award-winning writer best known for his work on *Que Pasa, USA?*, the groundbreaking 1970s' bilingual situation comedy, and for his long-standing contribution to *Sesame Street*, the children's educational program. He is also an accomplished playwright, whose funny, bittersweet dissections of contemporary Latino life have won him both Hispanic American and mainstream audiences.

Early life
Santeiro was born in 1947 in Havana, and grew up with his five brothers and sisters in the city's wealthy Vedado district. His mother was the granddaughter of former Cuban president Gerardo Machado (1871–1939); one of his uncles was a respected theater director. In 1960 the family fled Fidel Castro's communist regime. They took refuge in the United States, and settled in Miami, Florida, where Santeiro was educated at Christopher Columbus High School. He became a U.S. citizen in 1975.

University and early work experience
Santeiro received a bachelor's degree in sociology from Villanova University, Pennsylvania, and a master's degree in film and television from the Newhouse School of Public Communications at Syracuse University. In 1975, after working in a variety of jobs in the film industry, he became a television writer. Soon afterward, he was hired to write the script of the pilot episode of the Public Broadcasting Service (PBS) series *Que Pasa, USA?* Produced and taped in Miami, the show was a faithful, affectionate portrayal of a working-class Cuban American family. The success of the first episode spawned a series that ran from 1976 to 1980. Santeiro subsequently became the head of a team of writers on the show, and it was in that role that he won his first Emmy Award.

Between television and theater
In 1978 Santeiro moved to New York City, but continued to write for *Que Pasa, USA?* until 1979. He then became a permanent member of the writing team of another PBS program, *Sesame Street*. He has remained on the children's show ever since, and earned a further 14 Emmy awards for his innovative work.

Meanwhile, during the late 1980s, Santeiro established a parallel career as a stage dramatist. Among the best

KEY DATES	
1947	Born in Havana, Cuba, on October 9.
1960	Immigrates to the United States.
1975	Becomes a U.S. citizen.
1976	Begins a four-year stint writing on the bilingual television situation comedy *Que Pasa, USA?*
1979	Joins *Sesame Street* as scriptwriter.
1990	Premiere of his first successful stage play, *The Lady from Havana*.

known of his plays is *The Lady from Havana* (1990), a comical treatment of the generational and cultural barriers thrown up when a Cuban mother visits her daughter in Miami.

Some of Santeiro's plays have a sharp satirical edge. *The Lady of the Tortilla* (1991), for example, ridicules the common perception that Latinos eat only one kind of food. *Barrio Babies* (1999) is a musical farce about a Puerto Rican playwright trying to break into Hollywood. *Praying with the Enemy* (2000) deals with Pope John Paul II's much-criticized visit to Cuba in 1998. All three plays reflect their author's preoccupation with the Hispanic experience in the United States. Some critics have complained that Santeiro's writing is limited in its scope, and recommended that he broaden his range of subject matter; others, however, have recognized that his localized themes have universal applications. The latter view seems closer to that of the theater-going public. Santeiro's plays have been performed hundreds of times throughout the United States.

Accolades
Santeiro's work for both theater and television has won him wide acclaim. In addition to his Emmy awards, he has received the Hispanic Achievement Award (1991), the Hispanic Heritage Award (1993), and the National Hispanic Academy of Media Arts and Sciences Award (1995).

Further reading: Santeiro, Luis. *The Lady from Havana: A Play in Two Acts.* New York, NY: Dramatists Play Service, 1991.
www.hispanicmagazine.com/2000/jan_feb/Cultura (article about Santeiro).

SANTIAGO, Herman
Singer, Songwriter

Puerto Rican Herman Santiago sang second tenor with Frankie Lymon and the Teenagers. The U.S. vocal group leapt to fame in 1956 with its first single, "Why Do Fools Fall in Love?" The group was one of the foremost exponents of the rhythm-and-blues style known as "doo-wop" (so called because of the vocal harmonies created by the backing singers). Combining catchy, sweet-toned melodies with a wholesome, youthful image, the Teenagers won an enthusiastic young following and were hugely influential in the development of later teenage groups such as the Jackson 5.

Early life

Herman Santiago was born in 1941 in San Juan, Puerto Rico, and raised in New York City. By the early 1950s, Santiago, together with fellow Puerto Rican Joe Negroni and two African American friends, Jimmy Merchant and Sherman Garnes, were performing in an a cappella (voice-only) quartet named The Premiers. By 1955 they had been joined by another African American, Frankie Lymon, who initially provided the high-tenor backing to Santiago's lead. In 1955—at a time when all the members were still just 15 or younger—the group won a recording contract with Gee Records. Santiago became ill during the recording of the group's first single, "Why Do Fools Fall in Love?," which he himself had written, so Lymon provided the lead voice instead. The recording company liked the sound so much that the group's name was changed to Frankie Lymon and the Teenagers, and Santiago was relegated to second tenor. The record was a massive hit, reaching number six in the national singles chart.

The band's success proved short-lived, however. In the summer of 1957, Frankie Lymon quit The Teenagers to sing solo, and without his charismatic presence the group soon

▲ *Herman Santiago (left) sings with outstretched arms while fellow Teenagers' member Jimmy Merchant accompanies him on guitar.*

faded. Santiago made repeated attempts to revive the Teenagers, but had little success, and by the 1990s he was living in poverty. "Why Do Fools Fall in Love?," meanwhile, enjoyed a much more spectacular history, being successfully covered by singers as varied as The Beach Boys (1964) and Diana Ross (1981).

Legal dispute

Because the band members had apparently signed away their rights to the royalties, they received no income from their most famous song, despite its enduring popularity. In 1992, however, a federal court decided that the rights to the song belonged to Santiago, Merchant, and Lymon's widow (the singer had died in 1968). The ruling transformed the fortunes of Herman Santiago: After years of poverty, he finally became a millionaire. In 1996, however, his life again became precarious after the original judgment was reversed by a court of appeals. The song now belongs to EMI Music Publishing.

Further reading: Bogdanov, Vladimir, and others (eds.). *All Music Guide to Soul: The Definitive Guide to R&B and Soul.* San Francisco, CA: Backbeat Books, 2003. www.rockabilly.nl/artists/teenagers.htm (history of the group and biographies of its members).

KEY DATES	
1941	Born in San Juan, Puerto Rico, on February 18.
1955	Forms harmony group The Teenagers.
1956	"Why Do Fools Fall in Love?" reaches No. 6 in charts.
1992	Receives royalties from "Why Do Fools Fall in Love?"
1996	Rights to the song assigned to EMI Music Publishing.

SANTOS, Daniel
Singer

In the mid-20th century, Puerto Rican Daniel Santos was one of the best-known singers of *boleros*, the sultry, often bittersweet love songs popular throughout Latin America. Famed as much as for his rowdy private life as for his exquisite voice and music, Santos was widely regarded as the iconic Latin "macho man," and was often known by the nickname "El Jefe" (the boss). Santos was also a fierce Puerto Rican patriot, and during the 1950s he became closely associated with the revolutionary movement of Cuban Fidel Castro.

Early life
Santos was born in 1916 in the impoverished but musically vibrant district of Trastalleres in San Juan, Puerto Rico. At age 10, he and his family moved to New York City, where they were so poor that Santos had to give up school to work as a shoe shine boy. At age 14, he moved out of the family home, and went to live on his own in a run-down apartment. His professional career as a singer began a few years later, when he was overheard singing in the shower by a member of a local Puerto Rican *bolero* group and was invited to join.

Emerging talent
In 1938, the famous Puerto Rican *bolero* composer Pedro Flores (1897–1979) heard Santos performing one of his own songs, "Amor Perdido" (Lost Love), and was so impressed that he invited him to become a member of his singing group, the Quarteto (later the Sexteto) Flores. On joining, Santos sang alongside other leading Puerto Rican *bolero* singers, including Myrta Silva (1917–1987) and Pedro Ortiz Davila (1912–1986). It was with Flores that Santos recorded some of his best-known and most popular love songs, including "La despedida" (The farewell), "Tú serás mía" (You will be mine), "Esperanza inútil" (Vain hope), "Yo no sé nada" (I know nothing), "Bella mujer"

(Lovely lady), and "El último adiós" (The last goodbye). The song for which he became most famous, "Linda," was a jukebox standard throughout the United States in 1942. From time to time, Santos was also a guest singer with the orchestra of Xavier Cugat.

War and revolution
After serving in the U.S. Army during World War II (1939–1945), Santos became active in the growing movement for Puerto Rican independence. He drew his inspiration partly from the work of Juan Antonio Corretjer, Puerto Rico's national poet. In addition to love songs, Santos now recorded stirring political anthems, such as "Los patriotas" (The patriots). He also began to spend long periods in Cuba. There he became involved in the revolutionary movement of Fidel Castro, who adopted Santos's "Sierra Maestra" (named for Cuba's main mountain range) as his party's official anthem. Santos's politics frequently got him into trouble with the U.S. authorities, who were suspicious of his motives for traveling regularly between New York and Havana in the 1950s. Santos subsequently broke with Castro, however, when he discovered that the Cuban leader was using children in the armed forces.

Little devil
Santos continued to be a prolific songwriter for the rest of his life, and performed to large, enthusiastic audiences throughout the United States and in many countries of Latin America. His public success masked an unhappy, tumultuous private life, however. He was reputed to have married no fewer than 12 times, and was prone to bouts of drunkenness. He was detained at various times in jails in Cuba, the Dominican Republic, and Ecuador. His reckless behavior earned him a second nickname, "Anacobero" (Little Devil). Daniel Santos died in 1992 at his home in Ocala, Florida.

See also: Corretjer, Juan Antonio; Cugat, Xavier; Flores, Pedro

Further reading: Glasser, Ruth. *My Music Is My Flag: Puerto Rican Musicians and Their New York Communities, 1917–1940.* Berkeley, CA: University of California Press, 1995. www.musicofpuertorico.com/en/daniel_santos.html (biography with samples of music).

KEY DATES	
1916	Born San Juan, Puerto Rico, on February 5.
1938	Begins singing with the Quarteto Flores.
1942	Records "Linda," his most famous song.
1992	Dies in Ocala, Florida, on November 27.

SANTOS, Rolando H.
Media Executive

Rolando H. Santos is one of the most important Latinos in the media. As executive vice president and general manager of CNN Headline News, responsible for the development and overall operations of the business, Santos is a leading role model for Latinos pursuing careers in broadcasting. Santos is so proud of his Mexican heritage that he has a glass-encased Mexican flag, a present from former president Ernesto Zedillo (1994–2000), mounted above his desk. In 2005, *Hispanic Business* magazine named Santos one of the 100 most influential U.S. Hispanics. A talented conjurer and illusionist, Santos is also associate editor of *Linking Ring*, the magazine of the International Brotherhood of Magicians.

Early life
Born in Eagle Pass, Texas, Santos grew up in a family of four children. At age 15, he had his first experience of the media, sweeping the floors of a local radio station. He went on to become a disc jockey, presenting both English- and Spanish-language broadcasts. He fell in love with the media, and decided that one day he would manage a television station, an almost impossible dream for a young Hispanic at the time.

Achieving a dream
Santos studied journalism at Texas A&M University, graduating in 1978. He gained experience as a reporter, news anchor, bureau chief, and producer at several stations, including San Antonio's KMOL-TV, Salt Lake City's KSL-TV, and San Francisco's KPIX-TV. Santos's rise through the ranks of television and radio was not easy,

however. As part of the first major wave of Mexican American reporters on television, Santos experienced racism, and was once advised to change his name to something that sounded more "Anglo," advice that he ignored.

After working as the assistant news director of KTTV-FOX News in Los Angeles, Santos moved to Telemundo's flagship station KVEA Channel 52, where he oversaw international news coverage for all the U.S. stations. He improved the station's ratings significantly within the first six months of working there. In 1992, KVEA picked up an Emmy Award for best newscast; it was the first Spanish-language broadcast to achieve such an honor.

Rapid promotion
In 1993 Santos joined CNN in Atlanta, Georgia, as an executive producer. He was quickly promoted to become director of CNN en Español and special programming. In 1996, Santos was appointed vice president of CNN en Español; within two years he was president. In that position, Santos was also responsible for CNN en Español Radio, as well as CNNenEspañol.com and CNN.com.br, the CNN websites for the Spanish and Portuguese languages. In addition, Santos supervised the staff who worked on news-gathering and reporting in Spanish. His responsibilities included overseeing a large team of reporters as well as eight bureaus in such important Latino cities as Los Angeles, Miami, and New York. In addition, Santos helped create several international news networks.

In 2002, Santos became executive vice president and general manager of Headline News. His job involved maintaining viewer ratings and implementing experimental techniques in news broadcasting.

Honors
Santos is widely respected as a journalist and executive. News anchor Chuck Roberts commented that Santos's manner and method of business fostered a sense of unity and cohesiveness among his staff. Santos has won several awards for his work. He often speaks publicly about his experiences of being Latino, and about his impressive career in broadcasting.

KEY DATES

1978	Graduates from Texas A&M University.
1992	Wins Emmy for best newscast at KVEA Channel 52.
1993	Joins CNN in Atlanta.
1998	Becomes president of CNN en Español in Atlanta.
2002	Becomes executive vice president and general manager of Headline News.
2005	Named one of the 100 most influential Hispanics by *Hispanic Business* magazine.

Further reading: http://www.cnn.com/CNN/anchors_reporters/santos.rolando.html (CNN biographies).

SARALEGUI, Cristina
Television Presenter

Cristina Saralegui is a Latina journalist and television personality. Her effervescent screen persona is an accurate reflection of her character.

Early life

Saralegui was born in 1948 in Havana, Cuba. Her grandfather was the island's main newspaper distributor and a co-owner of three major magazines: *Bohemia*, which is still published by the Cuban government; *Cartéles*, a journal of opinion and current events; and *Vanidades*, a women's periodical. Saralegui left Cuba with her family in 1960 after the Castro revolution. Although much of their fortune was confiscated by Castro's government, they still lived comfortably in Key Biscayne, Florida.

While attending the University of Miami, Saralegui began her journalistic career as a college intern at *Vanidades*, which was now published in the United States by its exiled staff. In 1973, she was hired by editor Helen Gurley Brown to work on *Cosmopolitan*. Six years later, she became editor-in-chief of the magazine's Spanish-language edition, *Cosmopolitan en Español*. Over the next 10 years, Saralegui turned the publication into the second-best-selling Spanish-language women's magazine in Latin America, Europe, and the United States.

Also during the 1970s, Saralegui was married, had two daughters, and divorced. She later formed a lasting

▲ *Cristina Saralegui's TV show has been compared favorably with that of Oprah Winfrey.*

relationship with Marcus Avila, a founder of the band Miami Sound Machine. Avila became her personal manager, then her second husband, and the father of her only son.

Wider career

With Avila's support, Saralegui moved from print journalism to television stardom. In 1989, she gained world fame as the host of *El Show de Cristina*, a weekly talk show in Spanish. An immediate hit, it went on to attract 100 million viewers each week. Saralegui also hosted a successful radio show on ABC for 12 years. Meanwhile, she maintained her writing career as editor of *Cristina*, which she also owned. *Cristina* ceased publication after 14 years in 2005. Since then, Saralegui has diversified further, and now markets a range of products, including cosmetics and Casa Cristina furniture.

Further reading: Saralegui, Cristina. *Cristina!: My Life as a Blonde.* New York, NY: Warner Books, 1998.
http://www.cristinaonline.com (official Web site).

KEY DATES	
1948	Born in Havana, Cuba, on January 29.
1960	Leaves Cuba with her family after Castro takeover; settles in the United States.
1973	Starts work on *Cosmopolitan* magazine.
1979	Appointed editor-in-chief of *Cosmopolitan en Español*, which soon becomes the number two women's magazine in Europe, Latin America, and the United States.
1983	Marries Marcus Avila, bassist in the Miami Sound Machine.
1989	Starts her own television, radio, and magazine production companies.
1992	Begins publication of *Cristina*, a women's magazine.
2005	Named one of the 25 most influential Hispanic-Americans by *Time* magazine.

SCHIFRIN, Lalo
Composer

Lalo Schifrin is an Argentine American who is internationally acclaimed as a musician, composer, pianist, and conductor. Widely regarded as one of the most important film composers of the 20th century, he has written scores for more than 100 movies and television shows. His best-known works include the theme tunes for the TV series *Mission: Impossible* and *The Man from U.N.C.L.E.*, and the soundtracks to the movies *The Cincinnati Kid*, *Bullitt*, and *Dirty Harry*. Schifrin has also recorded almost 100 albums, conducted many of the world's most prominent orchestras, and recorded with some of the world's greatest performers.

Early life
Boris Claudio Schifrin was born in 1932 in Buenos Aires, Argentina. Lalo, a nickname derived from Claudio, spent his childhood surrounded by music. His father, Luis Schifrin, was conductor with the Philharmonic Orchestra of Buenos Aires, and regularly hosted evenings of chamber music at the family home. For Schifrin's fifth birthday party in 1937, his father arranged for his 100-piece orchestra to surprise the boy at home with a rendition of "Happy Birthday." Soon afterward the young Schifrin began to study the piano with Enrique Barenboim, father of the Israeli pianist and conductor Daniel Barenboim (1942–). Schifrin frequently visited the cinema, and quickly learned the importance of musical soundtracks in movies.

Emerging talent
At age 16, Schifrin began piano studies with Andreas Karalis, an expatriate Russian who had formerly been the head of the Kiev Conservatory. He also studied harmony with the Argentine composer Juan-Carlos Paz (1897–1972). Two years later, Schifrin began to study law and sociology at the University of Buenos Aires. In 1952 he won a scholarship to the Paris Conservatoire in France, where he studied under the French composer Olivier Messiaen (1908–1992). In Paris, Schifrin developed a passion for jazz music, and supplemented his grant by playing piano in nightclubs. He represented Argentina at the 1955 International Jazz Festival, which was held in the French capital.

Return home
On his return to Argentina in 1956, Schifrin formed a jazz orchestra, which was an immediate hit in a country that had had no previous exposure to the musical genre. The orchestra performed that year for trumpet legend Dizzy Gillespie, and Schifrin subsequently wrote the arrangement "Gillespiana" for Gillespie's big band. After a period as arranger for Xavier Cugat's orchestra, Schifrin accepted an invitation to join Gillespie's new quintet, and moved in 1960 to New York City. He began as the group's pianist, and soon became its musical director. In 1963 Schifrin was asked to score *Rhino!* (1964) for MGM Studios, and promptly moved to Hollywood, California, where he hoped to find greater opportunities to explore his interest in blending jazz and classical music.

Critical acclaim and popular success
In 1965 Schifrin wrote *The Cat*, a jazz album, for Paul Horn, and in the following year composed *Jazz Suite on the Mass Texts* for Jimmy Smith. Both albums won Grammy awards for Best Original Jazz Composition. Schifrin's distinctive theme for the television series *The Man from U.N.C.L.E.* was recorded in 1965. He followed that in 1966 with the theme to *Mission: Impossible*, which won Grammy awards in 1967 for Best Instrumental and Best Original Score. Schifrin's memorable television work also includes the themes to *Mannix* (1967), *Planet of the Apes* (1974), and *Starsky & Hutch* (1975).

Schifrin recorded numerous critically acclaimed movie soundtracks, including *Once a Thief* (1965), *The Cincinnati Kid* (1965), *Bullitt* (1968), *Dirty Harry* (1971), *Enter the Dragon* (1973), and *The Four Musketeers* (1974). *Voyage of the Damned* (1976), *The Amityville Horror* (1979), and *The Competition* (1980) received both Golden Globe and

KEY DATES

1932	Born in Buenos Aires on June 21.
1952	Wins a scholarship to the Paris Conservatory.
1960	Moves to New York City.
1967	Wins two Grammy awards for *Mission: Impossible*.
1987	Cofounds Paris Philharmonic Orchestra.
1990	Composition *Grand Finale* performed at event held to coincide with finals of soccer World Cup.

INFLUENCES AND INSPIRATION

Lalo Schifrin had several remarkable teachers, including pianist Enrique Barenboim and the composers Olivier Messiaen and Juan-Carlos Paz. Schifrin has described the profound influence on him of Argentine culture, his family (particularly his concert-master father), and his discovery of jazz as a teenager. Jazz drew Schifrin to the United States, where he had a significant influence on the direction of the form. His work challenged the rigid boundaries that remained in the 1960s between jazz and classical music. Schifrin's notion of combining the two forms was not always welcomed by purists, and the adverse criticism he received in New York influenced his decision to move to Hollywood, where his experimentation was embraced. Combining jazz, Latino, pop, and classical styles, Schifrin's arrangements inspired a generation of film and television composers, and helped create a new musical vocabulary.

Schifrin paid tribute to his influences in *Jazz Meets the Symphony*, a work that includes suites dedicated to Duke Ellington, Dizzy Gillespie, Miles Davis, Charlie Parker, and Thelonius Monk.

▲ *Lalo Schifrin's work is familiar to millions through the soundtracks of some of the most popular movies of the late 20th and early 21st centuries.*

Academy Award nominations. *The Fox* (1967), *Cool Hand Luke* (1967), and *The Sting II* (1983) also received Academy Award nominations.

International demand

In addition to his work as a composer, Schifrin has maintained a vigorous live performance schedule. He has performed both on stage and in the studio with some of the world's greatest musical talents, including Ella Fitzgerald, Count Basie, and Stan Getz. He has also conducted many of the world's leading orchestras, notably the Los Angeles Philharmonic, the Houston Symphony, the London Philharmonic, the Vienna Symphony, the Mexico City Philharmonic, and the National Symphony Orchestra of Argentina. In 1987 Schifrin was one of the cofounders of the Paris Philharmonic, and served for five years as the orchestra's musical director. His composition, *Grand Finale*, was performed by the Three Tenors (Plácido Domingo, José Carreras, and Luciano Pavarotti) at an event held to coincide with the 1990 soccer World Cup. The subsequent videos and albums of the performance, which was arranged by Schifrin, are among the best-selling recordings in the history of classical music history.

In 1988 Schifrin was honored with a star on the Hollywood Walk of Fame. In 1998 the Argentine government appointed him adviser to the president on cultural affairs. He has received honorary doctorate degrees from Rhode Island School of Design and the University of La Plata, Argentina.

Recent work

Schifrin remains active in the movie industry. His recent scores include the theme tunes and incidental music for *Rush Hour* (1998), *Tango* (1998), *Jack of All Trades* (2000), *Rush Hour 2* (2001), and *The Bridge of San Luis Rey* (2004). Schifrin's wife, Donna, runs Adelph Records, which has published many of Schifrin's recordings. They have three children.

See also: Cugat, Xavier

Further reading: http://www.schifrin.com (official Web site).

SCHOMBURG, Arturo Alfonso
Bibliophile

Arturo Alfonso Schomburg was a major collector of information documenting the historical achievements of African Latinos and African Americans. Schomburg's work helped combat racial prejudice by improving U.S. society's understanding of black history. The first Puerto Rican to be awarded the William E. Hannon Award for outstanding work in education, Schomburg was also a champion of Puerto Rican and Cuban independence.

Early life
Born in 1874 in San Juan, Puerto Rico, 1874, Schomburg was the son of María Josefa, a free-born black, and Carlos Féderico Schomburg, a mestizo of German descent. Schomburg described himself as "Afroborinqueño," meaning Afro-Puerto Rican.

A talented student, Schomburg's lifelong interest in history was sparked in the fifth grade when a teacher told him that "Black people have no history, no heroes, no great moments." He later studied English, history, and African American literature at college in the Virgin Islands.

The United States
At age 17, Schomburg moved to New York's Harlem, where he became involved in the political activism of the local Cuban and Puerto Rican immigrant communities. He held various menial jobs while attending night school. In 1897 he joined the American Negro Academy (ANA), where he met leading black intellectuals.

Although Schomburg worked as a paralegal clerk in the hope of becoming a lawyer, he was denied the opportunity to obtain the necessary qualifications on racial grounds.

▲ *Arturo Alfonso Schomburg's collection included books, manuscripts, prints, and other material relating to black history and culture.*

He joined the Bankers Trust Company in 1906, becoming supervisor of a mail section; he remained there until 1929.

Intellectual pursuits
In 1911, Schomburg helped establish the Negro Society for Historical Research, which published papers on black history. His essay "The Negro Digs Up His Past" expressed the belief that the study of black history and culture was essential for empowering communities.

By 1925 Schomburg had gathered 5,000 documents and artifacts from around the world. In that year, the New York Public Library opened the Division of Negro Literature, History, and Prints, and purchased his collection. After working as curator at Fisk University, Tennessee, Schomburg returned to New York in 1932 to oversee his major collection. He died in 1938.

KEY DATES	
1874	Born in San Juan, Puerto Rico, on January 24.
1891	Moves to New York on April 17.
1911	Cofounds the Negro Society for Historical Research.
1925	Writes the influential essay "The Negro Digs Up His Past."
1932	Appointed curator of the Schomburg Collection of Negro Literature and Art, the New York Public Library.
1938	Dies in New York on June 8.

Further reading: Sinnette, Eleanor Des Verney. *Arthur Alfonso Schomburg: Black Bibliophile and Collector.* Detroit, MI: The New York Public Library and Wayne State University Press, 1990.
http://www.nypl.org/research/sc/sc.html (Web page for the Schomburg Center).

SECADA, Jon
Musician

Jon Secada is a singer, songwriter, and producer who found fame with the Latino pop group Miami Sound Machine before achieving considerable success as a solo artist. He has sold 20 million albums, won two Grammy awards, and written hit songs for Gloria Estefan, Jennifer Lopez, and Ricky Martin.

Early life
Born in 1962 in Havana, Cuba, Juan Secada was nine when his family immigrated to the United States. Settling in Florida, where his parents managed a coffee shop, Secada grew up in the suburbs of Miami. After graduating from Hialeah High School, he went on to study at the University of Miami's Frost School of Music, where he completed a BA and an MA in Jazz Vocal Performance.

Musical career
In the late 1980s, Secada joined Emilio and Gloria Estefan's band Miami Sound Machine as a backing singer. He soon became a key member of the group, cowriting several songs, including Estefan's No. 1 hit "Coming Out of the Dark," featured on her best-selling album *Into the*

▼ **Musician Jon Secada believes in giving back to the community: He established the Jon Secada Music Scholarship at the University of Miami.**

KEY DATES	
1962	Born in Havana Cuba, on October 4.
1992	Debut album, *Jon Secada,* goes triple platinum.
1992	Wins Grammy for best Latin pop album.
1995	Wins Grammy for best Latin pop performance.

Dark. Secada took to the stage to perform solo during Estefan's tour "Coming Out of the Dark." His performance was well received by critics and fans.

In 1992 Secada released his self-titled debut album. It reached No. 15 in the *Billboard* pop album chart, and went triple platinum, selling more than three million copies. *Otro Dia Mas Sin Verte,* the Spanish-language version, was *Billboard*'s No. 1 Latin album of 1992; Secada also picked up a Grammy for best Latin pop album. His single "Just Another Day" reached No. 5 in the *Billboard* chart, and sold more than 500,000 copies.

In 1994, Secada's second album, *Heart Soul and a Voice,* went platinum. He also performed at the opening ceremony of that year's soccer World Cup. In 1995, he recorded with Frank Sinatra on the latter's *Duets II* album. His own third solo album, *Amor,* won a Grammy for best Latin pop performance.

After the release of a less commercially successful album, *Secada* (1997), the musician decided to focus on songwriting. His hits from that time include Ricky Martin's "She's All I Ever Had" and Jennifer Lopez's "Baila."

Secada established a successful career in musical theater, starring in *Grease* (1995), *Cabaret* (2003), and *Joseph and the Amazing Technicolor Dreamcoat* (2004). In 2004, he was invited by President George W. Bush to serve on the Advisory Commission on Educational Excellence for Hispanic Americans.

See also: Estefan, Emilio; Estefan, Gloria; Lopez, Jennifer; Martin, Ricky

Further reading: Firmat, Gustavo Perez. *Life on the Hyphen: The Cuban American Way.* Austin, TX: University of Texas Press, 1994.
http://www.jon-secada.com/ (Secada's official Web site).

SEGUÍN, Erasmo
Rancher, Politician

Erasmo Seguín was an influential upper-class Mexican rancher. The great-grandson of Guillaume Seguín, a French immigrant who came to Mexico in the 17th century, Seguín served as the postmaster and *alcalde* (mayor) of Bexar, and Texas's representative to the congress that developed the 1824 Mexican Constitution. He was also the father of Texan hero Juan N. Seguín.

Becoming a rancher

Born on May 26, 1782, Juan José María Erasmo Seguín was one of the seven children of Santiago Seguín and Maria Guadalupe y Fernandez Fuentes, who had settled near San Antonio de Bexar in the late 1770s. Seguín founded La Mora ranch with land inherited from his grandfather. He later purchased 9,000 further acres (3,642ha) north of present-day Floresville. La Mora became a cattle-breeding and trading operation that extended to southern Bexar County. Seguín built a magnificent home, La Basa Blanca, overlooking the San Antonio River. He lived there with his wife, Maria Josefa Augustine Becerra.

In 1807 Seguín became the postmaster of Bexar, an office that he held more or less continuously until 1835. In 1811, he helped bring an end to the Casas Revolt. On January 22, 1811, Juan Bautista de las Casas and his supporters arrested the governor, Manuel Salcedo. Casas was appointed the interim governor of Texas, but his government was overthrown in March 1811, after which Salcedo returned to power. Seguín served on the governing council until royalist officers returned, when he was accused of collaborating with Casas's rebels and

was removed from office as postmaster. His lands were also confiscated. Although Seguín was later exonerated and had his lands returned, he did not become postmaster again until 1822. He had already been *alcalde* of Bexar for two years.

Seguín backed Anglo-American settlement in Mexico. He befriended Moses Austin, a Missouri entrepreneur who had lost all his money in 1819. Austin wanted to establish an Anglo colony in Texas. In 1821, Austin's request was approved by Governor Antonio de Martinez, but Austin died before he could see the plan through. Seguín helped Austin's son, Stephen, carry out his father's plan.

In 1823, Seguín was the Texas representative at the Mexican National Congress that wrote the Constitution in 1824. He worked in Mexico City during this time, promoting the interests of both the colonists and Mexican residents of Bexar. Séguin supported a ban on slavery. He also worked on the 1824 National Colonization Law that placed immigration and land distribution in the hands of state governments. Disapproving of the union between Coahuila and Texas, he worked for Texas independence.

Texas independence

Following Antonio López de Santa Anna's election as president of Mexico in 1833, and his rejection of the 1824 Constitution and plans for a more centralist government, rebellions broke out in Texas. Santa Anna sent troops to deal with the problem.

Juan N. Seguín was a captain in the revolutionary army, and his father was removed from public office as a punishment for his son's actions. After that, Seguín returned to his ranch where he provided the rebels with meat and horses. In May 1836, the Treaties of Velasco, signed by Texas and Mexico, brought hostilities temporarily to an end. The Republic of Texas existed until its annexation by the United States in 1845. Seguín lived at his ranch until his death in 1857.

See also: Casas, Juan Bautista de las; Seguín, Juan N.; Texas, History of

Further reading: De la Teja, Jesús F. (ed.). *A Revolution Remembered: The Memoirs and Selected Correspondence of Juan N. Seguín.* Austin, TX: State House Press, 1991.
http://www.seguindescendantshp.com/family.html (biography).

KEY DATES	
1782	Born at Bexar (San Antonio), Texas, on May 26.
1820	Begins service as *alcalde* (mayor) of Bexar.
1821	Supports Stephen F. Austin in pressing for the concession of land granted to his late father, Moses, by the king of Spain.
1823	Serves as Texas deputy in the Mexican National Congress.
1824	Helps develop the Mexican Constitution.
1857	Dies near Floresville, Texas, on November 7.

SEGUÍN, Juan N.
Politician, Soldier

Juan Nepomuceno Seguín was a key political and military figure in 19th-century Texas. From a prominent Tejano family, he was the only Mexican Texan in the Senate of the Republic of Texas, serving in the second, third, and fourth congresses. A long-overlooked figure who played a vital part in Texas's fight for independence, Seguín was finally honored by the town that bears his family name, Seguin, Texas, in October 2000, when a huge statue was unveiled of him on horseback at the Battle of San Jacinto (1836).

This oil portrait by Thomas Jefferson Wright (1798–1846) was painted in 1838, while Juan Seguín was a Texas senator.

Early life
Born in San Antonio, Texas, on October 27, 1806, Seguín was the elder son of María Josefa Becerra and Juan José María Erasmo Seguín. Erasmo Seguín worked as a postmaster, and was for a time *alcalde* (mayor) of Bexar. In that role, he helped Missouri-born Stephen F. Austin settle more than 200 Anglo-American families in Texas in the 1820s. The young Seguín was influenced by his father's liberal politics, and also supported the policy of allowing foreign settlers in what was then still part of Mexico.

Erasmo Seguín was a member of the congress that drafted the 1824 Mexican Constitution. In his absence from the family home, Juan Seguín helped his mother carry out the duties of the postmaster. In 1825, at age 19, he married María Gertrudis Flores de Abrego, a member of one of San Antonio's most important ranching families; the couple had 10 children.

Political career
Seguín then held various political offices before he was appointed chief administrator of the San Antonio district in 1834. He advocated greater autonomy for Texas, and opposed Mexican president Antonio López de Santa Anna's attempts to centralize authority in Mexico (*see box on page 134*). When Santa Anna abrogated the 1824 Constitution in 1835, many Texans took up arms in protest, and several rebellions broke out in the region. Santa Anna sent troops under General Martín Perfecto de Cos to suppress the uprisings.

Military career
In September 1835 Seguín recruited a company of 37 Tejano ranchers and joined the Texan forces at Monclova. He fought with distinction at the Battle of Gonzales on October 2, 1835, and was promoted to captain by Stephen F. Austin.

Seguín provided essential support to the Texas revolutionary forces. He took part in the first phase of the siege of the Alamo in February 1836, and survived it because Colonel William B. Travis sent him to get help. He met up with General Sam Houston's army at Gonzales, and was told that the fortress had fallen to the Mexican attackers.

Seguín and his troops fought at San Jacinto, where Santa Anna's forces were defeated and the president himself was briefly captured; they were the only Tejano unit to take part in the battle. Seguín accepted the Mexican surrender of Bexar on June 4, 1836, and was the city's military commander for the next 16 months. He supervised the burial of the men who had died at the Alamo. He then resigned his commission to become a member of the Texas Congress.

Betrayal
Seguín was elected a senator from the Bexar District in the second, third, and fourth congresses of the Republic of Texas, serving between 1837 and 1840. He was a prominent member of the Committee of Claims and Accounts. In that role, he urged that laws should be written in both Spanish and English so that everyone could read them. (Seguín himself spoke little or no English.) In 1840 he stood down from the Senate. He was elected

INFLUENCES AND INSPIRATION

One of the greatest influences on Juan Seguín's life and thought was his political opposition to Antonio López de Santa Anna (c. 1795–1876), "the Napoleon of the West," who served 11 terms as president of Mexico.

Born into a middle-class family in Jalapa, Vera Cruz, Santa Anna joined the Spanish infantry in 1810. Under General Joaquin de Arredondo, he fought for Spain against Mexico's independence, but by 1821 had changed sides to join the rebel cause. Espousing a federalist platform, Santa Anna was able to secure the Mexican presidency in 1833. Once in power, he supported a centralist government, and formed a new congress that ignored the 1824 Constitution; he also dissolved state legislatures and limited state militia power. His actions led to mass protests and rebellions in Zacatecas and in Texas. In 1835, Santa Anna and his army defeated the rebels at Zacatecas. He then marched the army to San Antonio, the political center of Texas. Poor supplies, sickness, and the harsh climate badly affected his forces, but he still arrived in San Antonio with an army of 1,800 in February 1836. After a 12-day siege of the Alamo, Santa Anna and his army captured the fortress on March 6 of that year.

After defeating rebel forces at Coleto, Santa Anna met General Sam Houston's Texas rebel forces at San Jacinto. A surprise attack by Houston's men, including a charge led by Juan N. Seguín's Tejano unit, resulted in his defeat on April 21, 1836. Santa Anna was captured and, after surrendering to Houston, recognized Texas independence.

Santa Anna was overthrown in 1845 and replaced by José Joaquín Herrera. He was forced into exile. He later returned, poor and blind, to Mexico, where he died.

---

mayor of San Antonio in the following year. Seguín then found himself caught in the middle of growing hostilities between Mexicans and Anglo-American settlers.

Time of misfortune

After a land speculation deal went wrong, Seguín found himself in trouble financially. His problems increased when a Mexican commander referred to him as a loyal compatriot, a description that brought him under suspicion as a traitor to Texas. Amid mounting hostility, betrayed and embittered, Seguín was forced to flee Texas with his family.

KEY DATES

1806	Born in San Antonio, Texas, on October 27.
1834	Organizes opposition to the newly elected Santa Anna; appointed chief administrator of San Antonio district.
1835	Appointed captain in Texas forces.
1837	Elected member of the Senate of the Republic of Texas.
1840	Resigns from Congress.
1841	Elected mayor of San Antonio.
1890	Dies in Nuevo Laredo, Mexico, on August 27.
1976	Reburied in Seguin, Texas.

They took refuge in Mexico, where his record of armed opposition to the government made him equally unwelcome. Seguín wrote in his diaries that he was forced to seek "shelter amongst those against whom I fought; I separated from my country, and what was more from the institutions on behalf [of] which I had drawn my sword, with an earnest wish to see Texas free and happy."

In Mexican uniform

The Mexican authorities arrested Seguín, and offered him the choice between prison and serving in the army. He chose the latter, and took part in General Adrián Woll's abortive invasion of Texas in September 1842. Seguín spent the next three years guarding frontier posts along the Rio Grande, and repelling armed incursions by Native Americans. He then fought in the U.S.–Mexico War (1846–1848). At the end of the conflict he returned to the United States, but he eventually went back to Mexico in 1867. He died in 1890 in Nuevo Laredo. In 1976 his body was reburied in Seguin, the town that bears his name.

See also: Seguín, Erasmo; Texas, History of

Further reading: De la Teja, Jesús F. (ed.). *A Revolution Remembered: The Memoirs and Selected Correspondence of Juan N. Seguín.* Austin, TX: State House Press, 1991. http://www.tsha.utexas.edu/handbook/online/articles/SS/fse8. html (Handbook of Texas Online).

SET INDEX

Set Index

Set Index

Set Index

Picture Credits

c = center, t = top, b = bottom.

Cover: Corbis: Bettmann t, c; **Courtesy Indiana University:** b; **TopFoto.co.uk:** Revolution Studios/Phillip V. Caruso, SMPSP cb; **West Carolina University:** ct.
Arizona State University: 43; **Courtesy First Interstate Bank Oral History Project, Arizona Collection, Arizona State University Libraries:** 104; **Photo of Maria Ruiz de Burton is reprinted with permission from the publisher (Houston: Arte Público Press-University of Houston © 2005) from AAP Archive Files:** 94; **Photo of Dolores Prida is reprinted with permission from the publisher (Houston: Arte Público Press-University of Houston © 2005) from AAP Archive Files:** 11; **Photo of Luis Omar Salinas is reprinted with permission from the publisher (Houston: Arte Público Press-University of Houston © 2005) from AAP Archive Files:** 101; **George I. Sanchez Papers (Box 75 Folder 1), Benson Latin American Collection, University of Texas Libraries, The University of Texas at Austin:** 107; **Greg Bojorquez:** 64; **Used by permission of Special Collections, University of California, Riverside Libraries, University of California, Riverside, CA:** 46; **Photo Courtesy of the Citizens' Committee for Historic Preservation, Las Vegas Photographic Archive:** 82; **The Congressional Medal of Honor Society:** 58; **Corbis:** Steve Azzara 67, Bettmann 130, Brooklyn Museum of Art 36, Jan Butchofsky-Houser 35, Duomo/Steven Sutton 99, Jeremy Horner 6, Icon SMI/Andy Altenburger 60, Neal Preston 118, Roger Ressmeyer 70, Reuters 110, Reuters/Kimberly White 84, SABA/David Butow 33, Michel Setboun 129; **El Paso Herald-Post files, C.L. Sonnichsen Special Collections Department, University of Texas at El Paso Library:** 48, 100; **Empics:** AP 13, 22, 30, AP/Elise Amendola 57, AP/Christopher Berkey 62, AP/Joe Cavaretta 131, AP/Damian Dovarganes 81, AP/John Forschauer 23, AP/Yuri Gripas 78, AP/Tony Gutierrez 127, AP/Gerald Herbert 41, AP/Lawrence Jackson 91, AP/Marta Lavandier 108, AP/Krista Niles 108, AP/Kamenko Pajic 88, AP/ Rich Pedroncelli 56, AP/William Philpott 83, AP/Scott Sady 86, AP/Schwartz 115, John Buckle 28, Deborah Cannon 29, PA/ Yui Mok 114; **Photo courtesy of Foothills Magazine:** 24; **Getty Images:** 9, 52, 54, 103, 116, 122, 124; **Courtesy Houston Metropolitan Research Center, Houston Public Library:** 40; **Courtesy Denise Applewhite, Princeton University 2004:** 7; **Library of Congress:** 4, 73, repro.no.LC-USZ62-118274 10, repro.no.LC-USZ62-129147 44, repro.no.LC-USZ-71441 89; **John Rechy:** 31; **Retna:** Jennifer Graylock 27, Jak Kilby 106, Rahav Segev 17; **Rex Features:** BEI/Jim Smeal 102, John Dee 12, Everett Collection 80, Everett/©ABC Inc. 14, Patrick Rideaux 76, Sipa Press 93; **Chino Rodriguez/LatinMusicBooking.com:** 20; **Eloy Rodriguez:** 59; **Rudolph Projects/ArtScan Gallery:** 74; **Floyd Salas:** photo by Claire Ortalda 97; **John Samora:** 105; **Photo courtesy of Izzy Sanabria (SalsaMagazine.com):** 69; **Rik Sanchez:** 111; **Courtesy of the State Preservation Board, Austin, Texas. CHA 1989.96, Photographer P. Houston, 7/28/95, post conservation:** 133; **TopFoto.co.uk:** 68, 71, 75, ArenaPAL/Jak Kilby 15, Empics 61, PA 66, 121, The Image Works/Tony Savino 45, Ron James 18; **TQS Publications:** 77; **U.S. Army:** 112.

The Brown Reference Group has made every effort to trace copyright holders of the pictures used in this book. Anyone having claims to ownership not identified above is invited to contact the Brown Reference Group.